Not Much Improvement

Urban Renewal Policy in Birmingham

Not Much Improvement

Urban Renewal Policy in Birmingham

Chris Paris

Centre for Environmental Studies, London

Bob Blackaby

*formerly Centre for Urban and Regional Studies,
University of Birmingham*

HEINEMANN · LONDON

Heinemann Educational Books Ltd
LONDON EDINBURGH MELBOURNE AUCKLAND
HONG KONG SINGAPORE KUALA LUMPUR NEW DELHI
IBADAN NAIROBI JOHANNESBURG EXETER (NH)
KINGSTON PORT OF SPAIN

British Library Cataloguing in Publication Data
Not much improvement
   1. Housing—England—Birmingham
   I. Paris, Chris   II. Blackaby, Bob
   301.5′4   HD7334.B5

   ISBN 0–435–85950–1

Printed in Great Britain by
Biddles Ltd, Guildford, Surrey

Contents

List of Maps, Diagrams and Tables

Preface

Our research on urban renewal and the development of house improvement policy grew out of local involvement in one city, Birmingham, as well as interest in national developments in policy. The research which has informed this book was our project 'Urban Renewal in Birmingham', carried out at the Centre for Urban and Regional Studies of the University of Birmingham from 1974 to 1976.

Our previous research work and continued neighbourhood-based action in Birmingham provided us with the ideal opportunity to investigate the introduction of large scale 'improvement' policies. For some years we had been involved with numerous voluntary organisations facing a diversity of local housing issues and problems. Together with others, particularly John and Camilla Lambert, we had acquired some understanding of the relationships between neighbourhood associations, individuals in search of better housing, and the role of the city council in its management of the housing problem. While our academic base at the University was well known to those with whom we worked in the field, we also had well established bases within many of the inner city neighbourhoods which came to be included in Birmingham City Council's new proposals early in 1973. When the 'urban renewal policy' was announced in January 1973 we were still working on another project, reported in *Housing Policy and the State* (Lambert, Paris and Blackaby, 1978).

The urban renewal policy was one of many local authority policies which impinged upon the life chances of those with whom we collaborated. It was not at first our focus of concern, but it became increasingly apparent that it was being used by the city council as an attempt to coordinate and integrate diverse policies affecting Birmingham's inner areas. In that, it was part of the new Labour administration's first step towards 'corporate policies'.

But from its beginning, Birmingham's urban renewal policy encountered many difficulties and was met with a diversity of criticism. We decided to seek support for a study focusing specifically on this policy, and were grateful to receive a grant from the Centre for Environmental Studies to pursue this research.

Our concern in this book is specifically with the renewal of housing. As such we do not explore the redevelopment of central commercial and business districts. Conflicts over land between housing and business have been rare in Britain, with the possible exception of London (Mellor, 1977), although this has been a central theme of studies of urban renewal in the USA (see for example, Goodman, 1972).

We use the term 'urban renewal' to mean those activities of local authorities concerned with the replacement and improvement of older housing. Clearly, such practices have often been accompanied by other forms of action, notably in the provision of public facilities (educational establishments, leisure facilities, industrial infrastructure). But our central concern is with housing, and the working class residents of districts of older housing affected by policies of urban renewal.

Most research in Britain has focused on particular aspects of urban renewal, typically the relationship between local neighbourhood populations and local authority managers (see Dennis, 1972; Davies, 1972). These approaches, whilst useful in themselves, have often ignored wider issues in which the questions of urban renewal are located, and have focused on apparent 'inadequacies' of local government. This approach runs the risk of ignoring wider determinants of the local situation, in particular the impact of central government policies and the operations of the market. Thus the most powerful institutions in society do not come under scrutiny and, ironically, it has seemed 'that the middle dogs have been the chief target for champions of the underdog' (Pahl, 1975 edn., p. 268).

Some readers may be concerned that we might try to say more about general processes of urban development and change than can be sustained through a case study. However, whilst recognising the limitations inherent in any local study, we believe that there were also positive advantages to be gained.

First of all, Birmingham's urban renewal policy, announced in January 1973, was on a massive scale, attempting to affect 70,000–80,000 older houses. This represented nearly a third of the city's housing stock, and the vast majority of all pre-1919 housing. Thus it was intended that, in one form or another, state involvement in local housing should substantially increase, representing in an ambitious form developments that were occurring nationally.

The new policy also reflected the national switch from slum clearance and redevelopment to improvement, both of individual houses and neighbourhoods. The city council was also trying to come to grips, in advance of national legislation, with areas of older housing which were exhibiting forms of housing stress, which were neither suitable for declaration as general improvement areas under the Housing Act 1969, nor, as yet, bad enough for slum clearance. By signifying its intention to declare such areas as 'Renewal Areas' the city council was anticipating the concept of housing action areas; its early attempts to develop positive programmes of action in this way appeared to be of national significance. This early initiative also suggested that the experiences in Birmingham's renewal areas would give an early indication of the effects of the national policy initiative known to be forthcoming.

A second argument in favour of a local approach concerns the importance of national developments for ordinary people. We were in any case aware that others were collecting comparative statistical evidence and carrying out other studies which, together, would provide a fuller picture of the effects of improvement policies. But we wanted to explore the ways in which things actually worked out in practice, to put some flesh and bones on the statistics and to examine the aspirations and motivations of those involved—residents, councillors and officers—in the development and implementation of the policy.

In one sense, of course, every city is unique, with its own character and history. These can be extremely important and where we think Birmingham has special characteristics we specify particularly local developments. But our main concern was to use our understanding of a local study to generate insights into the significance of national developments in housing policy and processes of urban change.

It would be impossible to list all of the friends and colleagues who have helped us during the course of this work. Particular thanks, however, are due to Camilla Lambert who worked with us in a part-time capacity, to John Lambert, Phil Wells, and to all of our colleagues and students at the Centre for Urban and Regional Studies (CURS), Tony Travis, Director of CURS and David Donnison, whilst Director of the Centre for Environmental Studies

(CES), who encouraged our work and helped us prepare our project proposal; our link-person at CES, Michael Harloe, who provided continuous support and advice. Numerous community workers and other activists played important roles both in Birmingham's urban renewal story and in aiding our research; we are especially grateful to Mike Gibson, Rick Groves, Steve Jacobs and Jon Stevens. Many councillors and officers, both past and present, of Birmingham City Council, too, were of invaluable assistance; in particular councillors John Hannah and Ted Taylor willingly spent countless hours discussing urban renewal and local politics. The research on the private housing market, in which Camilla Lambert played a major part, would not have been possible without the willing and helpful co-operation of many building society managers and surveyors. Most of all, perhaps, we owe a debt of gratitude to those citizens of Birmingham's inner areas, as individuals and as members of residents' associations, who made this study possible.

Many secretaries have performed Herculean tasks in translating our handwriting. In particular we owe our thanks to Sue Buckley at the Centre for Urban and Regional Studies, and Judy Harloe who typed our final draft.

Numerous friends and colleagues have made helpful comments on earlier drafts of this book, in particular Alex Catalano, Simon Duncan, Ray Forrest, Fred Gray, Anthony Harrison, David Jordan, Valerie Karn, Bob Kraushaar, Gillian Lomas, Elizabeth Monck, Alan Murie, Chris Pickvance, Peter Williams, Peter Willmott and David Witham. This book has benefited greatly from their advice, even though many have disagreed with much of our analysis.

CHRIS PARIS
BOB BLACKABY
August 1979

1 Introduction

Urban renewal in the 1970s has increasingly become synonymous with improvement policy. Every British city now has an improvement programme of one sort or another, organised around powers and resources made available by central government. Our most modest ambition, therefore, has been to chronicle the development of such a policy in one major city. But our aim has never merely been to tell the story of one town and selected events in its inner city area. Rather we seek to locate that local history within a wider body of theory and analysis about urban change. The crucial task of this introduction is thus to outline the connections between what happened in Birmingham and the continuing debates about central and local government housing policy and the housing market and the relationships between the state and citizens in what remains substantially a private market in housing.

The relevance of theory to the practical concerns of councillors and local government officers, however, is problematic. Their concern is with action—getting things done (or at least presenting the appearance of getting things done)—not with the 'airy-fairy' concerns of academics. Theory is all very well in the university but it does not count for much in the council chamber or municipal offices. Who needs to bother with academic discussion, anyway, when there are slums to pull down, new houses to build and massive problems of continuing decay and dereliction in the inner city?

These are arguments which anyone familiar with local politics will have heard many times, and we have made similar points ourselves on certain issues at particular times. But the point of theorising is *not* to avoid action, quite the opposite, for theory serves the dual purpose of helping us *understand* action (and inaction!) and hence both to predict outcomes and offer alternatives.

A striking feature of urban renewal in Birmingham was the

theoretical vacuum within which a major new policy was conceived and implemented. To put it another way, there were few explicit statements about relationships or processes; rather there were a whole host of diverse assumptions, frequently couched in simplistic 'common sense' formulations. We shall refer to these in detail throughout the following chapters; our task here is to demonstrate the connections between the issues that we have selected for attention.

Our choice has not been an arbitrary one; neither is the manner of our exposition. The central theoretical concerns are the relationship between the state and working class housing and the nature of state policies. But state institutions and state policies are complex, and

Fig. 1.1   Birmingham: ward boundaries, 1971

operate at different levels of generality, from fiscal policies of central government right down to local control over the colour of council tenants' front doors or the details of an individual house improvement scheme. The state is also the locus, at both central and local levels, of political disputes and confrontations, and is thus an arena within which competing class interests seek to win gains and force concessions. The housing market is complicated by state intervention and the effects of market processes operating both within the housing market and external to it. These are just some of the complicating factors which require a framework for analysis: urban renewal policy is not separate from such processes and relationships, rather it has been forged from within them. So we cannot start with the same assumptions and assertions as policy makers; instead we must place them in their wider social, economic and political context. The changing nature of urban renewal in the context of state housing policy is the subject of our second chapter; that gives us a basis from which to examine specific features of urban renewal which provide evidence for the theoretical critique in our final chapter.

Chapter 3 examines the question of the relationship between housing policies and the structure of the housing market in inner areas. Overall changes in the structure of the housing market have had important effects in inner areas. Moreover, the housing stock currently being considered for improvement is much more heterogeneous in terms of physical type and conditions than the poor privately rented slums which were the subject of slum clearance action. The social structure of inner areas changed too, for during the 1950s and 1960s many inner urban areas had also seen substantial population changes, with out-migration to council estates, owner-occupied suburbs and new towns, and associated increases in multiple occupation, frequently resulting in the growth of ethnically mixed communities. Immigrants, whether from overseas or elsewhere in Britain, converged on the older housing areas to take the only housing opportunities available to them.

Such areas contained a combination of housing conditions and circumstances different from the forms of tenure now dominant in Britain—suburban owner-occupation or council housing. These complicated areas provided the context for the application of improvement policies, but they have varied tremendously both within and between cities. How much account was taken, then, of the peculiar characteristics of inner city housing markets in the development of a local policy? Moreover, to what extent was policy relevant to processes of residential segregation and market reorgan-isation which were taking place in inner areas?

The theme explained in the fourth chapter is that of the relation-ship between central and local government concerning policy formulation. Whilst housing policy is a subject of continuous political debate, both in Parliament and local councils and within political parties, the *context* of that debate varies enormously, as do the categories of analysis used. Frequently there is confusion between technical aspects of policy and its social and political implications and effects. The development of improvement policy was based on powers and duties deriving from central government, yet urban renewal policies were also the subject of local political initiatives and debate. But how realistic were 'local' issues in such discussions? In his revised version of 'urban managerialism', Ray Pahl (1975) stressed the tremendous importance of *constraints* affecting the power and influence of the 'urban managers'. How do these constraints operate? Many crucial decisions regarding the powers and resources to be made available to local authorities are frequently outside their control; to what extent, therefore, can local politics be viewed as an independent process?

Chapter 5 examines the management of Birmingham's urban renewal. In our earlier work we had come to redefine Pahl's concept of 'urban managerialism' and emphasise the limited autonomy of local decision-makers (Lambert *et al.*, 1978, Chap. 7). During the same period, however, others were arguing the case for the introduc-tion of 'better' management techniques in local government (Eddison, 1975). Central government, too, stressed the need for better management structures (Bains Report, 1972) and practices. Other local authorities had already begun to pioneer the develop-ment of 'corporate planning', for example, Coventry (Bennington, 1976) and Lambeth (Cockburn, 1977). The themes of corporate planning and 'area management' were actively being promoted by a variety of institutions, particularly Birmingham University's Insti-tute for Local Government Studies, the recently established School for Advanced Urban Studies at Bristol University and the Local Government Training Board.

The introduction of Birmingham's urban renewal policy was accompanied by the first steps towards the development of corporate management within the city council.

Ironically, as the local authority came to develop its new managerial structure, central government was embarking on a programme of cuts in public social expenditure. How far was it possible, then, to develop new management methods to cope with the complexities of inner city house improvement? Crucially, given the problems facing those responsible for the implementation of urban renewal policy in Birmingham, *what was being managed?* Very few houses were improved between 1972 and 1976; was management therefore more concerned with the management of people, and redefining political issues in technical terms?

Public participation provides the subject of the sixth chapter. The shift from comprehensive redevelopment to improvement policy took place during the same period that public participation was being encouraged by central government. The town planning profession, in particular, became obsessed with the concept of public participation, but other sections of central and local government also sought to develop community involvement—particularly in the social services, education and health. Whereas changes in the content of housing and renewal policies were a product of the cost of provision combined with the effect of previous policies and market changes, public participation, whilst related to the same global processes, was of wider ideological importance. As such, participation in housing issues should be considered as one example of centrally encouraged participation, rather than a special phenomenon in its own right.

Previously in Birmingham we had noted the reluctance of the local authority to engage in public participation. In one area studied in detail, a residents' group, assisted by a community worker, had been actively involved in discussions with the city council over the future of their area. Their influence, however, amounted to no more than 'technical cooperation', effectively legitimating decisions taken elsewhere (Lambert *et al.*, 1978, Chap. 6).

With the development of the urban renewal policy, however, new attitudes were expressed by councillors and subsequently by officers. Public participation was now to be *encouraged:* the exponents of the new policy and public involvement were not setting out to deceive. Quite the opposite; they genuinely believed in the objectives of the policy and in fostering residents' involvement. This chapter examines attempts made by residents' organisations to participate in the urban renewal policy, and to seek to compare these experiences with other research on public participation in planning and housing issues.

The limited scope for, and effects of, public participation which we describe, however, raise important concerns about the relationship between citizens and state, and about democratic theories of politics and decision-making.

The issues discussed in chapters 3–6 are re-examined in the last chapter, but in a wider context. This involves both consideration of recent developments in state policies for housing and inner city areas, and also a critical analysis of the nature of state policy during a period of economic recession.

2 Housing Policy and Urban Renewal

Housing Policy and the Housing Question

For every housing question there is a different answer—it all depends on who is asking the question, what they ask and of whom an answer is expected. Our question may be different from yours, indeed the notion that there is a housing question in contemporary Britain has been increasingly criticised for obscuring more problems than it raises:

> . . . we no longer have a single 'national' housing problem: we have a large number of local problems of great variety. It is, therefore, essential that local policies be based on a well-informed understanding of the problems of individual areas and the context in which they arise.
>
> *(Central Housing Advisory Committee, 1969, para. 448)*

Local housing problems may indeed take on a variety of forms. There may be a dwelling shortage in some areas which manifests itself through sharing, overcrowding and multi-occupation. In other areas there may be a crude surplus of dwellings, but households in need through an inability to gain access to housing of the kind and at the price they require. In other areas, whilst needs and supply may be in balance, large numbers of dwellings are unfit for human habitation or lack basic amenities.

However, whatever the scale of local problems, there can be little doubt that the housing conditions of all classes in British society have improved considerably since Engels' exposure of the slums of the mid-nineteenth century industrial cities. The period since the Second World War, especially, has seen dramatic improvements in both the quantity and quality of housing. In part this has reflected continuing economic growth, but changes in the availability and standard of housing have also been profoundly affected by public policies, principally determined by central government but mainly executed by local authorities.

In *The Housing Question*, written a hundred years ago, Engels maintained that:

> It is perfectly clear that the state as it exists today is neither able nor willing to do anything to remedy the housing calamity. The state is nothing but the organised collective power of the possessing classes . . . If therefore the individual capitalists deplore the housing shortage, but can hardly be moved to palliate even super-ficially its most terrifying consequences, the collective capitalist, the state, will not do much more. At most it will see to it that that measure of superficial palliation which has become customary is carried into execution everywhere uniformly.
>
> *(Marx and Engels, 1973 edn., p. 347)*

Yet the last hundred years have seen a growing and massive involvement of the state in housing problems. So much so, in fact, that 'we now take for granted the government's ultimate respon-sibility for the success or failure of housing policy' (Murie *et al.*, 1976, p. 235). Moreover, the form and content of housing policy has been a constant subject of debate both within Parliament and at the local level; profound party political differences of opinion have resulted in many changes of policy. This applies particularly to attitudes towards council housing, but also to the growth of owner-occupation and the future of the privately rented sector. Engels' notion of unitary 'state' policies, therefore, can no longer apply in the light of important differences within government over what policies to adopt.

State housing policies have brought about significant changes in the structure of British housing markets. In the early years of this century the vast majority of the population lived in housing owned by private landlords; less than 2 per cent of all houses were rented from local authorities and a mere 10 per cent were occupied by their owners. The situation today is completely different. The amount of property owned by private landlords has dramatically fallen as a proportion of the total housing stock to below 20 per cent. The major forms of tenure are houses and flats owned by and rented from local authorities (including New Town Development Corporations), constituting about a third of the total stock and owner-occupied properties comprising just over half of all dwellings (Murie *et al.*, 1976).

The main concern of this book is the development and application of state policies for older housing, particularly since the Second World War. Before we can examine the question of older housing, however, it is helpful to summarise briefly some of the main features of housing policy, and associated changes in British housing, which led to the introduction of urban renewal in the 1950s and 1960s. The reader interested in a comprehensive discussion of British housing policy should consult *Housing Policy and the Housing System*, by Alan Murie, Pat Niner and Chris Watson (1976). (See also: Bowley, 1945; Community Development Project, 1976a and b; Cullingworth, 1966; Donnison, 1967; Nevitt, 1966; Harloe *et al.*, 1974.)

The inter-war period
The two decades between the First and Second World Wars saw major social and political changes in British life. These were reflected in, and the cause of, the rapid growth of state involvement in housing provision. Legislation during the First World War had established the principle of rent control, to be followed by the 'Addison Act' of 1919 which granted generous subsidies to local authorities, requiring them to survey local housing needs and enabling the introduction of programmes of house building.

In spite of variations of policy during the 1920s, resulting in tremendous variety of both style and quality of municipal housing, especially under the Housing Act 1924, council housing became established as a form of tenure during the decade. By the outbreak of the Second World War over 1,100,000 publicly owned houses had been built in England and Wales. Variations in quality within the sector have also been significant. Whereas nearly all council housing during the 1920s, particularly in the immediate post-war period, had been built to high standards, much of the 1930s building was to a lower standard, aimed not so much at extending housing provision for 'general need' as to provide accommodation for families displaced by slum clearance. This reflected government belief that the worst crisis was over, and also the growing support for owner-occupation.

New building was cheaper than ever before in the 1930s, so that better off workers, who had been occupying relatively expensive council housing, could afford to buy a speculatively built house at little extra cost. The Conservative dominated 'National Government' was politically opposed to further growth of the public sector, and saw this owner-occupation as an alternative to 'general needs' council housing. The public sector would be a residual coping only for those 'unable to compete'. Most additional building during the 1930s was for owner-occupation, then, rather than council housing. (See Cullingworth, 1966, Chap. 1; Dickens, 1976.)

By the outbreak of the Second World War far greater complexity had been introduced into British housing. Initial workers' militancy after the First World War over their housing problems had been reduced by rapid building of council houses (at rents only better paid workers could afford). Then, after 1932, the principle was established that council housing was a residual form of tenure. Increasing numbers of people from the middle and upper sections of the working class had to look to property ownership, buying their housing on mortgages provided by the rapidly expanding building societies.

Much of this is criticised by the Community Development Project (1976a). In particular, as evidence of the ideological nature of inter-war policy, the report refers (p. 15) to a statement of Viscount Cecil, who was quoted in the *Daily Telegraph*:

> the ownership of property cultivates prudence. Clearly it encourages thrift, fosters the sense of security and self dependence, and sensibly deepens citizens' consciousness of having a 'stake in the country', and the influence is surely one which, spreading from the individual to the community and linking all classes, must contribute appreciably to national stability.

Ironically, during the later years of the decade, those local authorities whose control had just been gained by the Labour Party and which were dedicated to programmes of slum clearance built some of the worst council housing of the whole inter-war period. It was thus 'those local authorities who did get to clear their slums and relieve overcrowding who contributed most to the devaluation of council housing itself' (Community Development Project, 1976a, p. 15).

Housing policy in post war Britain—production and renewal
Many cities had not begun to undertake slum clearance on any substantial scale before the Second World War. Birmingham, for example, had concentrated on new building, mostly in the outer ring of the city, and while 94,000 houses were built between the wars (approximately half by the city council) only 8,000 had been demolished during the 1930s. Increasingly, the older housing areas in the 'inner ring' around the city centre were characterised by decay and obsolescence.

The immediate post-war years saw, however, not the rapid introduction of slum clearance, but instead a continuation of peripheral
development. Usually within post-war administrative boundaries,
local authorities sought to catch up on five years of neglect, bomb
damage and a standstill of building. The housing problem was seen
as part of larger conurbation-wide problems, and the proposed
solutions are now all too familiar: urban areas would be contained
by 'green belts', inner areas were to be redeveloped and 'overspill'
population was to be rehoused in 'new towns'. Those policies were
to include elements of inter-regional movement of industry so that
economic development could rejuvenate those areas which were in
need of assistance.

Slum clearance and the comprehensive redevelopment of residential areas did not really get underway until the late 1950s. Massive
inner areas of all the major cities and towns of Britain were changed
as a result of this process. Moreover, the process of comprehensive
redevelopment always took longer than expected, almost invariably
blighting adjacent areas. In anticipation of future redevelopment,
those people who could afford to move, did so. Often their place was
taken by others in the least favourable market situation, for
example, newcomers, frequently immigrants from the Caribbean,
Asia and Africa. Such areas of rapid change are typically areas in
which private landlords still thrive, often packing large numbers of
tenants into inadequate rooms and flats.

Opposition to comprehensive development grew rapidly during
the 1960s and the cry went up for the improvement of older housing
rather than clearance and new building. Government, faced with
increasing costs, the unexpectedly slow progress of previous schemes
and local opposition to comprehensive redevelopment, saw improvement—both of houses and neighbourhood environments—as a
cheaper way to solve housing problems. Elected representatives,
social workers and others who were working in areas affected by
redevelopment, witnessing the delays, frustrations and privations of
the populations affected, hoped that improvement would retain
communities and lead to an increased commitment on the part of
residents to involve themselves in their areas.

Housing policy and the private sector
In addition to the direct provision of housing and encouragement of
the improvement of poorer owner-occupied housing, the state has
played a critical role over privately rented accommodation. Since

the First World War state controls have directly affected rent levels and hence the profitability of the private landlord. Subsequent governments have changed the basis on which this control has been exercised but the principle has remained: tenants should not bear the full 'market rents' for their dwellings. This has contributed to the decline, both relative and absolute, of the privately rented sector. However, evidence also suggests that disinvestment in the sector had begun *before* the introduction of rent control, as better investment opportunities became available, especially abroad (Murie *et al.*, 1976, pp. 187–88).

Increasingly, the stock of privately rented accommodation has come to comprise older housing, and the best option for many landlords in the light of taxation, subsidies and rent control has been to sell to an owner-occupier rather than seek to improve their properties and recoup the cost through rents (Murie *et al.*, 1976). Attempts by the Conservative Government of the 1950s to stimulate investment in private renting by abolishing rent control failed to achieve any such effect; rather, they resulted in the growth of harassment and intimidation of tenants (Samuel *et al.*, 1962).

State involvement in the owner-occupied sector takes a variety of forms. Some local authorities build houses for sale. Many authorities provide mortgages for people to buy houses, particularly those which are unlikely to attract an advance from a commercial source. Renovation grants are also available to those wishing to improve or repair older dwellings. State intervention in the provision of finance for private housing is, however, limited in extent. The building societies have played the most significant role in lending money for house purchase, particularly since the 1930s, and this has stimulated building for owner-occupation. Building societies are private institutions outside direct public control, although they are supervised by a state appointed registrar whose principal responsibility is to ensure that the societies adequately serve the interest of the people who invest their money with them (Harloe *et al.*, 1974).

In one critical way, though, government policy has affected the growth of owner-occupation. By a series of special tax arrangements the market position of building societies, and owner-occupiers, has been privileged. The rate of income tax levied on investment income from building societies is lower than that in the rest of the money market. This, therefore, makes the societies more attractive to the investor. In addition, mortgage payers receive tax relief on the interest they pay on their loans and this is a direct way in which the state grants subsidy to the owner-occupier. Recently, government has intervened to prevent the building societies raising their rates of interest. This has been achieved by persuasion and by the government making loans which have augmented the societies' funds, allowing them to continue to lend money for house purchase without having to raise their interest rates to attract investment from the open market. The concern of government has been to keep down the rate of interest paid to investors since any raising of rates is normally reflected in subsequent increases for borrowers who find their mortgages more expensive to service. The function, therefore, of such intervention by government, as well as serving as a counter-inflationary measure, has been to maintain cheaper owner-occupation in the interest both of those who have already bought their houses and those who are seeking to buy.

Housing Policy and Inner Urban Areas

Most new construction since the First World War has been in peripheral urban areas or, with redevelopment, in neighbourhoods adjacent to central business districts. The effect of macro-scale changes in tenure, and their impact on the spatial structure of metropolitan areas (Hall *et al.*, 1973; Paris and Lambert, 1979) has resulted in changes in the social composition of areas of older housing, as well as to the kind of housing to be found in contemporary inner areas (see also Rex and Moore, 1967). As Cullingworth (1973) has shown, the comprehensive redevelopment drive of the 1950s and 1960s took with it very poor privately rented dwellings and, by the end of the sixties, local authorities were facing quite different areas compared with ten to fifteen years earlier. These areas now had a higher proportion of owner-occupied properties, whose occupants would be more likely to resist clearance proposals than would private tenants and absentee landlords, and also the very nature of the stock was different, being more substantially built and, in physical terms, lending itself more suitably to improvement.

Rosemary Mellor (1973) has outlined the relationship between different processes of change affecting older housing which have created three different kinds of 'twilight area'. What such areas have in common, she suggests, is poor housing, often associated with other indicators of social stress, but the social relations involved and the social consequences of alternative policies which might be adopted are quite different.

The first type of area can be thought of as a central zone of slums, where 'the buildings on the land are not only physically decrepit, but also socially and economically obsolete . . . a hopeless slum to which only those with absolutely no choice drift'.

Secondly, and today much more common, are the 'grey areas of so many towns and cities':

> There are terraced houses, cramped at front and rear, often without bathrooms and with outside lavatories, but sufficiently sturdily built not to be classed as slums, yet . . . elderly households, long resident and attached to house and neighbourhood, coexist with younger households vainly endeavouring to brighten up their drab house . . . large areas of our cities built between 1875 and 1914.

Finally, Mellor talks of 'areas of special need', with:

> appalling housing conditions, measured in terms of space, facilities and management, in structures that while economically and socially obsolete are not considered slums as the structures are relatively sound. The population is characteristically heterogeneous, comprising young households, with or without young children, as well as the older households who have remained in the area. A diversity of ethnic groups, English, Irish, West Indian, Pakistani and Greek, might be found in the same area; these groups are very mobile. Many of the households will only recently have arrived in town, many others are moving in and out of the lodging houses of the area, and many others seek to move away. It is a rootless population with no allegiance to the area, and no sense of a community of interest.
>
> *(p. 55)*

During the 1960s, as Mellor points out, many areas which formerly were of the second kind were transformed into rooming house districts. The study by Rex and Moore of Sparkbrook in Birmingham (1967), remains the classic British example of such processes of transition.

Meanwhile, during the 1960s, comprehensive redevelopment policies tended to concentrate on the first type of area. Thus an important spatial manifestation of redevelopment has been the concentration of municipally owned housing in many of our cities and towns, particularly in the central areas. In cities such as Birmingham, Manchester and Leeds there developed areas for which Peter Norman coined the description 'Corporation Town':

Vast areas of the old inner suburbs are being bulldozed and replaced by council housing. The agency of both destruction and redevelopment is almost always the local authority . . . the provision of new housing in the inner areas is largely a public enterprise. The net result is to transform the inner city into a corporation town in which the assumptions of a free market no longer apply.

(Norman, 1971, p. 361)

This process was an important subject of political debate, as the changing tenure structure potentially had electoral effects and was also of itself an issue over which the two major parties disagreed.

As well as bringing about changes in tenure structure, the redevelopment process also has its effects on the cost of housing in particular areas, tending to replace poor quality but cheap housing by better but more expensive dwellings for rent. The effects of this change on the housing opportunities of households affected is hard to determine although a national rebate scheme introduced in 1972 cushioned the impact for those low income families who claimed.

However, some effects of the tenure changes resulting from redevelopment are clear: increasing numbers of households depending on the local authority for housing and decreasing opportunities for those who typically were denied access to the public sector (single people and transients) and where some of the housing (cheap private renting) was rapidly being removed by the clearance process.

With the introduction of improvement policies, the second and third types of area as described by Mellor have been the subject of various local policies. There is, however, a danger in arguing that improvement strategies for such areas are a rational and obvious response to the changing structure of the inner city since there can be no fixed and self-evident definition of different kinds of physical house conditions. Many would argue that dwellings in these areas are slums, that they should be pulled down and that there is indeed no neutral, technical solution to decision-making in this field.

The work of Davies (1972) and Dennis (1970 and 1972) shows the importance of economic rather than technical imperatives. In the case of Sunderland there was wide disagreement on what, given the set of house conditions which then obtained, should be done:

So long as there was agreement on what constituted 'unfit property' the ends served by housing replacement were 'given'. They were given by public opinion itself. In Sunderland . . . this consensus has evaporated; and the end of consensus ends also the pre-eminence of the technical expert. In housing replacement the situation is no longer that of a set of agreed goals which the technical officer is commissioned to reach with as much expedition and with as little cost as possible.

(Dennis, 1970, p. 361)

Thus it is an oversimplification tö·view the change of policy from redevelopment to improvement simply as a rational response to a changing situation. The issue of owner-occupation versus council renting, for example, remains a political one (Harloe, 1977).

By the end of 1977, comprehensive redevelopment had been almost totally abandoned, and improvement policy had come to be considered as the 'best' approach to the problem of older housing. But recent empirically based research on the effects of improvement policy, particularly Trevor Roberts' book *General Improvement Areas* (1976), has raised many doubts about the effectiveness of the Housing Act, 1969. We need to examine the shift from redevelopment to improvement in some more detail, therefore, both to understand more fully how the change in policy came about, and to set the context for our study of urban renewal policy in Birmingham.

From Comprehensive Redevelopment to Improvement

There was a continuing debate over policy towards older housing through the 1960s and early 1970s. Much discussion concerned the effects of renewal policies, and there was a reaction against comprehensive redevelopment in favour of improvement and 'gradual renewal'. We have already referred to the critical effects of restraint on public spending, which was the single most important reason why the comprehensive clearance schemes involving massive acquisition and rebuilding costs fell from favour. But this alone was not sufficient cause for the switch, since a truly successful improvement based policy, that would produce the same comprehensive increases in housing quality which former policies claimed to pursue, would also have been an expensive operation involving large commitments of financial and manpower resources from the public sector. Foremost among other reasons put forward were those claimed to be 'social' in nature.

The social arguments against redevelopment

While many people undoubtedly agreed with Paul Channon, then Minister for Housing and Construction, when he said in 1973 that the time had come to stop large-scale redevelopment projects, it is equally true that some ten years previously there was widespread agreement that comprehensive redevelopment was an urgent necessity (Samuel *et al.*, 1962). At this time Richard Crossman had been convinced that the only solution for the immediate housing problems of major metropolitan areas was a large-scale, sustained programme of comprehensive redevelopment:

> We have to concentrate on six or seven places, Liverpool, Manchester, Birmingham, Glasgow, London, where the local authorities simply can't grapple with the job . . . A Labour Minister should impose central leadership, large-scale state intervention, in these blighted areas of cities, the twilight areas, which were once genteely respectable and are now rotting away.
>
> *(Crossman, 1975, p. 44)*

What happened during the intervening years to change opinion so much? For one thing a vast number of dwellings had been cleared (86,000 a year during the 1960s) and much of the worst housing removed. Critical too were the effects of the process of redevelopment in human terms. In terms of social criticism of redevelopment we can now make a broad distinction between the process of clearance and the various subsequent effects. The process of redevelopment has been described by Barry Cullingworth (1973, p. 173) as a problem of management, complicated by the different levels of concern—central government and local government:

> The lengthy nature of the whole process results from the inherent complexities, the multiplicity of departments involved, the time taken for objections to be made by owners and for these to be considered by the local authority and . . . the time taken in arranging, holding and deciding upon a public inquiry.

In human terms, the delays and consequent dereliction of large inner areas have been recorded and publicised many times. Shelter's (1974) report on *Slum Clearance* emphasised three kinds of problems facing families affected: (a) The repeated postponement of the date when people are to be rehoused in satisfactory accommodation. (b) The appalling and continually deteriorating living conditions both within houses themselves and in the surrounding neighbourhood. (c) The despair felt by residents of clearance areas who feel that they have very little contact with the authorities carrying out the programme.

We could also add the problems generated by much housing which replaced the slums and to which many former slum dwellers were rehoused. Many central area redevelopment sites are now character-ised by multi-storeyed flats and low rise, but high density, flat and maisonette developments. Much of this stock rapidly became unpopular with tenants and created management problems for the housing authority. For many, slum clearance came to mean a forcible displacement to an unfamiliar high rise flat—a 'prison' in the sky—without friends and relations nearby and with little prospect of a move to the type of accommodation they wanted (for full discussion of high rise living see Sutcliffe, 1974).

The process of clearance and rebuilding was also itself a source of complaint. Frequently clearance proposals created uncertainty which led to anxiety and in some cases fear on the part of residents affected. In Ungerson's (1971) work on clearance programmes there were few instances of local authorities in her survey adopting procedures to alleviate anxiety; there was a misleading and inaccurate set of information being conveyed and re-conveyed to and by residents and no mechanisms for updating a reliable and consistent information flow.

It was precisely these kinds of criticisms, which were voiced not only by critics of local authorities, but also by elected members and officers, that contributed to the growing opposition to comprehensive redevelopment. In addition, comprehensive redevelopment has frequently been accused of the 'destruction of communities' and established neighbourhoods. This argument is often used, but what is not demonstrated is the extent to which redevelopment caused as opposed to contributed to ongoing processes of social change. For example, the 'loss of community' is also lamented in areas which have not been affected by redevelopment. 'Communities' would have been partly dispersed anyway through generational change; some children would have had to move out on household formation, whether to local authority housing or owner-occupation on the urban peripheries.

Changes in job markets, culture and the relationships between the two can easily lead to memories of a past that is romanticised and distorted, as Seabrook (1971, p. 26) found in Blackburn:

Most old people remember the coercive and crushing discipline imposed by the old industrial structure—first through the mills and weaving sheds, and then, as these decayed, through the threat of unemployment and poverty. These social disciplines were internalised by individuals, who then dutifully reflected them in authoritarian family structures: parents were unwittingly united in blind complicity with the owners of mills and money to ensure that the personalities of their children were systematically deformed and repressed, in order to provide an unceasing stream of unskilled labour. But the restricted social matrix of the working class subculture could not hold them all; and at length it burst like a ripe fruit. And it is this dispersal that the old now mourn in the bricked-up streets.

We are sceptical of the image of 'the happy slum' so often conjured up to describe urban working class communities in early twentieth century Britain. Frequently, such abstractions join the search for lost but golden ages, as such they amount to little more than '. . . a deep desire for stability, served to cover and to evade the actual and bitter contradictions of their time' (Williams, 1973, p. 60). Redevelopment for many people, particularly young married couples, provided the opportunity to escape precisely these restrictive social structures described by Seabrook.

In their examination of residents' attitudes to moving from redevelopment areas, English *et al.* (1976) cite a number of studies which show that there is not a simple case to be made either way for the relationship between redevelopment and the breakdown of communities. Frequently large proportions of affected populations, from areas studied in Liverpool, Leeds, Nottingham and Sunderland, did not want to move—but usually between 30 per cent and 50 per cent of residents did want to leave the area rather than be rehoused locally. As they comment: 'In none of these studies is there any evidence of a clear cut and overwhelming majority favouring one simple course of action' (op. cit., p. 158).

The critical factor that their research highlighted was that of age, with younger couples wanting to leave and older people not wanting to be disturbed. Significantly, in exception to this general rule, were young couples who owned houses in good condition, the factors of tenure and house condition being considered by the researchers as crucial in the influence of attitudes.

We should also consider the extent to which traditional urban working class community structures have been affected by changes in racial balance—both within and outside redevelopment areas. There is abundant evidence available that successive waves of working class immigrants have sought, and only had access to, housing in older inner metropolitan areas. For the last fifteen to twenty years many of these immigrants have been from the West Indies, India and Pakistan, and already it is clear that the housing opportunities open to them are different not only from the indigenous population but also from other immigrants who happen to be white. The difference is most marked after the first generation, by which time the children of white immigrants are usually able to pass unnoticed amongst the majority population. Low average income, combined with discrimination in both job and housing opportunities and, to an extent, choice has continued to concentrate the black population into older poorer housing. Of course, there are many variations within and exceptions to this rule, but the principle has obtained in both the private and public sectors. In particular, Valerie Karn's (1977–8) work on the housing market and immigrant areas has demonstrated the extent to which many blacks are forced to become owner-occupiers of low quality, and in relation to quality, high cost older property.

The most significant issue in the context of renewal policies is the extent to which comprehensive redevelopment largely missed areas of substantial immigrant concentration. With reference to their national sample, English *et al.* (1976) noted that it 'confirms the widely held view that slum clearance procedure does not deal with transitional areas of multi-occupation and immigrant housing' (p. 185). Many such areas are immediately adjacent to previous clearance areas, and thus, almost by definition, potential areas for future action. Often this can be explained in terms of the date at which areas were selected for clearance action, compared to the time that different groups moved in. Indeed, the survey conducted by English *et al.* was carried out in the summer of 1970 and the profile of areas more recently treated has frequently been different. In addition, local authorities had avoided treating areas of multiple-occupation partly because there was little chance of 'housing gain'; that is, almost invariably the redevelopment of such areas resulted in fewer units at lower densities. The clearance of terraced housing offered greater scope for maintaining or even increasing the number of housing units on a site. The central point, though, is that areas adjacent to redevelopment areas were often characterised more by change and heterogeneity than by stability and homogeneity (see for example, Rex and Moore, 1967).

The exclusion of substantial racial minorities from earlier clearance schemes meant that they would eventually have been affected by the bulldozer had comprehensive redevelopment continued as an active policy into the areas they now occupy. This would have been highly problematic for local authorities who would have faced hostility from some members of the minority groups anxious to retain their owner-occupation and wary of council action and, perhaps even more problematic, hostility from the indigenous population and from those within the authority itself who feared large-scale incursion of black families onto council estates as they were displaced as a result of clearance action. Improvement was in that sense justified in terms of meeting the desires of many immigrants for owner-occupation and as a way of minimising racial tension by preserving much of the public sector stock for whites (though such considerations were rarely if ever made explicit).

On balance, the 'social' arguments against comprehensive redevelopment, whilst fully justified and today uncontroversial, were *criticisms of the way in which policy was carried out—not the objectives of the policy itself*. That is to say, they were criticisms of a particular administrative device which was itself the product of the political and economic conditions prevailing at its conception and during its operation. If, indeed, it can be argued that the dwellings which were removed were fit only for clearance (and public health inspectors' reports from the period make this abundantly evident), then one policy alternative was a different process of clearance and rebuilding, not necessarily for the retention of obsolete, unfit housing. In order to arrive at a fuller understanding, therefore, of the shift in policy at government level one must look at wider political and economic influences on renewal policy.

Political and economic considerations
During the early 1950s the emphasis of state housing policy had been on the construction of new council housing. Macmillan, as Conservative Minister of Housing, boasted of the achievements of 300,000 new houses in 1954. In fact, the Conservatives had proceeded on lines organised by the previous Labour administration, with the critical exception that the Conservatives changed the emphasis between 1954 and 1964 away from council housing to private house building for owner-occupation. This period saw a continuation of the political distinction between Labour and Conservative party approaches to housing policy, especially between Conservative central government and Labour controlled local councils. Central subsidies limited the standards to which councils could build

after clearance, so that radical commentators have suggested:

> Unable to build good houses without drastic increases in rents the
> shift of emphasis was marked, as in the thirties, by a further
> reduction in standards. Once again Labour-controlled councils
> trying to represent the interests of the poorly housed found
> themselves building houses described as slums from the time they
> were built.
>
> *(Community Development Project, 1976a, p. 19)*

During the 1950s the annual total of new housing built declined
and the balance of policies and subsidies increasingly favoured
owner-occupation. The General Election of 1964 saw the return of a
Labour Government pledged to the development of the nation's
economic base. The means were suggested in the Party Manifesto in
1964: 'a deliberate and massive effort to modernise the economy, to
change its structure and to develop with all possible speed the
advanced technology and the new science-based industries with
which our future lies'.

The incoming Labour Government of 1964 was also pledged to a
programme of slum clearance and the construction of 500,000 new
houses a year. However, as David Coates emphasises, the Labour
Party 'entered office equipped to run a high growth economy,
anticipating that the barriers to growth would be technological and
scientific. They, in fact, inherited a low-growth economy, where the
barrier to growth was primarily a financial and competitive one'
(Coates, 1975, p. 100). House building fell well short of the target.
Slum clearance, however, was a major priority in 1964, and the
1960s saw an acceleration of slum clearance and new house building.
Much of the latter, however, was for owner-occupation, by then
considered the 'normal' trend. By 1967 the Labour Government was
faced with severe and deepening economic problems. The 1965
'National Plan' was abandoned, the government finding itself
critically influenced by outside forces. Labour politicians found that
'their ability to initiate changes in domestic and foreign policy was
tightly restricted by the international payments situation that they
persistently faced. For, because the Labour Government was so
dependent on foreign loans, the institutions which linked Ministers
with international financiers occupied a strategic position from which
to influence policy, and possessed immediate sanctions against
recalcitrant Parliamentarians.' (Coates, op. cit., pp. 105–6). As again
was the case in 1976, the Labour Government was forced to borrow

from the IMF on terms dictated by the latter. The financiers were not stupid, irrational or merely 'anti-socialist'; rather their analysis of the crisis of British capitalism emphasised the contradiction between high levels of 'non productive' investment and private sector confidence and profit. They demanded a reduction in Government spending, which came to mean a decrease in public sector house building by the end of the decade.

Increasingly government policy favoured the expansion of owner-occupation. The 1965 White Paper on the Housing Programme 1965–70 envisaged 'the stimulation of the planned growth of owner-occupation by financial measures to widen its economic basis'. The effects of the new strategy were slow to materialise and indeed, whilst there was a consistent decline in public sector house building in Great Britain since 1967, this was not matched by a consistent upturn in private sector completions. Nevertheless it was the objective of the government to encourage home ownership and this goal was pursued with even greater vigour by the Conservative Party when it resumed power in 1970.

Whatever changes were occurring in policy towards new building, a strategy towards the older housing stock was becoming increasingly necessary. The 1967 House Condition Survey clearly demonstrated continuing decay of the housing stock. Richard Crossman, who three years earlier had so strongly advocated extensive redevelopment, was also impressed by some early attempts at rehabilitation:

> it was really a pleasure to see how happy old people are when their old traditional slum houses are transformed by being given a bathroom and a skylight in the attic and a proper dry roofing and modern kitchen.
>
> *(op. cit., p. 12)*

Crossman also decided that:

> It is far better to give thirty years more life to some of this existing central property than to let it become a slum and then have to pull it down. In Salford I found that for £200 they were making people happy. Since I don't like the idea of people having to live in huge blocks of high rise housing, I found the Salford efforts extremely attractive.
>
> *(op. cit., p. 124)*

Although there was much debate about the relative merits of comprehensive redevelopment versus improvement, the government was crucially concerned about the high cost of redevelopment programmes, and willing to see a reduction as a saving. Not only was it argued that improvement policy was cheaper than redevelopment, although that debate was never finally resolved (see, for example the debate between Needleman and Sigsworth and Wilkinson, 1967–70) but also that improvement would slow down decay whereas redevelopment, through 'blighting' adjacent areas accelerated and actually induced their decline. But at the time of the Housing Act 1969 the debate usually turned around how much improvement, and it was rarely suggested that improvement was an alternative to redevelopment, rather that both policies should be pursued in different kinds of areas (see, for example Spencer and Cherry, 1970; Duncan, 1974). What remained in some doubt was the actual kind of area which would be most suitable for improvement and how the process would be accomplished. The Housing Act 1969 thus sought to stimulate and concentrate improvement action in parallel with continuing programmes of comprehensive redevelopment and new building (Cullingworth, 1973).

During a period of marginal economic recovery, Labour went out of office nationally to be replaced by a Conservative majority, whose housing policies concentrated on raising the levels of council rents and stimulating owner-occupation. Julian Amery, Minister for Housing and Construction, announced the imminent end of the slum problem '. . . we can beat the problem of slums and unsatisfactory housing within a measurable time . . . there is light at the end of the tunnel'. This statement was in an annex to *Slums and Older Housing: An Overall Strategy* (DoE Circular 50/72), in which local authorities were required to develop strategies to deal with existing problems of slums and older housing by 1980.

Amery's successor, Paul Channon, indicated the Conservative Government's growing preference for improvement at the 1973 Annual Conference of The Housing Centre:

> We must think about homes, not dwelling units. This fundamental requirement lies at the heart of our proposals in the White Paper,* and underpins, for example its statement that, in the majority of cases comprehensive redevelopment is no longer the answer to problems associated with bad housing.

On the question of the kinds of policies which would in future be appropriate, he went on to argue for greater sensitivity to local

---

*Cmnd. 5280, *Widening the Choice: the Next Steps in Housing*.

problems and the importance, where clearance was still necessary, of approaching in a 'gradual and sympathetic manner . . . redeveloping in smaller units and using improvement in a complementary way to keep those houses not yet ready for demolition in as decent a condition as possible in the meantime'. This approach was built on the work of the Denington Committee (Central Housing Advisory Committee, 1966) which had reported some seven years earlier. The Committee had urged local authorities to develop comprehensive policies towards the older housing stock and implement a national target of eliminating slums within seven, and in some cases fifteen years. Areas would be designated for clearance, for full improvement and for limited improvement and eventual clearance.

The Conservatives' Housing and Planning Bill was not changed substantially by the incoming 1974 Labour Government, and the emphasis on *improvement* not redevelopment was retained. In their book on slum clearance, English *et al.* (1976, Chap. 3) argue that one major reason for this shift of policy during the early 1970s had been the growing awareness that most big cities were clearing slums faster than they were rebuilding. Thus, as a stop gap measure at least, slum clearance should be slowed down to give local authorities the chance to catch up on a growing backlog of new building (see also, Stones, 1972). There was, however, no indication that the shift of emphasis was merely a temporary measure. On the contrary, as English *et al.* argue, the Housing Act 1974 and its accompanying circulars 'make it quite clear that slum clearance is now definitely a second best' (op. cit., p. 38).

The concept of 'gradual renewal' was very much in vogue, and in the context of a range of policy measures concerned with housing (stimulants to local authority building, increased municipalisation and extension of security to furnished tenants) there was widespread support for those new developments in urban renewal policy. In a *Housing Monthly* Editorial the Act and its accompanying circulars (DoE 13/75 and DoE 14/75)* were triumphantly welcomed as the dawning of a new era:

> It is at last being accepted, and propounded officially, that urban renewal must be a gradual process, not a wholesale clearance. This policy has been advocated in these columns for many years

---

*(a) DoE 13/75, WO 4/75 *Housing Act 1974: Renewal Strategies.*
 (b) DoE 14/75 *Housing Act 1974: Housing Action Areas, Priority Neighbourhoods, and General Improvement Areas.*

because housing managers know that satisfying the many and varied needs in housing is a gradual, continuing problem, and that a concern for people before bricks and mortar is all important and fundamental to any solution of our housing problems.

(Housing Monthly, *April/May 1975, pp. 2–4*)

This near-euphoric reception, however, was based upon the assumption that the levels of commitment—both in political and resource terms—to gradual renew would continue. This assumption was soon to prove highly questionable. For, within six months of the 1974 Housing Act becoming operative, against the claim that housing action areas could 'go a long way to give new hope to people suffering from the accumulated neglect and indifferences of the past', some important concerns were being raised. The editorial of the March/April 1975 edition of *Housing Review* emphasised the great dangers involved in viewing improvement as a cheaper, easier alternative to redevelopment:

. . . it may well be quite as expensive in resource terms, if not human terms, as the earlier policy, and there must be some suspicion that it is seen as a cheaper alternative to a continued new building programme rather than a changed strategy.

With reference specifically to Circular 14/75, the same leader argued:

If more resources are not made available many councils will be trapped as large scale slum landlords and the prospects of decent housing for many families will be set back for a generation.

Improvement Policy in Practice

Improvement policies, then, had originally been developed in parallel with those concerned with comprehensive redevelopment; each had either tackled a different kind of older housing stock, or improvement was seen as a stop-gap measure to enhance the last few years of a dwelling's life until its time came for the bulldozer.

This began to change with the Housing Act 1969, which envisaged the long term improvement of dwellings for a life of thirty years or more. The Act gave a great spur to improvement by raising the level of grants, attempting to concentrate grants in general improvement areas (GIAs) by adding resources for environmental improvement and widening their area of application.

The Housing Act 1974 consolidated the switch to improvement by raising the level of grant aid for house improvements, introducing a new form of grant for repairs and establishing the 'housing action area' (HAA) and the 'priority neighbourhood'.

General improvement areas were to consist of areas of basically sound dwellings but where a significant proportion of properties lacked basic amenities. Declaration of an area by a local authority was to be a two stage process—the second stage could only proceed after sanction by the Department of the Environment had been received. Once an area was declared, dwellings eligible for grant aid could receive a 60 per cent rate of grant on the eligible expense for restoration work.

Housing action areas were to be in areas where housing stress was combined with social problems. Such areas were thought to be characterised by overcrowding, multi-occupation, harassment of tenants by landlords, low incomes and a racially mixed population. The purpose of declaration and subsequent local authority action to achieve a rapid improvement in the housing stock as the area was to be substantially improved within five years of declaration (although this could be extended to seven). The emphasis was to be on house, rather than environmental improvement and after five or seven years an area could be re-declared a GIA. A 75 per cent rate of grant was to be available.

Priority neighbourhoods could be declared in a district adjacent to an HAA to prevent the 'rippling out' of problems from the HAA. Such a neighbourhood was to receive more intensive treatment when a local authority had sufficient resources to re-declare it an HAA.

A number of features in the progress of improvement policy during the 1970s need emphasising. Firstly, a considerable number of renovation grants approved were for the improvement of local authority housing—mainly council built pre-war dwellings rather than acquired property. In the years 1969–73 some 31 per cent of all grant approvals were for local authority dwellings (DoE, 1977a, Tech. Vol., Part 3, p. 118). Secondly, the rate of grant approvals, whilst rising after the 1969 Act, started to fall quite dramatically after 1973. In that year approvals to private owners totalled some 240,000 but this had fallen to under 73,000 in 1976 (op. cit.).

A third feature is the extent to which the improvement campaign was tackling the worst housing. The 1977 Housing Green Paper (DoE, 1977a) noted that, in spite of the payment of 550,000 grants to private owners during the period 1971–75, only a relatively small drop in the number of unfit dwellings had occurred. Progress in the treatment of *areas* of older housing had also been slow. A sample of

GIAs between 1969–70 found that only 35 per cent of dwellings which needed improvement at the time of declaration had in fact been improved (DoE, 1977a, p. 125) whilst, by mid-1977 in twenty-six declared HAAs, only six had achieved a grant take-up rate of 25 per cent or more (Wintour and Van Dyke, 1977). This latter figure, moreover, represented take-up in terms of grant *approvals*, not completed work. In the same areas the efforts of local authorities and housing associations were apparently more successful. In the twenty-two areas where public agencies owned houses the 25 per cent level of house improvement starts had been achieved in fourteen.

Central government directives have, since 1969, always stressed the importance of *voluntary* house improvement with the use of compulsory powers as a last resort. The approach is simple, in theory at least. Cash grants are available to the owner from public funds, which, combined with investment from his own funds, should increase the quality of the housing stock, enhancing use values for the owner-occupier and tenant, rent for the landlord and exchange values for owners generally.

In practice it has been far more complex. There is a close relationship between incomes and private sector housing conditions in older areas; in general terms the poorest live in housing of poorest quality. As Barry Cullingworth (1973, p. 83) noted, 'There is more than a growing suspicion that the quality of an area is related more to its socio-economic character (and changes in this) than to physical features'. Even so, levels of grant aid vary with house condition up to a maximum percentage of 'eligible expense' and not in accordance with the householder's income. Thus, the poorer the house in terms of quality, the more the householder has to meet from his own resources and, because the poor tend to live in the worst housing, the greater in relative terms is their contribution to house improvement. This regressive effect of the house improvement subsidy has been one of the major reasons for the slow start in the house improvement drive in the worst housing areas since the Housing Act 1974.

Further reasons for the private owner's reluctance to improve lie in the level of costs that he will need to bear in relation to the post improvement value of his house. On occasions costs, even allowing for a grant, exceed any enhancement in value that may occur after renovations have been completed. Furthermore, the immediacy of the expense and the disruption that full scale renovation bring have provided an additional barrier to action, with many owners preferring to carry on doing 'patching' improvements and repairs at their own cost but, and this is important, in their own time and in their own way.

A further problem concerns the private landlord. Poor house condition, low levels of rent following improvements and, in some cases, near impecunity have deterred many from seeking grant aid. Others, particularly in housing stress areas, have sought to exploit local housing shortages by providing multi-occupied lettings at relatively high rents to those who have no choice. In these circumstances total rent income could well exceed that which they would derive if their houses were improved, converted into self-contained flats and let at lower densities.

The slowness of the landlord's response can also be explained with reference to frequent reluctance on the part of local authorities to use compulsory improvement procedures (Hadden, 1978). Outside of declared GIAs and HAAs tenants anyway have to make the first move. Ignorance of their rights, fear of landlords' reprisals and reluctance to accept changing modes of life, particularly amongst the elderly, have prevented many tenants from acting. In GIAs and HAAs a local authority can take the initiative. The procedure however is extremely complex and a further deterrent to a local authority is the landlord's right to 'counterserve' a purchase notice requiring an authority to buy his unimproved dwelling—a commitment which many authorities would not welcome. A further restraint on the local authority's use of its powers lies in the need to respect the wishes of tenants, many of whom are elderly and who are willing to tolerate substandard living conditions rather than face the disruption that improvement frequently brings.

This problem for the private tenant reflects basic property relations, tenants being unable to force an improvement in living conditions without recourse to complex legal procedures involving the local authority. Indeed, Wintour and Van Dyke's analysis (1977) suggests that the lot of tenants will not improve unless they become a tenant of a local authority or 'social housing agency'.

The relative failure so far of the improvement drive cannot wholly be explained in terms of a failure of the economic incentive, for there are also social reasons. Many HAAs and some GIAs were once proposed redevelopment areas and the years of blight and uncertainty have not, in the eyes of many residents, been counteracted by subsequent improvement proposals. Councils have changed their minds in the past, the argument goes, so how can people be sure that they will not do so again in the future? Furthermore, contrary to popular assertion, many older housing areas are not settled homogeneous neighbourhoods. Racial tension and 'urban leapfrog' (Rex, 1968) have split black from white, 'stayers' from 'goers' and a residual indigenous population has often been left, wishing to move out but unable to, and whose last thought would be to spend money on improving their homes. Such improvement would almost certainly guarantee to make their stay more permanent than at present.

The National Context: A Summary

The acceptance of improvement as an alternative to comprehensive redevelopment is now fairly general. The 1977 Green Paper confirmed the approach of the government in terms of the gradual renewal of the housing stock through improvement and selective clearance and foresaw growth in renovation activity over the next ten years. Improvement was, in general terms, seen to be cheaper than clearance and redevelopment and carried with it the social advantage of maintaining within parts of our towns and cities 'a familiar neighbourhood which most people prefer to large-scale slum clearance and redevelopment' (DoE, 1977a, p. 91).

An important concomitant to the growth in improvement strategies has been the development of policies to assist owner-occupation. To an extent, improvement has been seen not only as an alternative to redevelopment but also to public sector house building and now both major parties, whilst differing in their approach to council housing, favour the growth in owner-occupation. Indeed, the most recent policy statement by the Labour Government tends to view council housing increasingly as a residual form of tenure (DoE, 1977a; Harloe, 1977).

The growth in owner-occupation, both aided by government policy and as a consequence of 'natural' change such as disinvestment by private landlords, has brought about distinctive effects in the older areas of our towns and cities. As we shall discuss later on in this book, in these areas owner-occupation does not wholly conform to the rosy picture conjured up by home ownership of a 'semi' in the suburbs. Many former tenants became owners through lack of choice or, in a situation of limited choice, ownership offered a slightly better prospect compared with a long wait for a council tenancy or poor conditions in a diminishing private sector. 'Marginal owner-occupation', as we shall later refer to it, frequently means incomes squeezed by rising mortgage costs leaving little, if any, cash left for necessary repairs. The problem of disrepair in the private sector in the older areas is a growing one, particularly affecting low income households and the elderly. These problems, as we shall see in chapter 3, are further compounded by lack of mortgage finance. The purpose of this chapter has been to set the context for the Birmingham study. At this stage we would wish to stress three points. Firstly, improvement has come largely to replace redevelopment and is to be a growing feature of housing policy. Secondly, reaction against redevelopment can be accounted for both in terms of the heavy costs involved and adverse social effects, the latter arising more from the way the process was managed rather than the policy itself. Thirdly, the development of improvement policy is to be seen both as a part of, and consequence of, a growing trend towards owner-occupation in the housing market.

Urban Renewal in Birmingham

The next four chapters of this book are devoted to the analysis of recent developments in urban renewal in the city of Birmingham. During the 1960s inner Birmingham was transformed by comprehensive redevelopment, as vast areas of older housing were cleared and replaced by new council owned tower blocks, maisonettes, and, to a lesser extent, low rise housing. In the early 1970s Birmingham was one of the first local authorities in Britain to embark on a new urban renewal policy based on improvement, rather than redevelopment, of the city's older housing.

What happened in Birmingham is both interesting in its own right, as Birmingham is one of Britain's largest and, in many ways, more progressive local authorities. But, and this is of more importance for our final chapter which seeks to draw some general conclusions about improvement policy, our case study provides detailed evidence about the realities of policy making and development which puts meat on the dry, albeit necessary, statistical overviews which are already available elsewhere.

3 Older Housing in Birmingham

Change in the Inner Areas

Britain's inner urban areas have changed dramatically during the last twenty-five years. The most obvious process of change has been comprehensive redevelopment. While the slums were being cleared and replaced, however, other changes were occurring in inner areas, particularly in neighbourhoods adjacent to clearance areas.

In part such changes were the result of deliberate state policies, but more often they were produced by the combination of state interventions and the market. Chapter 2 discussed some of these changes, and noted that many areas were characterised more by heterogeneity and rapid change than by homogeneity and stability. It is therefore difficult to talk of 'typical' inner area housing, rather it is better to examine the processes at work, and to see how different combinations have produced apparently different kinds of neighbourhood.

This chapter looks at the ways in which Birmingham's inner areas changed during the 1960s and early 1970s. Of particular interest are the roles of public and private institutions as they have affected housing in inner areas.

Comprehensive redevelopment had a direct and immediate effect on house conditions, even though delays in implementation often meant that the timing of change was uncertain. The effect of comprehensive redevelopment was also predictable, so that it could be assumed that eventually new housing of the type planned, in areas deliberately laid out by the council, would replace the former neighbourhoods. The effect of redevelopment on adjacent areas, however, was less certain. 'Blight' is a well recorded phenomenon (Dennis, 1972; Lambert *et al.*, 1978), but many areas adjacent to clearance areas were changing anyway, so that it is difficult to be certain that clearance in one area was the major cause of decay elsewhere. Indeed, in Birmingham many areas which were *not* adjacent to clearance areas exhibited signs of rapid change and housing stress (see Lambert *et al.*, 1978, Chap. 3).

The introduction of improvement policies relied heavily on state initiated, but essentially voluntary action. Minor public works and the availability of improvement grants were expected to stimulate private investment in older housing. But little consideration was given in Birmingham to the organisation of the housing market in inner areas. There appeared to be roles for landlords and property companies in the actual improvement of dwellings, estate agents in facilitating property exchange and building societies and banks through the provision of funds for the exchange and improvement of dwellings.

These institutions have received scant attention from 'urban academics' until fairly recently. Several studies have, however, now been published in recent years, in particular Harloe *et al.* (1974) examined both private and public institutions in London. Others have focused on financial institutions, notably Harvey and Chatterjee (1974), Karn (1977/8), Duncan (1977), Boddy (1976), Green (1976) and Williams (1976).

The concern of much of this work has been to examine the basis for, and consequences of investment decisions affecting mortgage lending. Both Harloe *et al.* and Duncan examined building society mortgage lending criteria and the consequences of the operation of such criteria for particular geographical areas. Harloe *et al.* noted the export of capital from one of the inner London boroughs through the reluctance of building societies to relend money collected from savers in the form of mortgages in the area. Drawing on the work of Harvey and Chatterjee, Duncan studied mortgage lending policy in Huddersfield and noted how the refusal of building societies to lend in certain parts in the city, characterised by poor property, lower socio-economic groups and, in particular black immigrants, led to the creation of sub-markets. This was because the withholding of funds from particular categories of people and types of housing, located in certain areas, created the need for, and growth of, particular kinds of finance institutions, whether it be the 'backstreet' finance company described by Duncan, the fringe financier discussed by Green (1976), or for that matter the local authority in its role of specialist lender on older housing (Karn, 1977/8).

The creation of sub-markets—the existence of particular categories of people occupying and restricted to particular kinds of housing stock—through mortgage lending policy tends to support and cement the existing relationship between housing quality and market power of different house occupants. We have referred in chapter 2 to market forces which lead to a fairly close correlation, at least in private sector housing, between income and class position on one hand and housing status on the other. Because housing of particular quality and status tends to be located in different areas the consequence is the creation of distinct spatial units. The practices of restrictive mortgage lending in both class and area terms reinforces this pattern in that it locks in the poor, unskilled workers and immigrants into particular sub-markets in the housing market, through an enforced reliance on fringe, or local authority sources of lending. This does not necessarily mean, however, that such areas are uniform internally, rather they may be characterised by diversity, albeit of identifiable and recurrent nature.

We can now examine Birmingham's housing market, and in particular the market in the inner and older areas, in order to set the scene within which urban renewal policies were formulated and developed.

Housing in Birmingham 1960–70

The 1960s was a decade of massive and extensive local authority involvement in both the demolition and construction of housing in Birmingham. The peak years were 1966 to 1969. Eighteen thousand slums were cleared (compared with twenty thousand, 1946–65) and thirty thousand new homes built (compared with 47,000, 1946–65). This acceleration was greatly helped by the 1964 Labour Government which allowed the city council to develop a large site at Chelmsley Wood, outside the city boundaries. Ten thousand of the homes built between 1966 and 1969 were in this development (Sutcliffe and Smith, 1974).

Partly because of this substantial local authority involvement in housing there were numerous important changes in the structure of the housing market in the city during the decade, as well as within the conurbation of which Birmingham city council's jurisdiction formed but one part. The *total* amount of housing in the city was little different, because demolition offset new building, but critical changes took place in terms of the structure of ownership and the use of the housing stock (Table 3.1).

The most striking changes, purely in terms of tenure, concern the

Table 3.1   Household tenure in Birmingham, 1961–71

Tenure	1961	1971	% change 1961–71
Owner-occupied	117,000	141,100	+ 21
Rented from local authority	116,600	127,600	+ 10
Privately rented and not stated	99,500	65,100	− 35
All tenures	333,100	333,800	+ 0.2

(*Source:* City of Birmingham, 1973.)

increase in the owner-occupied sector and decline in the privately rented sector. We shall examine the three major tenure groupings during this period, with special reference to the older housing stock which has come to be included within the urban renewal policy.

Council housing

At the beginning of the 1960s there were, crudely speaking, two types of municipally owned dwelling. First, there were substantial council estates in the middle and outer rings of the city, with subsequent post-war additions mainly built to similar design and levels of amenity. Secondly, the city council owned many older properties which had been acquired from private owners specifically with the intention of demolition (later, if not sooner). The basic distinction was between *purpose built* council properties and acquired slum properties.

Whilst there was continued use of the latter stock, it had become a much smaller part of the local authority's stock by the late 1960s. In 1965 the city council owned 30,000 properties in slum clearance and redevelopment areas, but the total had dropped to 10,000 by 1970 (Murie, 1975, p. 87).

From 1966 until the end of the local Conservative administration in May 1972, the city council also pursued an active policy of selling council houses. A total of more than 10,500 dwellings were sold between 1967 and 1972, comprising both dwellings built specifically for sale, but also, increasingly, large numbers of council houses built originally for rent under the housing acts. In his study of council house sales, Alan Murie suggested 'that the number of council houses sold in Birmingham was, in spite of publicity and the pioneering role, very small in proportion to the whole stock' (1975, p. 86). Even so, the number of such properties sold, by 1971, accounted for 30 per cent of the absolute increase in owner-occupation in Birmingham during the 1960s. Sale of council owned stock to owner-occupation, excluding properties specifically built for sale, had accounted by 1971 for 4 per cent of the city's purpose built stock.

Most sales were of more popular property in the most sought after estates; very few low rise flats and no tower block flats went into owner-occupation, so we can see that there were a number of selective elements in the policy (Murie and Forrest, 1976). First, only those tenants who could afford to buy, even after favourable financial arrangements had been made, could do so. Secondly, as Murie pointed out, the stock from which the sales came was an increasingly important part of the city's annual available tenancies. There was also, during the 1960s, an increase in the numbers of people wanting a transfer *within* the council stock. Whereas continued growth of the council sector, despite the policy of sales, tended to require an increase in flexibility of allocation (to compensate for reduced opportunities in the privately rented sector), council house sales directly reduced management flexibility, taking better properties out of the city council's ownership (Murie, 1975, p. 91). In relation to movement *within*, as well as into and out of the council's stock, the policy acted as a brake on attempts to increase mobility and develop sensitive management strategies; this affected those who were still waiting to get into the council sector, by reducing the number of 'relets' available each year, and altered the balance between types of property. The policy continued to operate even after Labour took control of the city council; due to the 'pipeline effect' a record number of houses was sold in 1972, with an increasing proportion being newer properties. Subsequently, the policy was reversed by the Labour administration.

By 1970 the council was responsible for large numbers of inter-war and post-war estates throughout the middle and outer rings of the city. More important in terms of inner city housing, the council was now the landlord of the redeveloped inner core, with the first phase of the programme virtually complete and work ongoing in the second generation of comprehensive redevelopment areas (Fig. 3.2).

Throughout the 1960s there was gradual extension of acquisition into those areas where the council intended to undertake comprehensive redevelopment but where compulsory purchase orders had not yet been made. A steady trickle of older housing, adjacent to slum clearance areas, was thus coming into municipal control. Progress was being made on slum clearance and housebuilding in the late 1960s, but this often meant that acquired property was let to homeless families who would otherwise have been allocated to a hostel or

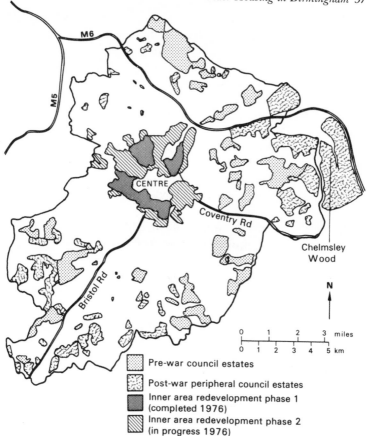

Fig. 3.2 Birmingham: the development of council housing (pre-1974 city boundary). (*Source:* City of Birmingham Planning Department)

'half way house' (Sutcliffe and Smith, 1974, p. 246). Such acquisition extended beyond even these areas in the second phase of the redevelopment programme, however, and there was the possibility that, once again, the amount of city owned slum property would begin to increase.

The Conservative group in power in the late 1960s, however, was opposed to increasing the authority's involvement in the housing market. There was constant debate about the ratio of local authority housebuilding to private development, as well as concern over the costs of such activities. Rather than increase public ownership they sought ways to *reduce* it. In addition to the sale of council houses, the

Conservatives planned to slow down the rate of acquisition of older property. They wanted to preserve inner area owner-occupation and slow down the decline of the private landlord.

The private sector—landlordism and the marginal owner-occupier
Whilst the proportion of households renting from private landlords had been declining since the First World War, the process accelerated during the 1960s. The proportion had, of course, fallen dramatically when the city council compulsorily purchased the first five redevelopment areas, but after relative stability during the 1950s not only did the proportion decline at an accelerating rate, but the absolute amount of privately rented accommodation plummeted.

Table 3.2   Tenure by household in HAAs and selected GIAs (proposed and declared)

Tenure	Housing action areas		General improv. areas		HAAs and GIAs		City totals	
	Total	%	Total	%	Total	%	Total	%
Owner occupied	6,550	39	14,000	49	20,550	45	141,050	42
Rented from local authority	2,250	13	4,700	16	6,950	15	127,600	38
Privately rented:								
furnished	4,350	26	6,700	23	11,050	24	45,350	14
unfurnished	3,650	22	3,450	12	7,100	16	19,600	6
Total	16,800	100	28,850	100	45,650	100	333,600	100

(*Source:* 1971 Census, ED data.)

The 1971 census revealed a pattern of ownership adjacent to the redevelopment areas which was substantially different from the city average (see Table 3.2). Municipal ownership was low comprising both pockets of pre-war infill, replacement of bomb damaged properties and small redevelopment projects; there was relatively little acquired property. Improvement policy was still oriented towards voluntary improvement by owners, with no immediate prospect of acquisition by the city council in order to improve. The band of neighbourhoods selected as suitable for GIA or 'Renewal Area' declaration was characterised more by an increase in owner-occupation, the residual elements of private landlordism (frequently in the form of multiple occupation) and, increasingly after 1970, housing association activity.

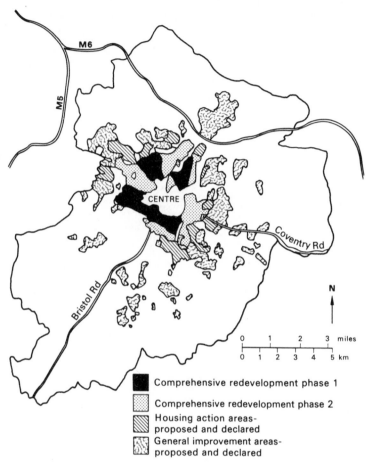

Fig. 3.3   Birmingham: housing redevelopment and improvement, 1976 (pre-1974 city boundary). (*Source:* City of Birmingham Planning Department.)

The ring of enumeration districts (EDs) which comprised the bulk of the originally scheduled renewal areas* and most of the proposed GIAs is shown in Fig. 3.3. We have omitted including a number of GIAs which we can roughly term the 'outer improvement areas' as these tend to have much lower levels of housing stress than any of

---

*The ED analysis was conducted in the summer of 1976 by which time the term 'Renewal Areas' had been dropped and the city council was programming activity in terms of GIAs and HAAs. We selected EDs to correspond most closely with HAAs and GIAs, though the former cover very similar areas to the previous renewal areas.

the 'inner improvement areas'. Most of these outer areas were not scheduled for declaration until well into the life of the urban renewal policy.

It is immediately apparent from Table 3.2 that these neighbourhoods had very high proportions of households renting privately, as well as a substantial amount of owner-occupation (although this was lower in the renewal areas). We should also note that the majority of properties were built before the First World War and, with the

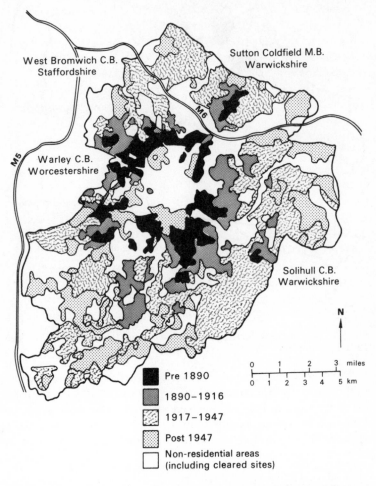

Fig. 3.4 Birmingham: age and distribution of dwellings, 1971 (pre-1974 local authorities). (*Source:* City of Birmingham Planning Department, 1973.)

exception of some previously free-standing village centres, these areas comprised the bulk of the city's older housing (see Fig. 3.4).

This ring of older housing, then, contained about 60 per cent of all households renting privately in the city, as well as the bulk of older owner-occupied property. Further, it comprised *poorer* older housing and the bulk of low income private renting. There was, indeed, other pre-1919 housing in areas such as Moseley, Harborne and Edg-baston, but it was predominantly of a different size, quality and condition; even such areas, too, had their share of private tenants, but typically these were from different social class positions than the tenants of Sparkbrook, Balsall Heath, Saltley, Handsworth or Aston.

The privately rented sector was becoming increasingly polarised throughout the 1960s. First, in social terms, it was possible to identify an impoverished group of tenants, excluded both by income and access to finance from owner-occupation and also from council housing being either ineligible for consideration or still low down on the waiting list. These tenants sharply contrasted with better-off tenants of purpose built or converted high quality property at higher rent in Edgbaston or Harborne. With the rapid growth of student numbers, another category of tenant emerged which many landlords particularly favoured—they were mobile, willing to live at high densities and unlikely to seek security of tenure. Often students were directly in competition with less advantaged groups in the areas of most acute housing stress, in Balsall Heath and Handsworth, as well as forming distinctive student markets in parts of Selly Oak, Edgbaston, Aston and Erdington.

A major feature of the change in the privately rented sector during the 1960s was the growth in multiple occupation, particularly in districts where council policy was aimed both at control over the numbers of multi-occupied houses and their location. In the mid 1960s Birmingham sought additional powers to strengthen its policy and, under the Birmingham Corporation Act 1965, most private owners of multi-occupied houses had to register with the city council.

At the end of 1972 it was estimated that in the areas affected by the urban renewal policy, there were some 2,700 houses *registered* in multi-occupation—2,000 in general improvement and 700 in renewal areas (Millar, 1972, p. 210). The total number of houses in multiple occupation was certainly larger than this as some owners had evaded the 1965 Act by failing to register their dwellings. In addition, other dwellings which would count as multi-occupied under the housing acts were not registrable under the scheme.

In many ways the council's approach was caught up in a crucial contradiction—the growth of multiple occupation was frequently the source of complaints from established residents, but it was a *necessary* development for meeting certain kinds of housing need. The declining privately rented sector was the repository of those ineligible, or still waiting for council accommodation and unable to afford owner-occupation. If the city council had actively pursued its stated policies of control and enforced the housing acts, then many families would have been evicted and become the *de facto* responsibility of the city council. A large proportion of those who would have been so displaced were black, and the growth of multi-occupation was frequently linked with issues of race relations and immigration.

Rex and Moore (1967) have already emphasised the effect of structural processes at work in the housing market which, combined with local authority housing eligibility and allocation criteria, concentrated newcomers to the city in twilight area lodging houses. They argued that the second phase of comprehensive redevelopment *deliberately* avoided concentrations of immigrants, thus obviating the need to rehouse large numbers of blacks (op. cit., p. 35). This, however, left undecided the future of such areas. Theoretically, the local authority was 'policing' the growth of multi-occupation, but strict application of its policies would also result in a rapid increase in the number of black families rehoused. This, correspondingly, would have meant fewer families rehoused from other categories of need. It is difficult in practice to discern the extent to which there was a calculated avoidance of areas of multiple occupation.

A leading Conservative committee chairman from their late 1960s administration claimed that the shift from redevelopment was *not* a product of the problems of rehousing from areas of multiple occupation, although he conceded to us that it was a 'convenient by-product'.*

He also made the link between the growth of multi-occupation and immigration. When asked specifically about the kinds of problems caused by the growth in multiple occupation, he suggested that the greatest exploiters of tenants were West Indians, Pakistanis and Indians, who 'came from dreadful conditions to what they thought of as fantastic conditions'. Most important, he suggested that rigid enforcement of the public policies was, in practice, undesirable, as many more people would have to be rehoused. There

---

*In an interview with the authors.

were, of course, many prosecutions and the Pakistani Welfare Association representing landlords, was frequently at odds with the public (now environmental) health department.

The structural point, however, remains: those 'pariah' landlords who let poor accommodation, overcrowded and underserviced, actually helped the city council maintain its claim to be solving the housing problem. First, they provided accommodation (of a sort) to those excluded from the dominant form of desirable tenure. Second, they could be blamed for *causing* the problem of which they were also themselves victims (Rex and Moore, op. cit., especially chapter 5). We should not want to romanticise about the many bad landlords, to minimise the unpleasantness or obscure the instances of malicious exploitation. Rather, we emphasise that this kind of landlordism is a symptom of the problem, and could exist only in conditions of general shortage or inequitable relations of ownership and control of housing.

It is difficult to obtain comparative data for changes in the extent of owner-occupation in older areas, but it is evident from Table 3.2 that the level of owner-occupation in such areas was remarkably similar to that in the city as a whole. Indeed, even in the worst areas there was a substantial minority of owner-occupiers. Many, however, might be thought of as 'marginal' owner-occupiers; their status being determined by the continued availability of cheap, usually, therefore, old housing for sale. Many older terraced houses had gone from the privately rented sector into owner-occupation, often as the result of sale to sitting tenants. Others were sold at the termination of a tenancy, often by the death of the tenant.

For many of these owners, their property has had the effect of tying them to an area. Too old or on too low an income to get a mortgage elsewhere, and ineligible for local authority housing, they were rarely able to leave. They became owner-occupiers relatively late in their lives, the opportunity being produced by their particular status as protected tenants and the poor investment that their houses represented to their landlords.

Many other new owners, including those from the New Commonwealth, were also marginal in the sense that they were excluded from other forms of tenure (by local authority eligibility criteria and discrimination from private landlords) and unable to purchase better, newer property (both on income grounds and through discrimination). As Valerie Karn has argued on the basis of her research on immigrant owner-occupation in Birmingham:

Considering their relatively modest incomes and the extent of their family commitments, the people who bought in Saltley, Soho and Sparkhill might have been expected to rent or at least to have tried to rent. There has, in the past, been considerable difference of opinion between academics as to whether Asians and West Indians buy because they prefer to own rather than rent, or because they are unable to rent and so are forced to buy. To polarise the argument in this way is in itself a distortion . . . their very choices are constrained without their necessarily being aware of it, and many choices are unconsciously made on negative rather than positive grounds.

The crucial point is that Asians and West Indians have predominantly moved into the inner cities at a time when the housing there is changing from renting to owner-occupation. In particular, each vacant property that appears is likely to be sold rather than let. Far from being able to swim against this tide, they are in many respects even more vulnerable than the indigenous population to the type of pressure which is producing the switch to owning.

(Karn, 1976, pp. 27–8)

Other owner-occupiers, of course, represented the kind of 'first-time buyer' that are conventionally expected to 'move up the ladder'. For them, usually young childless families, an older terraced house was the first step towards suburban owner-occupation.

All groups of owners, however, were affected in one way or another by changes in the structure of Birmingham's housing market during the 1960s and by the policies pursued by the city council. Owner-occupation remained a major and, in some areas, growing form of tenure. The first redevelopment areas, which the city council had acquired shortly after the war, predominantly consisting of privately rented accommodation, had effectively become vast municipalised slums before clearance. Areas that became included in the 'second phase' of the redevelopment programme, and many other neighbourhoods adjacent to them, contained housing not just of more mixed quality, but with more complicated tenure and social structures.

In the main, however, the latter were areas of local authority neglect. With the end of the second phase of redevelopment (theoretically at least) in sight, and the attempted implementation of the Housing Act 1969 with its emphasis on 'improvement', these were the areas within which the next chapter of Birmingham's urban renewal story was to be written.

Older Housing in Birmingham 1970–76

All attempts to evaluate processes of change within local housing markets are bedevilled by the lack of readily available information. In areas of housing stress census data may be out of date even before it is published. Local authority records, if carefully and systematically organised, may contain much valuable information but pose problems over issues of confidentiality or over the sheer time and effort involved in working through disparate and often badly organised raw data. Private institutions operating in the housing market are notoriously reluctant to release any but the most global aggregate information (Williams, 1976), and many of the 'fringe' private sector 'operators' thrive in a climate of secrecy and even deception.

Sub-markets

With owner-occupation there were signs pointing to the existence of at least one major differentiating factor discriminating against much older housing, namely the availability of mortgages from building societies. In addition, private renting was largely confined to older property, certainly houses in multiple occupation are almost entirely confined to the pre-1914 stock. The majority of acquired council owned property, too, was to be found in older areas.

Whilst there were indications, then, that the combination of public policies and private investment had produced distinctive, spatially structured patterns of housing opportunity, it would be misleading to think of these as fixed in any way. The pattern of opportunities that existed during the early 1970s in Birmingham was both relatively recent as well as substantially unstable. Much depended on council policies, which could have the effect (through redevelopment) of removing these patterns entirely, though they might, of course, also have the effect of 'moving them on'. Some areas, perhaps nearer Birmingham University, might even be candidates for 'gentrification' as house prices rose generally and the cost of commuting increased. Crucially, areas of older housing were in need of greater maintenance than the majority of the more recent stock. Without improvement, every indication was that this older property would continue to deteriorate.

At the same time, there was wide diversity both within and between areas of older housing. In some areas this took the form of a slow gradation in quality, radiating outward. In other areas there were sharp contrasts between poor older housing and nearby areas of substantial, albeit older housing, often still in single family residence. The contrasts between Balsall Heath and nearby Moseley or Rotton Park and Harborne illustrated such distinctions vividly even to the casual observer.

Rather than think in terms of sub-markets (Harvey, 1974; Duncan, 1974) with their implied geographical base, we decided to focus on processes of change and explore these in greater depth. Such processes, naturally enough, were apparent to, even if not fully understood by, local residents and their elected representatives.

In particular, the Birmingham Labour Party set out its intentions in the manifesto for the 1972 local elections: 'A strategy for progressively renewing the older areas of our city will be undertaken . . . it is hoped to concentrate on improvement, only redeveloping where it is absolutely necessary.'

This, however, begged questions about the processes affecting such areas, and about the ways in which the inner areas might have been expected to change anyway. A city-wide decline in house-building was rapidly becoming apparent, slowing down the redevelopment programme, with a consequent increase in the council's housing waiting list. By 1973, council house building had slumped from the 1967 record of 8,500 to 1,500 completions. Private house building had fallen almost as rapidly, and house prices for both new and older property had sharply increased. At the same time the decay of the inner areas continued, and the viability of any form of investment there remained uncertain.

Areas such as Balsall Heath, Handsworth, Saltley and Sparkbrook had clearly been changing in character since the middle 1950s. Older residents typically referred to neighbourhoods having 'gone down' as their neighbours left to be replaced by newcomers whom they could not relate to. Large properties were subdivided, often illegally, into bedsits; the stable working class community appeared to be disintegrating around them.

Often by the early 1970s older areas contained elements of Mellor's second and third kind of area side-by-side (Chap. 2 pp. 13 to 14), the status variations between streets, which on a cursory glance might appear identical, being carefully preserved. Some areas were in the process of being transformed from white twilight areas into black ones: for example parts of Saltley, so well described by the local Community Development Project, exactly fitted this category.

Some areas of older housing, particularly those spatially removed from existing redevelopment areas, were inhabited by settled, often ageing populations, which still merited a description as in Mellor's second kind of area. These were not unlike Norman Dennis' beloved Millfield in Sunderland, established patterns of relationships were highly valued, as was location relatively near to city centre. In Birmingham parts of Small Heath or Selly Oak were like this.

For our purposes, the most important points are the increasing diversity to be found in and between many areas, their transitional status and the processes which both cause and are a product of these changes.

The most visible change occurring was residential ethnic segregation. In Birmingham, as throughout the Midlands, there were signs during the 1960s of substantial racial discrimination. Ken Newton (1976) drawing on earlier work by Rex and Moore (1967, pp. 218–9), argued that 'the zones of transition shared by whites and coloured people alike, turn out over the longer run to be developed into ghetto-like areas which are losing their white population and rapidly gaining coloured people'. The areas that Newton mentioned were among those areas featured in the urban renewal policy: Handsworth, Soho, Sparkbrook and Rotton Park.

The extent to which fears of 'ghettoisation' may be countered by the strength of the internal solidarity within immigrant communities is doubtful. First, there were signs that, particularly amongst second generation West Indians, family ties were frequently breaking down. Whilst many Asian communities exhibited patterns of mutual assistance which in many ways resembled the model of the classic English working class community, such communities, paradoxically, frequently also became subjects of abuse and objects, even, of fear. Seabrook's insightful comments illustrate this point in his discussion of the role of immigrants in Blackburn:

> It was ironical that the very things which the townspeople object to in the immigrants are precisely those aspects of the old communal working-class way of life that used to be considered so valuable—the sense of community, the system of mutual help, the sense of duty to kinsfolk, and the extended family structure. In their often vengeful and punitive attitude towards the immigrants, it is as though the working class were confronted by a spectre of their own past which they are anxious to banish.
>
> *(Seabrook, 1971, p. 49)*

Valerie Karn's research in Saltley, Soho and Sparkhill has shown that the vast majority of people who bought homes during the previous two years in these areas were Asians. As vacancies arose, it was rare for a white purchaser to move in; rather, white people seemed to move out faster as black people moved in. She suggested that, whilst not accompanied by institutionalised 'block busting' as in the US, 'white flight' was part of a rapid process of racial change (Karn, 1976).

Just as visible as changes in skin colour was the process of physical blight and obsolescence. Repairs, particularly in the privately rented sector, were usually kept to a minimum; many owner-occupiers simply could afford to do no more than the absolute minimum.

Throughout the middle ring, but particularly in some notorious areas, prostitution became an everyday fact of life. Deeply offensive to both 'respectable' whites and immigrants, blatant soliciting and accompanying organised protection services added to the general sense of neighbourhood decline. Council services were a source of frequent complaint; bins were not emptied regularly, street sweepers rarely seen. Repairs to road surfaces and pavements were the subject of major local campaigns. There was little evidence that the city council saw any future other than clearance or neglect for these areas.

It was officially estimated that in 1972 there were still at least 15,000 houses statutorily unfit in Birmingham. In 1971 there were still 26,000 households without a hot water tap. As the housing section of the city's structure plan *Written Statement* pointed out, the worst housing conditions were concentrated in certain inner and middle ring areas.

So far we have described the effects of the process of obsolescence, rather than sought to explain its causes. Whatever their original quality, houses require some level of maintenance at all times and an increasing level of maintenance, including major repairs and improvements, as time goes on. Thus, in one sense, all houses can have indefinite lives, so long as their owners consider it worthwhile to invest in their upkeep and repair. At the most simple level of analysis, many property owners in Birmingham's inner and middle rings decided that such investment was not worthwhile. Others, often owner-occupiers of small properties, had not been able to afford the necessary levels of work, particularly as for many years their property was not considered suitable for grant aided assistance. Many 'marginal' owner-occupiers, on low incomes with proportionately high housing costs and often with large families, had to defer any thought of further expenditure on their houses.

The extent to which any investment was worthwhile in terms of increased house value was also uncertain. For many residents this was not very important—they expected to remain where they were for the rest of their lives and so exchange value did not count in their calculations. But it *was* a critical consideration for those institutions which mediate property exchange, and for private landlords in their investment decisions.

Closely related to population loss or changes in the structure of neighbourhood populations is the process of neighbourhood economic decline. As established communities moved out, shops and jobs moved out also. But it has not been a process internal to the inner areas: public policies on shopping have facilitated the growth of central and outer suburban shopping districts financed by private investment. Whilst employment in Birmingham was relatively abundant during the 1960s, workers increasingly had to commute either into central industrial areas or to the peripheral industrial estates. There was some local revival, as thriving Asian communities established their own shops and small production units. Ironically, these usually contributed to the growing alienation of longer established white residents.

From mid 1973 onwards, however, there were increasing signs that economic decline was affecting inner areas in more significant ways, with major long term implications. Symptoms were not so much the loss of jobs locally as the replacement of skilled workers by unskilled in the same neighbourhood, which correspondingly increased the probability of unemployment.

It should not be assumed that industries located in the inner areas necessarily provided work for local people, as many small inner city firms employed substantial numbers of workers from outside their neighbourhoods. High unemployment in inner areas resulted from the relationship between housing and job markets: the residents of such areas were typically there for housing market reasons, but were affected by city-wide job availability. Usually dependent on public transport, with high proportions of unskilled and semi-skilled workers, during the last few years unemployment levels would have risen in inner areas *regardless* of the closure of local plants.

At the same time, youth unemployment was disproportionately high in both older areas and inner council estates, particularly among young blacks. This factor, combined with unemployment amongst older workers created a situation where certain areas combined both lower than average incomes, poor older housing and the likelihood of continued or increasing structurally determined unemployment above the national average. Since 1970 this has been, in broad terms, an increasingly critical aspect of life in areas of older housing.

The short lease problem

Many houses built in Birmingham during the latter part of the nineteenth century were originally offered on long leases (usually ninety-nine years) at a ground rent. By 1970 many leases had nearly run out and occupiers anticipated the time when they would become the weekly tenant of the freeholder. Short leases created three main problems for an improvement programme. First, local authorities could not allow applications for improvement grants where leases were shorter than five years. Such dwellings were not likely to be improved, therefore, at least until the lease had expired and the freeholder had assumed full ownership rights. Secondly, lease-holders nearing the expiration of their tenancies, even though grant aid was available, were unlikely to contemplate spending their own capital on a house which would belong to the landlord once the lease was expired. Thirdly, many leaseholders would require a mortgage to meet their share of improvement costs and most mortgagees were unwilling to lend to someone with a short interest in a dwelling. Those that would, often charged high interest rates. Furthermore, local authorities were prohibited by law from granting mortgages unless all repayments could be made within ten years of the expiry of the lease.

Difficulties also affected those who had purchased the freehold interest of their property. Many had used up their only capital in this purchase and had none left to meet their share of improvement costs. Many who had borrowed money to enfranchise the freehold faced a level of repayments (perhaps together with those on a loan taken out to finance their purchase of the leasehold interest) which would prohibit them from borrowing further sums to finance the cost of improvement.

There were further difficulties connected with the leasehold issue. Many of these have been highlighted by the Birmingham Community Development Project (CDP) as part of their work in Saltley. Through contacts with local residents, CDP staff witnessed many of the consequences of the leasehold problem on the financial position of many tenants in their area (see, Green, 1975). Their work, too, focused on the workings of the Leasehold Reform Act 1967 and the way in which land owners and their advisers effectively prevented leaseholders from exercising their rights to purchase the freehold interest in their property. Under the Act, most leaseholders could buy their freehold or extend their lease for fifty years *as of right* if the lease was originally granted for over twenty-one years, the rateable value of the dwelling was not more than £200 (£400 in Greater London) as at 23 March 1965 and the leaseholder had occupied the house as his only or main residence for the previous five years or for a total of five years of the previous ten. The Act thus denied recent leaseholders the right to purchase or extend their lease so their only hope of buying was by voluntary negotiation with the freeholder who could, of course, refuse to sell.

The CDP discovered that leaseholders who qualified under the Act were experiencing difficulties in exercising their rights. First, freeholders were often uncooperative and refused to respond to notices served on them by leaseholders intending to purchase the freehold. Second, many solicitors were unwilling to act for lease-holders or were quick to abandon their efforts to assist him to purchase once difficulties were encountered. Third, many would-be purchasers were deterred by the cost of enfranchisement. Lease-holders were in a weak position in relation to the freeholder. He could name his own price; the shorter the lease the more he could demand. Many original freeholders and their successors had granted leases to others and so there could be, beneath the freeholder, a chain of interests—a head leaseholder and a number of under-leaseholders all of whom also had to be paid for a resident to become a freeholder. In addition to the cost of buying the interest, lease-holders would have to pay the costs of their own solicitor and valuer as well as fees of those employed by the holders of the other interests, including the freeholder, greatly inflating the cost of purchase.

Under the Leasehold Reform Act 1967, if a leaseholder and a freeholder failed to agree a price for the freehold, the former could apply to the Lands Tribunal to fix the amount. However, the CDP discovered further problems. Gaining access to the Tribunal was costly because of the lawyer's time spent in arguing his client's case; thus, if recourse to the Tribunal was necessary, this added to the costs of purchase, deterring more people from taking action. Unless several leaseholders shared the same freeholder and could jointly sponsor the making of one application to the Tribunal to provide a 'test case', many leaseholders would be effectively denied their rights.

Most of the CDP's work related to Saltley but short leases were also to be found in other parts of the city. One neighbourhood in particular, eventually declared a GIA, was singled out by the council as an area where the problem was particularly marked. In the mid-1960s, the area's major freeholder had approached the council with a view to selling its interest. The council agreed to purchase but was thwarted by central government which did not provide loan sanction due to cuts in public expenditure. A full survey of the area had not been carried out so the extent of the short lease problem was not fully known but council officers knew that many houses only had between four and twenty years remaining on the leases—later plans for comprehensive house improvement were therefore severely constrained.

Institutions, Organisations and Older Housing

In terms of the housing market, and its sub-divisions, the most striking feature to emerge from our discussion of Birmingham's twilight areas is their *complexity* compared to the dominant form of tenures: suburban owner-occupation and the municipal stock.

Access to council housing, and transfers within the stock, are complicated (see Lambert *et al*, 1978), but despite differences between estates in terms of status and amenities, the essential unity of tenure position parallels that of the other major form of housing, owner-occupation. Again, regarding the latter, there are important variations in quality, levels of provision and accessibility, further complicated in part by leasehold interests. But the dominant route of access to owner-occupation is through mortgage finance from building societies. Some properties are bought outright, others inherited, and local authorities (particularly during the early 1970s) have played an important role; but the building societies are still the major institution controlling access to owner-occupation, particularly for the purchase of new housing (Williams, 1976).

The growth of council housing in Birmingham in the later 1960s and continued new private building both within Birmingham's boundaries and, most significantly, within its larger metropolitan sphere, reinforced the dominance of two major types of housing situation. These sharply contrasted with the fragmentation of proprietary interests in areas of older housing.

Birmingham's urban renewal policy was based on the assumption that retention and improvement strategies were cheaper, more humane and sensitive ways of approaching problems of housing shortage and decay. But success in this depended to a considerable degree on the cooperation of both private owners and the institutions concerned with financing and controlling the private housing market. If owners did not wish or were unable to improve their properties, the council might have to become engaged in a much more complicated process, involving the use of compulsory improvement and repair procedures or the threat and use of compulsory purchase.

The viability of any renewal policy based on attempts to influence private owners, then, would be crucially affected by the attitude and policies of those institutions which control investment in housing, in particular the building societies. For, without access to finance to facilitate property exchange and contribute towards improvement costs, even with the far reaching claims of Birmingham's urban renewal policy, it was unlikely that confidence could be reborn, and improvement as a policy might have been merely a short term stopgap pending comprehensive redevelopment at some future date. Thus we contacted a cross-section of building societies operating in Birmingham, in order to understand better their 'normal' activities with regard to older housing, and, specifically, the ways in which their policies and practices were affected by the switch in council policy from redevelopment to improvement (Lambert, 1976).

Recent studies in Lambeth, Islington, Newcastle and Loughborough have confirmed the view that building societies avoid lending in inner city areas (Harloe *et al.*, 1974; Williams, 1976; Boddy, 1976; Ford, 1975). Their caution in lending to lower income groups and on older or unconventional types of property resulted from their financial structure, their history, their recruitment policies and internal organisation, all of which continued to reinforce a distinctive ideology and way of perceiving potential clients. An area of profitable 'gentrification', such as Islington, was clearly an exception but, even there, changes in building society policy were slow and apparently did not entail a complete change of view—the two storeyed new suburban house remained the safest bet.

We did not expect building society behaviour to be very different in Birmingham. Valerie Karn's work on owner-occupation in immigrant areas had involved a study of the financing of recent house purchasing in three inner areas. This showed that only in one area, Sparkhill, which contained more English and Irish families and less Asians than the other two areas, did building societies make as many as 36 per cent of recent loans. In Saltley and Soho, the societies lent on 7 per cent and 10 per cent of purchases respectively and the clearing banks were the most important sources of mortgages. The local authority lent to 20 per cent of purchasers in Soho but on only 8 per cent and 12 per cent in Saltley and Sparkhill (Karn, 1975). Clearly, whilst there were local variations, building society investment was minimal in these areas.

During the course of our interviews with building society managers, we were told that they were guided in their attitude to neighbourhoods and specific properties in them by the professional advice of chartered surveyors. It was, therefore, decided that additional interviews be sought with a selection of surveyors working in estate agent offices to examine their relationship with the building societies, and their understanding of trends in the private market and of the likely effect of local authority attempts at renewal.

Little work has been published on estate agents in Britain. There is little evidence of American style 'blockbusting', though Elizabeth Burney (1967) suggested that some estate agents actively steered black purchasers away from certain areas by giving false information. Stuart Hatch (1973) attempted to establish the extent to which discriminatory instructions from vendors were accepted by estate agents operating in the older areas of Bristol. Despite conflicting data, he concluded that estate agents were not powerless intermediaries, acting only on behalf of their clients (a view they liked to project), but that they played an active role interfering in the processes of supply and demand.

Peter Williams, in his work in Islington, also agreed with this interpretation, seeing them as important actors in the 'gentrification' of the area, persuading building societies to become more involved, encouraging the trend in rising prices, at least partly as a means to earning higher commissions. The most active salesmen were the newer 'entrepreneurial' agents who went out of their way to advertise the attractions of the neighbourhood and to persuade existing landlords and owners to sell (Williams, 1976). The less legal activities of agents who forced tenants out of property in order to sell with vacant possession for renovation has been described elsewhere (see, for instance, Counter Information Services, 1973).

Estate agents can also act as 'filters', facilitating or restricting individual or group access to building society funds (Harloe *et al.*, 1974; Ford, 1975). In their capacity as surveyors, however, and in combination with policies of building societies, estate agents can play a crucial role in the 'redlining' of inner areas, fundamentally affecting subsequent investment opportunities in such areas.

Building societies, surveyors, and Birmingham's older housing

The building society managers, who represented a cross-section from local branches of big national societies, through regional societies down to small local societies, conformed very much to the established model. They were unanimously cautious about lending on older property, particularly in extensive areas of old working class housing. Some managers explicitly acknowledged that whole neighbourhoods were excluded from consideration.

Their explanation for this policy emphasised the lack of security in such areas and, they claimed, the limited demand for dwellings (at least, compared with more suburban areas); they also worried about the effects of redevelopment and other local authority action. Older areas housed poorer, riskier people, more likely to be unemployed during times of economic difficulty. One manager summed up their attitude:

> Both individuals and property in the older areas are poorer risks. Ultimately the solution to not losing money is good property . . . the problem in Birmingham is that here is a modern affluent city with thousands and thousands of houses built since the Second World War. Money is always limited—then how much more sense it is to lend it on those modern houses rather than in the riskier areas.

The building society managers claimed to rely heavily on their surveyors' advice about the marketability of property. If 'redlining' occurred, they suggested, this was determined by the advice of surveyors who, the managers stressed, knew the city and the various housing markets much better than they did. In cases of doubt they would defer to a surveyor's advice.

Several managers suggested that surveyors were possibly over-cautious, thereby preventing people from buying property which might well turn out to be good security. However, they stressed that the surveyor had to be certain about the future market and the possibility of resale as he had a professional reputation to lose if things went wrong. Most managers were happy to let the surveyors take the decisions. The interviews with surveyors, however, revealed a somewhat different picture, for it became clear that both groups shared a conception of the relative merit of investment on older property. Surveyors and building society managers alike had a similar picture of property and people in terms of market risks.

The surveyors agreed with the building society managers that houses in the older areas were poor risks because of 'limited demand' (mainly from coloured immigrants and others who could raise their own finance and from housing associations) and because of the uncertainties created by local authority involvement in these areas.

One said that building societies did stipulate certain areas where they would not lend and that these were 'where the city's plans have been changed in the past, where they fear they may be involved in slum clearance, where there's risk' and went on through much of the rest of the interview to talk about the uncertainty created by local authority action. Another distinguished the 'twilight' areas of Balsall Heath, Sparkbrook and Handsworth, where there was little building society lending, from the 'fringe' areas a little further out, where 'better' properties might be eligible. Several pointed out that it was normal practice for the societies to clamp down on older areas when funds were low and that this was sensible management of investors' money.

The surveyors, then, had a clear idea of building society policy as it related to areas of Birmingham, but this was not the result of explicit instructions. Rather, it was built up from the experience both of trying to get finance for clients wanting to buy, as most had an agency with a particular society, and from observing that they received few instructions to survey housing in older areas. This, of course, was part of the vicious circle referred to by one surveyor: because building societies did not lend on houses in those areas, they were no longer readily saleable; because they were no longer readily saleable, they were not good security; and because they were not good security, then surveyors did not recommend them for a loan. No surveyor went on to argue that building society finance should be more readily available in order to break this cycle. Only one stated explicitly that the ease of borrowing money on a particular property was a factor to be considered when making a valuation. Most seemed to hold, in other words, a conception of 'demand' and 'desirability' which was in some way independent of the availability of finance for purchase.

What emerged clearly from our discussions, therefore, was that building society managers and surveyors tended to share definitions about 'good' and 'bad' areas. It would be misleading to see this as a deliberate conspiracy. Rather, the two groups shared a consensus because of their concern for the maintenance of values and their views about 'rational' behaviour in the housing market. This had the result that both could say that the other set the definitions. The managers claimed to rely on surveyors since, in practice, all property for which a loan is required had to be surveyed by a professionally trained man, and the surveyors who did this work were themselves handling property transactions and knew current prices. In their valuation work, they had some influence in turning managers for or against a property, but ultimately it was the building society manager who granted or withheld the money. On the other hand, surveyors were rarely asked to survey property which fell into the 'unsafe' category as far as the societies were concerned, and they were not likely to disagree fundamentally over what this category meant. So, only on 'borderline' cases did surveyors have any real influence, and these formed a minute proportion of all building society mortgages.

Valuations were supposedly based on the actual prices at which houses changed hands. All of the surveyors stressed that they were making comparisons between different properties which they had seen and allowing for differences between them. They stressed, too, the imprecision of the process and the extent to which it relied on their own fund of experience built up over the years:

> There are only two factors to be taken into account when doing valuations, supply and demand, and our own experience. It's not something you can learn from a textbook, or quickly, it takes at least five years.

And again:

> Valuation is purely and simply a matter of experience and comparability and requires a large degree of instinct or acquired knowledge . . . it's all a question of opinion, there's no fact about it.

In practice, however, surveyors used a check list, beginning with the dwelling's condition and facilities, including environment and location of the house and the existence of plans for development or road widening. These latter factors were actually more crucial in determining value than the style, size and state of the property itself, so that the 'same' house in Balsall Heath would fetch far less than its twin in Harborne. 'You can't divorce a house from its location. A house is where it is in a road in a district . . . You know your district, you stand back and look at it . . . In a sense it's so much part of your make-up that you're not conscious of doing it, but unquestionably you do it instinctively.' It seemed to be a well-worn adage in the surveying profession that, 'the best house in a road is the worst to sell, and the poorest house is the easiest to sell because the road lifts it'.

The impression gained from our discussion was that the job of a surveyor was not to look for the positive aspects of a property, but always to look for negative factors which might endanger its value in either the near or the more distant future. For example, one of the textbooks on valuation gives the following advice on mortgage valuations: 'The valuer should err on the side of safety when making his valuation, for it is likely that, if the power of sale has to be exercised, it will be at a time when conditions are unfavourable . . . (he) must always look to the worst possibilities, for the lender on mortgage can never profit by any enhancement of value which may occur in the security, but he may lose by depreciation' (Mustoe, Eve and Anstey, 1960). Road widening plans, for instance, might or might not happen, but the assumption is that they would be carried out. This stress on negative factors was stronger in valuing older property in the inner areas, which was approached with the assumption that there would be problems. Newer suburban areas, almost by definition, were going to be safer but, even there, the surveyor needed to check whether there might be any indications that the value would not be maintained.

Surveyors claimed to assess 'the market price' for each particular property. They saw the housing market, however, as being divided into different sources of demand with the result that different areas appealed to various population groups. Most frequently mentioned were Handsworth for West Indians and Asians, and Sparkhill for the Irish. The valuers agreed that these differential appeals explained price variations, but maintained that, for each area, there would be a top price which reflected willingness and ability to pay, although their confidence in the continuing strength of market levels affected the valuations they made.

The perspective on older housing shared by building society managers and surveyors was conservative and cautious, and had been nurtured in them throughout their careers. The managers were imbued with an ethic of safe investment which enabled them to regard the financing of mainly newer housing as the only fair course open to them given the trust of their investors. The surveyors had been taught to fear the worst and assume that, unless there were absolutely no signs to the contrary, values and house prices might not be sustained. For both, the older areas spelt potential trouble;

the combined effect was to 'redline' vast tracts of Birmingham's inner areas and to exclude many properties within the line from funds. We have sought to illustrate the effect of 'redlining' graphically, based on these interviews and on maps we were shown by different building society managers. As Fig. 3.5 shows, whilst not every property was ruled out, all of Birmingham's HAA programme had come to be included within the redline, as were many of Birmingham's GIAs.

This finding should give rise to little surprise; after all, building societies have never been substantially involved in these areas. When they were first developed (before 1914) the dominant form of tenure was private renting. The growth of building societies since the 1930s did not result in their involvement in pre-1914 property, rather they focused on new property, and that emphasis has been maintained. Clearly, during the 1950s and 1960s, many mortgages were granted on older property, facilitating the process whereby landlords sold their stock into owner-occupation. But that was the exception. It was the growth of marginal owner-occupation of properties with lower investment potential (and, the possibility of relative negative investment potential) which was the innovation.

In his useful introductory essay on building societies and owner-occupation, Martin Boddy (1976) refers to 'fringe and "irregular" mortgage finance which steps into the place of building societies in the inner city'. We see it somewhat differently, in terms of fringe and 'irregular' mortgage finance responding to a vacuum created by the withdrawal of the private landlord and to the fact that building societies do not charge differential rates of interest on properties which (whether correctly or not) they consider to represent greater risk, though they do reduce the percentage they will lend or the period over which repayment is made.

It would thus be misleading to consider 'redlining'—which undoubtedly takes place—as a positive discriminatory practice. Instead, the problem to be explained was how owner-occupation was sustained in areas which did not, and rarely ever had received any significant volume of credit from these major institutions.

Secondary sources of institutional finance—'merchants, dealers, and friends'
During our discussions with surveyors we asked them about their knowledge of, and attitudes towards, various 'fringe' estate agents and mortgage brokers. These included those without 'professional' qualifications and those who actually bought and sold property

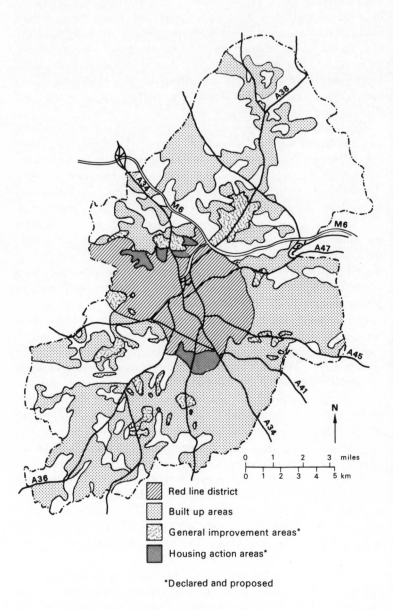

Fig. 3.5 Redline district in Birmingham and its impact on the Council's inner area improvement programme, 1976 (post-1974 city boundary). (*Source:* Discussions with building society managers and surveyors and examination of their maps.)

rather than acting simply as an intermediary. One surveyor was keen to see the registration of all agents to protect the public, but it became clear that he was thinking less of preventing exploitation of innocent customers than protecting estate agents from competition from unqualified people. Most said that they did tell people about 'fringe' sources of money when asked, but would also try to explain the pitfalls, so that it was the customer's fault if he ended up paying more than he needed. On the other hand, some considered the high interest rates justified in that the 'fringe' banks were taking more risk than conventional institutions, and filling a gap in the money market. There was agreement that it was ethically wrong to play on the ignorance of ordinary individuals about the complexities of real interest rates, and to deal in property and finance without disclosing an interest in the transaction.

Geoff Green (1976) has described the process whereby the less scrupulous estate agents, solicitors, surveyors and mortgage brokers, whom he terms 'merchant professionals', control the process of access to owner-occupation. He makes his point vividly by reference to a particular house in Saltley:

> At the beginning of 1973 the house got caught up in a system controlled by Gandhee, a Birmingham estate agent, financed by Cedar Holdings, the fringe bankers, and greased by Standard Properties (Gandhee) Brokers, together with George Mitchell Coleman, solicitors. Potential buyers, often in desperate circumstances, were seduced into the system by the offer of 100 per cent mortgages. Generally working class people do not have a solicitor and were recommended George Mitchell Coleman in Gandhee's office. Gandhee is also a broker for Cedar Holdings so it was in his interest to arrange a mortgage with them to get commission. He dissuaded buyers from using alternative funds which they may have had access to. Gandhee, George Mitchell Coleman and Cedar Holdings each made a lot of money and artificially boosted the prices of houses caught up in their system. They made money by creating unstable mortgages which led to frequent buying and selling at higher and higher prices. The system was underpinned by Cedar's willingness to lend on artificially high house values. Gandhee made his share by brokerage and estate agents' fees: George Mitchell Coleman made theirs by conveyancing fees on buying and selling: Cedar Holdings made theirs by high fixed interest rates (from 17 to 25 per cent over the last two years) and large penalty clauses (up to £750) for those who want to redeem their mortgage early.
>
> *(Green, 1976, pp. 54–5)*

The underlying forces behind this kind of arrangement were the search for profitable investment and the physical decay of the housing stock. The conjuncture of the two, in Birmingham's older areas as throughout Britain, created a situation in which the major source of profitability was to be found in the circulation and exchange of property. The profiteers were in effect 'merchant capitalists' exploiting the special nature of the local housing market:

> In the community as a whole residential property still provides income in exchange for housing services, but in certain areas— special situations the Stock Market would call them—it becomes more like a commodity for exchange.
>
> *(Green, op. cit., pp. 50–1)*

It was, however, difficult to establish the extent and importance of 'fringe' agents and finance companies on the basis of our interviews with surveyors and of Green's research in Saltley. The surveyors agreed that clearing banks had little involvement with older housing, especially after one bank had financed several deals where ownership was confused, houses changed hands rapidly and valuations had been careless. In so far as banks did loan on houses, it would only be for a short term, usually up to a maximum of ten years.

The only work available on patterns of housing finance in inner areas is Valerie Karn's study of recent purchasers (Karn, 1976). Whilst in one area nearly 50 per cent of purchasers had obtained finance from clearing banks, this was both exceptional and specific to the period 1972/3. As she explained, their lending policies changed after that period so that the clearing banks would not be expected to play such an important role.

An important finding of her work was the extent to which properties had been bought using loans from friends and relatives. The surveyors we interviewed assumed that most of the people who could manage to do this were coloured immigrants, particularly Indians and Pakistanis who would often overcrowd houses in order to charge enough rent to enable them to buy another house—the stereotype of the lodging house landlord. Although the surveyors were careful in their comments, it was obvious that they concurred with the view that such activity had a direct effect, lowering the tone and dignity of areas and discouraged white purchasers. One pointed out that many of the sales to Asians which he had managed were done through a middle man, and there was frequently confusion because reference was made to cash purchase when really the intention was to raise a mortgage. Vendors, therefore, agreed to a sale thinking it would be quicker than it turned out to be. However, on the whole, Asians seemed to have a reputation for raising money quickly and would be the majority of customers at an auction of pre-1919 houses. Another firm held a monthly sale of 'dealer-type' properties, for improvement and resale, and over the last two years, 90 per cent had gone to immigrant dealers.

Local authority mortgages
The extent to which local authority mortgage lending differed from established patterns of building society lending has been one of Karn's principal concerns. In her surveys in Saltley, Soho and Sparkhill she found a surprisingly low proportion of local authority mortgages; rapid growth in city-wide council mortgage activity in 1974 and 1975 was actually matched by a relative decline in lending on older property. Many of the council's mortgages were going to people and property that the building societies could have dealt with. She concluded that by June 1975, when central government sharply cut back on local authority mortgage lending, there was little evidence that the city council was a major source of finance for older property, although other local authorities had much heavier lending.

Housing associations and older housing
As in most cities, housing association activity grew rapidly during the early 1970s within areas of older housing. Their effect on the market was difficult to establish. Certainly, they had facilitated continued disinvestment by private landlords, but during 1975/6 about half their acquisition had been from owner-occupiers; indeed this was the only way that they could acquire with vacant possession.* Thus it can be argued that they were coming into competition with owner-occupiers—something that had never been declared policy. On the other hand, the lack of available finance for owner-occupation of older properties must be considered, and it is probable that many properties they acquired would have been difficult to sell otherwise.

Clearly, though, the extensive government support to housing associations ensured one source of continued investment in older housing which would otherwise have been lacking.

---

*Information derived from discussions with the managers of Birmingham's three largest housing associations.

Public Policy and Private Practice in the Older Housing Market

The most striking feature of the building society managers' attitude towards Birmingham's urban renewal policy, was that it was irrelevant to most aspects of their work. The future of older housing was, in their eyes, still shrouded in doubt, and local authority sponsored improvement excited little interest or enthusiasm. We met the same response when talking to surveyors, although some were prepared to admit that, in a few areas, improvement policies could be seen to be working. Both groups were ignorant of, unconcerned about or distrustful of local authority plans. Some accused the city council of attempting too much; others made more detailed criticisms about administration and the improvement grant system. As with more general attitudes about older areas, the two groups shared basic assumptions which led them to define the problems in very similar terms. Most of the surveyors had better knowledge of what the urban renewal policy involved but, as the building society managers pointed out, that was the surveyors' job.

The council's plans for improvement were of limited importance to the building societies, they argued, because improvement would only affect a small number of properties compared with the vast numbers of new houses where there were no problems involved. As long as overall demand for mortgages remained well above what they could satisfy (and their assumption was that this would continue for some time), there was no reason to switch resources towards older housing.

Moreover, they complained that previous policies of improvement had not yet had any visible effect on areas of older housing. They were also concerned about the legal requirement that improvement grants may be repayable if the owner sold within five years of having a grant, and by the fear that the high costs involved (caused partly by high standards demanded) would not be met by a rise in value. They were, therefore, reluctant to commit themselves further until they saw how well the local authority implemented its policy. If anyone took risks, it should be the council, not them.

Both building society managers and surveyors felt strongly that a lot of harm had been done by previous council plans which had either taken much longer to complete than originally promised or had been altered, even cancelled. Any council activity created uncertainty for them rather than reducing it. They were primarily going on their experience of the effect of comprehensive redevelopment on areas and house prices, and they were sceptical of the idea that general improvement areas were safe places to buy. Fears were expressed that there might still be clearance; unless and until there was firm evidence of the council spending money in older areas, helping owners improve and encouraging more owner-occupation, they saw no reason to take extra risks. Some were indignant about such a suggestion, saying 'Why should we do the council's job?'

Any 'softening' of attitudes towards older areas, involving less stringent lending policies was extremely unlikely in advance of major house and area improvement achieved by local authority action alone. In other words, both ideologically and from the point of view of good business sense, the building societies, supported by the surveying profession, had no inducement to make any alteration in their policies.

The unwillingness of building societies to lend in areas of older housing meant that other sources of finance, however disreputable, were all that was available. Only those with least choice in the housing market, then, would be willing to buy poorer housing at higher rates of interest than better, and relatively cheaper, suburban housing. Exploitation has remained the prerogative of smaller operations: the 'fringe' institutions and their attendant 'merchant professionals', and the 'pariah' landlord of multi-occupied property.

The housing market in areas of older housing had been affected by a variety of forces which had left it starved of investment from both institutional and individual sources. Particularly important were the declining profitability of rented housing, the increasing profitability of suburban developments for owner-occupation compared with investment in the older areas and the greater security of financial investment in newer rather than older dwellings. This left the housing stock ageing and decaying, occupied by an increasingly poor and powerless population. Some had managed to keep pace with decay and obsolescence but any improvements were piecemeal. The result was that the late nineteenth century building boom had yielded a large stock of dwellings which, by the 1960s, was rapidly wearing out and which, following years of neglect, urgently needed attention.

The city council's approach to urban renewal, which was developed in the early 1970s, only partially grasped the processes described in this chapter and ignored the roles and attitudes of building societies and other mortgage lenders (see Karn, forth-coming). Many of the problems came to light only over time, emerging apparently as problems of policy implementation. It was assumed all along, first, that improvement would be welcomed by those living in the older areas and those concerned with property exchange as making sound economic sense and, second, that a modernised house was a good investment. As we have argued here and shall show later, these assumptions were not valid.

4 The Development of Policy in Birmingham

Policy Change

Explaining change in public policy is a difficult task. To what extent do changes reflect fundamental changes in the social structure? How much are they a response to local politics, and as such marginal reforms? Do political institutions exercise a degree of power independent of economic interests; does it matter who is 'in charge' of the local council—or would things have been the same whoever was apparently exercising political power?

The first chapter discussed reasons for the national policy change from comprehensive redevelopment to improvement. Birmingham was one of many major cities which had pursued substantial redevelopment programmes during the 1960s, and became the first major metropolitan authority to develop a large-scale policy for house and neighbourhood improvement. The timing of policy change in Birmingham, and the scope of the city council's proposals were important—new policies were discussed earlier, and at a scale in excess of most other urban authorities. Were these especially *local* developments, to be explained in terms of factors unique to Birmingham, or were there more fundamental reasons underlying the change, so that what happened locally was little more than a minor variant of national changes and developments?

During our research we interviewed several members and former members of the council together with some of the senior officers who were concerned with policy development in the late 1960s and early 1970s. Our purpose was to discuss the crucial decisions and discussions which were held within the council in the period, as well as to learn about their views on the effects of the urban renewal policy some two or three years after it had been launched. We also examined minutes of council meetings and committee meetings, as well as reading numerous officers' reports to various committees.

The theoretical perspective from which we started stressed the importance of structural features underlying social change, accounting for changes in state policy in terms of economic and social forces working outside the control of individuals. We were, therefore, somewhat sceptical of the claims of some of our informants who maintained that they were personally responsible for much of what happened by way of urban renewal in the city. Some, however, whilst not sharing our perspective, explained local developments in terms of processes that were operating at a national level and which were consequently relevant to Birmingham. The growing capital cost of clearance and reconstruction, the changing nature of the older stock and the reactions of residents were typically offered as the three most important reasons for the shift from redevelopment to improvement.

But how much were these peculiar to Birmingham? Other big cities have shared many of the problems that local housing policies seek to confront. Whilst local authorities are the actors, is it not central government that directs? Rosemary Mellor has recently said that the role of central government is most important in housing renewal:

> . . . the future of older housing is not a matter which will be locally determined. Decisions as to the level of investment in housing are primarily national policies taken with an eye to the desired level of public expenditure, the rate of housing investment considered desirable in the national economy, and the conditions and requirements of the building industry.
>
> *(Mellor, 1977, p. 78)*

This chapter is concerned to explore her thesis by an examination of the development of Birmingham's urban renewal policy, particularly during 1972.

Launching the New Policy

Birmingham's urban renewal policy was publicly launched at a meeting held in the council chamber in January 1973. Leading committee chairmen and senior officers presented the new proposals to invited representatives of voluntary organisations, the press and professional bodies.

The *Evening Mail* immediately announced the 'City's seven-year plan to save old homes' (*Birmingham Evening Mail*, 31 January 1973) as the city council claimed to be embarking on 'a mammoth task and a new concept of urban renewal' (City of Birmingham, Urban Renewal Conference, 1973). In publicity associated with the policy, the council emphasised that a new and distinctive phase had been entered in council policies for older housing:

> . . . the urban renewal problem has now reached a new threshold. Today the task is to prevent dwellings becoming slums . . . the old slums were so worn out and outmoded that the only solution was to demolish the houses whilst the preventive measures necessary today to arrest the social and physical decline of dwellings and large areas of the city call for a different technique.
> Unless these dwellings and areas are dealt with in the next decade . . . they will become slums. The cost to the city, the destruction of communities and the hardship to individuals would be unacceptable.

The council presented its proposals as a major break with previous policies. Comprehensive redevelopment was to be phased out and replaced by a programme of house and area improvement. With an emphasis on 'public participation' and 'community development' the policy was of a magnitude staggering even by the standards of Birmingham's past redevelopment exploits. Initially some 75,000 houses in the city's middle ring were included in areas requiring action within a ten-year period. Sixty-eight general improvement areas, comprising 60,000 houses, were to be declared in the period 1972–78, and twenty-six potential renewal areas were identified where a mixed policy of clearance and improvement would be undertaken. Without doubt, this was an ambitious and far-reaching set of intentions, with a potentially massive programme of local authority action and resource commitment.

Even critical commentators accepted the city council's assertion that a substantial change was taking place. They reckoned that the development had been influenced by residents' views of previous policy: 'This represents a remarkable shift in policy, a shift which is due in part at least to constant pressure both formal and informal from community groups.' (Gibson, 1972b).

Voluntary associations welcomed the new policy, mainly responding to the decision to end comprehensive redevelopment, which one association referred to as '. . . an inevitable cause of social squalor and no longer appropriate to the mixed condition of the remaining older housing stock' (quoted in Gibson, op. cit.). Such organisations with experience of comprehensive redevelopment had campaigned for a change in policy, and had been encouraged by the priority given to urban renewal by the Labour Party since regaining control of the city council in May 1972. Clearly, the policy statement was just a beginning and, although many reservations were expressed about the new policy, there was virtually no public opposition to it.

It would, however, be misleading to overstate the unanimity and the extent to which the new approach resulted from well articulated community campaigns. There were few well developed community groups in the city at the time when crucial policy decisions were taken in the late 1960s and early 1970s; the effect of central government directives and pressure to hold down expenditure were much more important. Furthermore, the apparent consensus over the new policy was at most temporary and confined to agreement over what was self-evident: that the old policies had brought with them severe problems and that something different should be done.

Most Conservative members of the council welcomed Labour's policy initiative in principle but many had reservations about the scale of what was proposed, and there was party disagreement about the degree of local authority commitment of resources. For most residents affected by the policy change, as was demonstrated at the public meetings held during 1973, the typical reactions were scepticism, disbelief and uncertainty rather than any immediate sense of relief.

There was also heated debate about urban renewal within the leading political parties in Birmingham. Much of this discussion focused on the cost effectiveness of different policies and the social distribution of such effects.

The Background to Improvement
Despite the apparent novelty of the 1973 urban renewal policy, a close inspection of the relationship between previous developments and the new policy suggests that much of what was proposed was far from new. During the 1960s the city council had initiated small scale improvement policies. After the House Purchase and Housing Act 1959, which introduced grants of 50 per cent of the costs of the provisions of 'standard amenities', there was an increase in voluntary improvement in Birmingham, at first by owner-occupiers, and later mainly by landlords (Langstaff, 1972). Such voluntary improvement was scattered widely throughout the city's middle ring, and although the city council tried to concentrate improvement by declaring improvement areas under the Housing Act 1964, this had virtually

no effect. Very little work was undertaken in the twilight areas adjacent to areas which were being redeveloped during this period.

Chapter 3 discussed how the combination of market processes and local authority policies had affected the social composition of areas adjacent to inner redevelopment areas. One council policy, namely 'deferred demolition', had an important effect on popular attitudes to improvement:

> Unlike most authorities, Birmingham has pursued a policy of buying up unfit property several years ahead of the date of phased demolition . . . many of these acquired dwellings are improved for their remaining years before demolition, expenditure on improvements generally being related to the life span of the dwelling.
>
> *(Spencer, 1970)*

'Deferred demolition' or, as it is more popularly known, 'patching', can be traced back to the immediate post-war period, when the city council took advantage of a war-time measure, the Town and Country Planning Act 1944, to declare five inner areas 'Comprehensive Development Areas' (CDAs). This act enabled local authorities to acquire privately owned land and property. Shortly after the war the city council compulsorily acquired nearly 1,000 acres in the inner ring, becoming, at the stroke of a pen, the largest 'slum landlord' in the city. Initially, because of post-war shortages, little clearance took place. Systematically these old unfit properties were repaired to minimal standards—made 'wind and weather proof'—particularly after the Housing Repairs and Rents Act 1954 which brought together powers for this kind of work. As Roberts (1976) comments in his recent work on general improvement areas, deferred demolition 'is a policy which has been frequently and sharply criticised, since it can be seen as the authority committing itself to clearance at an unspecified time, and deplorable conditions can result' (p. 8).

There is little point in chronicling yet again the effects of the process on family and communal life; but we should emphasise the critical relationship between the city council's ability to rehouse people (which is the key to the rate at which Birmingham's slums were actually demolished) and the development of this peculiar form of 'improvement'. Furthermore, these properties were often used by the city council to rehouse families who had been judged as 'poor housekeepers', and therefore not fit for decent accommodation (Lambert *et al.*, 1978). Whilst deferred demolition was never considered as a long term policy, many properties were left for ten, fifteen or even twenty years, particularly where they were purchased well in advance of statutory action. What is astonishing in retrospect, was the credit given to the city council by radical commentators for these practices! (Samuel *et al.*, 1962).

As the redevelopment programme progressed, it became clear that other housing in the city's middle ring consisted of more varied housing stock than the older back-to-backs of the original redevelopment areas. Whereas the earlier clearance areas had been inhabited mainly by single family tenants of private landlords, the 'twilight areas' of the middle ring contained a much more varied tenure pattern—more owner-occupiers, a sprinkling of council-owned houses bought from private owners, and the poorer part of the privately rented sector. Increasingly, it was a different kind of private renting, with concentrations of multi-occupied properties, rooming houses, often over-crowded and inadequately serviced, housing those who could neither afford better nor get a foothold in the local authority sector. These were the kind of areas described by Rex and Moore's *Race, Community and Conflict* (1967) and in which we worked before embarking on our study of the urban renewal policy.

The Housing Act 1969 did not have an immediate impact on the council's approach to house and area improvement. No special agency was set up to implement the legislation. Attention was still focused on the second phase of comprehensive redevelopment. Slum clearance and rebuilding continued to dominate the council's approach to the renewal of older housing.

A working party of council officers had been set up to examine the scope for house improvement after the Housing Act 1969. It recommended a 'buffer zone' approach to the declaration of GIAs:

The Working Party was instructed primarily to concentrate on areas which comprised groups of houses, which, after improvement and repair and the upgrading of the surrounding environment, would be likely to stand for at least thirty years . . . old, worn-out and overcrowded houses which ought to be pulled down should not be included in GIAs. The Working Party was asked to devote their main effort to consideration of areas containing the better type of house built between the turn of the century and the first world war. One of the important matters for consideration in choosing general improvement areas was the desirability that they should act as a buffer between the present stock of good suburban houses and those properties which had deteriorated too far to the

point where slum clearance and total redevelopment would be necessary.
(Birmingham City Council Minutes, Report of the Health Committee,
November, 1971)

This approach was based on naïve implicit assumptions about the nature of house decay. It argued that deterioration of housing was part of a spatial process, which 'spreads' until arrested by a physical barrier of better housing. Also, by definition, the relationship between neighbourhoods was conceptualised in terms of the physical condition of the housing stock and it was presumed that a spatial gradient of quality would somehow contain the spread of decay, with improvement of housing in this 'buffer zone' stemming the tide of deterioration. The processes whereby housing comes to be used in different ways, and the underlying causes of housing stress, remained unexplored; the expected success of a policy of physical improvement of older housing, which in turn would act to prevent further decay elsewhere, was also presented as beyond doubt.

A further problem lay in the consequences of leaving certain areas undeclared. The 'buffer zone' policy left high and dry those areas of housing which were multi-occupied, overcrowded and in poor repair. These areas, without the security of GIA status, were in a policy vacuum; there were no clearance proposals and, at least until 1973, no proposals to call them GIAs. It was not until late 1974 that legislation existed which could define the way in which they could be treated (as HAAs), in the meantime there was little available evidence to indicate how much voluntary improvement would be forthcoming.

The 'buffer zone' approach was criticised locally (Gibson and Langstaff, 1972) and similar local authority policies have also been condemned elsewhere (Duncan, 1977). However, the city council did not adopt this approach spontaneously, rather it followed central government advice:

We had already been looking at other areas in the city and had delineated those areas that were thought to be suitable for general improvement areas. Circular 65/69 suggested that you choose an area that won't give you too many difficulties to begin with, the idea being that you could gain experience, and get public participation going without too much conflict.
(Interview by the researchers with a senior official from the former public
health department)

Discussing the question of the balance between improvement and redevelopment, MOHLG Circular 65/69 recognised that local authorities might have difficulty deciding which areas to choose as their first general improvement areas. One way to avoid the problem was suggested:

> Local authorities may well think that it is best to defer such a difficult choice where they can be given priority to the clearance of areas which must obviously be cleared and the improvement of areas which will obviously repay attention of that kind. Areas where the physical condition of housing makes the choice difficult should on the whole be tackled later when more experience has been gained.

It was therefore claimed that continuing housing problems were so complex that local authorities needed to learn the best approach to such problems. The impetus coming from central government, though, was that local authorities should give increasing priority to policies of improvement, even if the content of such policies for the more 'difficult' areas had yet to be determined.

Locally, the circular allowed the council to avoid decisions about the future of the very areas which contained the greatest concentrations of housing and social stress. Indeed, the approach sustained what one officer called a 'sort of planned obsolescence' in areas adjacent to the programme of redevelopment then underway.

Powers to implement the Housing Act 1969 remained with the health committee, and the emphasis continued to be on purely physical aspects of house and area improvement; by the beginning of 1972 Birmingham's GIA programme had had little impact on the twilight areas and, like redevelopment, had avoided almost all concentrations of immigrants and multiple occupation.

The Politics of Improvement
There had been remarkably little political debate nationally about the shift from redevelopment to improvement. Roberts, in his analysis of the White Paper preceding the Housing Act 1969, says that it 'should have been a political bombshell' (1967, p. 17) particularly as it 'unambiguously implied a substantial cut in the target of 500,000 new completions per year which the Labour government had made as a solemn election pledge in 1964, and which had only been slightly modified in the post-devaluation

economies of 1967' (*loc. cit.*). That it was not a bombshell, he claims, was due to the 'political irrelevance' of improvement policy:

> . . . improving old houses had a certain basic social and economic sense which appeals to politicians of all parties. Party political squabbles over improvement legislation have been mainly restricted to its implications for the privately rented sector; in other respects, it has been outstandingly uncontroversial.
>
> *(Op. cit., p. 18)*

Many Labour Party politicians had opposed cuts in council house building, but there was strong pressure against such criticism being made public with Labour in office nationally. With the Labour Party suffering a particularly severe rout in Birmingham's local elections in 1968 and the party under threat nationally, opposition tended to be 'cooled out' in local party or Labour group meetings. By appealing to party loyalty the national leadership was able to sustain a programme of cuts in public expenditure to which rank and file members and elected representatives were personally opposed. Many members, however, supported the trend towards improvement since it was hoped that its effects would be less disruptive and protracted and that their constituents would be able to remain living in the area they liked.

Among Conservatives, improvement was welcomed as a cheaper housing policy, and one which cut down the need for council building programmes. Whereas Birmingham's Conservatives had previously been divided over housing policy, particularly regarding the cost of redevelopment and level of council house building, the shift to improvement brought them together as it appeared cheaper than previous policies.

The 1968 White Paper and Housing Act 1969 caused some internal division within Birmingham's Labour group, then in opposition; many members feared that a 'second-best' solution was being forced upon the areas which they had expected would be cleared. They echoed W. S. Hilton, MP for Bethnal Green, whose views Roberts quotes as an example of 'demolition socialism' opposed to improvement policy:

> No matter what one does with some of the houses in (older areas), nothing can be done that will elevate the ceilings or extend the walls. The houses will still be cramped and small.
>
> *(Op. cit., p. 18)*

When we remember the long experience of 'deferred demolition' in Birmingham, it is hardly surprising that many councillors who had pressed for a better programme of comprehensive redevelopment were concerned that 'improvement' was a euphemism for perpetuating the problems of slum housing. Ironically, they often found themselves disagreeing with other members of their own group, who were also concerned with the social costs of redevelopment, but who hoped that improvement policies might provide a better alternative. Most of all the supporters of improvement stressed the delay, uncertainty and long term dereliction of comprehensive redevelopment.

There was even a growing body of protest about the new housing which had been produced to *solve* the slum problem. High rise flats and maisonettes dominated central comprehensive development areas and even some new peripheral estates. To many people these were synonymous with redevelopment after slum clearance and were regarded as one of the failures of that policy, as if it was inevitable that slum dwellings had to be replaced by high rise flats.

Most protest about redevelopment came from voluntary associations working in areas affected by the city council's redevelopment programme, from Christian ministers such as Canon Power, author of the well known tract *The Forgotten People* (1965), and from the residents themselves. Often attention was focused on the plight of those families who were only deemed suitable to live in the oldest and worst properties, and the frequent family breakdown and homelessness resulting. *Cathy Come Home*, the TV documentary partly filmed in Birmingham, had considerable impact on the national conscience, and was also influential in the development of Birmingham's programme of 'Family Advice Centres' associated with the redevelopment programme (Means, 1977).

Inner city areas traditionally returned Labour councillors who were faced with a barrage of problems at their advice bureaux. Frequently they bore the brunt of complaints from long established residents, awaiting removal from the area, who felt that their neighbourhood was used as a 'dumping ground' for 'problem families'. 'Communities', it was argued, were being destroyed.

Improvement policy, it was hoped, would cause less disruption to communities. In their critical review of Needleman's work, Sigsworth and Wilkinson agreed that modernisation produces less social disturbance than replacement. 'People stay where they are and maintain neighbourly and kinship ties unbroken where otherwise they might be sundered as a result of rehousing' (1967, p. 115). They also said, however, that comprehensive redevelopment did not necessarily cause unwelcome disturbance anyway, and that there were social factors in favour of redevelopment:

> The desire for clean surroundings, open space, greater privacy, the feeling that children will have a 'better chance', physically and educationally, awareness that the rundown neighbourhood has a poor reputation in the community at large and that to live in it is to be associated with social inferiority and failure are all 'social factors' which are as relevant in determining a positive desire to move, as the possible fear of social disturbance.
>
> *(Op. cit., p. 116)*

Ironically, in Birmingham, both the supporters and opponents of improvement policy referred back to the worst features of redevelopment policy as evidence of their case. If redevelopment had been quick, well managed and had produced well appointed pleasant housing at reasonable rent, then the entire structure of local debate would have been different. As it was, rather than debating the reasons why redevelopment was unpopular and unsuccessful, the major concerns were over the way in which improvement policy should be carried out. Several petitions were presented to the city council from residents' groups requesting that their area should become a GIA and the only policy issue which remained in contention was the 'buffer zone' approach favoured by the Conservatives.

Some Labour members of the city council were concerned that this approach failed to tackle the problems they perceived as most pressing, and an amendment to the report of the health committee to the council in June 1971 was carried to the effect that the committee should further report on 'the considerations which they have laid down, to be taken into account in choosing GIAs' (Minutes of Birmingham City Council, 1971).

Government policy on improvement had changed very little since June 1970 (when the Conservatives came to office nationally), except that added emphasis was given to improvement rather than redevelopment. Certainly, it can be shown that government policies were also acting to reduce the amount of council house building but the main thrust of the Conservative Government's housing policy lay in its Housing Finance Bill (Lambert *et al.*, 1978, pp. 155–7).

This was taken up as the central 'housing issue' when it came to Birmingham council elections in 1972. At the Birmingham Labour

Party policy conference, held in March 1972, it was argued that if the Labour group came to power it should 'refuse to operate the Tory government's "Unfair Rents" policy'. Most debate centred on this controversial Bill, which was thought likely to have a far reaching impact on both council tenants and owner-occupiers.

Urban renewal was never given the same priority by the major political parties, though there was some discussion in the local press. One Labour councillor, discussing 'our plan for housing' claimed that 'squalor, misery and fear predominate in all our redevelopment areas'. He then went on to outline how things would change:

> . . . we shall mount an immediate all-out attack on the dereliction which disfigures these areas . . . Improving older houses and their environment is far better than wholesale redevelopment, for it keeps communities together . . . we hope to concentrate on improvement, redeveloping only where absolutely necessary.
>
> (*Birmingham Evening Mail, 27 April 1972*)

He blamed the process of comprehensive redevelopment, which had never been a major political issue, for past social problems. Improvement was preferred, in order to minimise social disruption, but it was never shown how this preference was peculiar to the Labour Party; indeed, the Conservatives also claimed to be in support of improvement.

The local elections of May 1972 resulted in an overall majority for Labour in Birmingham with nineteen seats gained from the Conservative Party. At the first meeting of the general purposes committee after the election, it was agreed to set up a 'Standing Conference on Urban Renewal' to coordinate various departmental contributions to urban renewal. The conference represented, in part, an attempt to break down the rigid departmental structure of the local authority; and was to be served by officers from existing departments through the newly created post of urban renewal officer. Specifically a non-executive body, the conference was given responsibility to develop a strategy for urban renewal, coordinate all works involved in the implementation of an urban renewal programme 'relative to the social and environmental development of communities' (Millar, 1972, p. 203) and also to encourage public participation.

Policy making and implementation continued to rest with existing committees and their officers: the conference was a place where some of them met to discuss new initiatives. Without its own officer structure, and with the continuing importance of the existing committee, it had a liaison function but little else. Just before the first meeting of the conference a DoE circular was published requesting that local authorities with central government, undertake '. . . a *concerted* and decisive drive on the problem of slums and older housing'. Circular 50/72 *Slums and Older Housing: An Overall Strategy* had been keenly anticipated in Birmingham and senior officers in the local authority were in contact with the DoE prior to its publication. The circular was accompanied by a speech from the Rt. Hon. Julien Amery, Minister for Housing and Construction, who was launching 'a new and decisive attack on the problems of older housing'. Like others before him, the minister claimed to see an end to slums for all time. It was his conviction that:

> . . . if we, together, really set our hands to it we can beat the problem of slums and unsatisfactory houses within a measurable time. That is why I have described this drive as a decisive one. For the first time there is light at the end of the tunnel.
>
> *(Appendix to Circular 50/72)*

Whereas in general terms the requirements contained in the circular had been expected in Birmingham, what was surprising was the timescale laid out for action: local authorities were expected to determine housing conditions and housing need in their areas and develop strategies to deal with problems of older housing by 1980. All the preparation had to be done by 1st October 1972! Not only were authorities expected to prepare their strategic policies, but they were also expected to consider 'the needs and wishes of those now living in slums and older housing'.

Residents' Action and Policy Formulation

The urban renewal conference was not in a position to undertake large-scale surveys of the views of people living in older housing; it had neither the personnel nor the financial resources for such a task. Some voluntary organisations made representations to the conference, mainly advocating improvement as a preferred alternative to redevelopment, but few took up the suggestions in a local community action journal, *West Midlands Grass Roots*, that local groups should seek a meeting with the chairman of the conference or that groups should make a submission regarding the kind of policies they preferred for their area (Gibson, 1973). One simple explanation for this lack of response was simply that there were few groups able to make one. There was a dozen or so well established neighbourhood-based voluntary organisations, but these were almost invariably composed of people originating from outside of the areas concerned—typically 'community professionals' though often with a base of some kind in the neighbourhood, whether teacher, social worker or cleric.

A number of these associations had wide experience of advisory and advocacy work within the neighbourhoods likely to be affected by any new policy, and local residents frequently joined in their activities. But there were no organisations structured in any formally representative way which could have rallied members to make collective proposals. When groups did try to do this the most successful medium was the public meeting where councillors and officers were exposed to residents' comments and criticisms.

Secondly, there was virtually no publicity associated with the city council's response to Circular 50/72. Local authorities had not been asked specifically to publicise the exercise, rather they had been asked to compare housing conditions with 'their assessment of housing need in their area, in particular, the needs and wishes of those now living in slums and older houses'. *West Midlands Grass Roots* never had a very wide circulation, and the mass circulation local newspapers made no attempt to stimulate interest.

Time was not on the side of public consultation. The circular was published on 25 May 1972 and authorities had to report as soon as possible, and in any case, by 1 October 1972. That left barely four months to collate information, assess 'needs' and prepare a draft strategy. The members of the conference, and particularly its first chairman, had every intention of bringing in those affected by the policy, but that would have to come later, once an outline was prepared.

The Formulation of the Draft Strategy, Summer–Autumn, 1972
The urban renewal conference had to coordinate departmental suggestions in the development of a strategy for the city's older housing stock. Coordination itself, however, presented problems quite separate from the object and purpose of urban renewal. First, there was still opposition from some members and officers to the idea of any 'corporate planning', and powerful departmental interests sought to counter any reduction in their autonomy. In particular, officers in the massive public works department opposed the growing importance of the public health department in urban

renewal. The housing department, which had played a major role in policy implementation through the latter half of the 1960s and which had been critically concerned about the long-term reduction in the amount of properties acquired under the Housing Act 1954, sought also to gain a major say in policy formulation.

These departmental differences were expressed in the various submissions to the urban renewal conference following Circular 50/72, and were to reappear a couple of years later when an assessment was made of the policy by the new performance review committee (see chapter 5). The immediacy of the task, however, forced a pragmatic approach, and a report of officers from the major departments was produced, entitled 'Strategy for dealing with slums and older housing within Birmingham up to 1980'. This and other reports were never made public.

The report from the housing department examined the problems facing further slum clearance and redevelopment; its assumptions as well as its analysis merit consideration. Two levels of constraints were identified—national and local. At the national level, the report identified four problems: financial restrictions on acquisition and administrative delay over CPO procedures; the building cost yardstick was too low, thus the council could not fill contracts for new building; loan sanction did not cover 'social facilities' that should accompany redevelopment; and, whilst powers existed to enable retention of suitable properties, it was not possible to compel owners to improve to the required standard.

At the local level the council had experienced problems relocating small businesses displaced by redevelopment. Fears were expressed about the increased staff load that would be required for house inspection in GIAs. There seemed to be few firms available for council work. Land availability was also identified as a problem, and what sites existed were smaller than in previous years. Additionally, the social and age balance of older areas did not match the council's policies for allocation, nor the pattern of relets likely to be available—high proportions of small, old and also young, large families would prove difficult to rehouse. Finally, high overall costs were seen as a major constraint. We should add that the report assumed that comprehensive redevelopment would continue in some areas, and also that improvement would never be more than one part of an overall strategy. The 'Chief Officers Working Party' reported to the urban renewal conference that the proposed programme was 'substantial', adding:

> . . . the working party is of the opinion that it is reasonable and feasible *appreciating that the city council is responsible only for the implementation of environmental works—the physical improvements of the dwellings occur if and when the owners decide that the time is appropriate—* subject to a policy review should the rate of improvement be considered unsatisfactory.'
>
> *(Our emphasis)*

This statement was naïve as, based on experience of improvement in the 1960s, there was reason to expect that substantial local authority involvement would be necessary to stimulate house improvement. As later events were to show, at the very least an improvement policy would require a massive house inspection effort. Much work would also need to be done in assessing improvement grant applications, advising the public, inspecting the work and enforcing improvement to tenanted property.

The report claimed that progress in the GIAs declared to date had been inhibited by the initial decision not to employ more staff, and suggested 'limited acquisitions' in GIAs where owners were unwilling to improve. A map was presented which showed the physical conditions of older housing, and introduced the concept of 'Interim Amenity Area' (IAA). This was a new idea and unique to Birmingham, implying an area where short term environmental improvements would reduce the blighting effect of proposed clearance. Those areas of 'retention properties' within the IAAs, once identified, would probably be reclassified as GIAs at a later date.

The IAA label was merely a locally invented administrative device aimed at designating areas where certain environmental action was proposed, and, more important, where intensive house inspection to determine 'lifing' would take place. It had no basis in law, and in order for action to be taken, areas would have to be 'redeclared' either clearance areas under the Housing Act 1957 or general improvement areas under the Housing Act 1969.

In accepting these recommendations in its report to the general purposes committee, the urban renewal conference established a number of precedents which were later to appear as issues of central importance. The four most critical were, (a) the acceptance of the principle of *voluntary* improvement, (b) the assumption that there would be a *mix* of redevelopment and improvement, (c) the need for administrative and organisational *change*, and (d) the need to take *positive* action in the areas of greatest uncertainty (IAAs) as well as *accelerating* progress in GIAs. We return to all four of these issues throughout our analysis of subsequent developments in the policy.

A broad strategy was announced in the *Birmingham Evening Mail* as an 'Eight-year new look plan for city suburbs' (6 October 1972). The plan would mean:

> tearing down unfit houses, building new homes and improving existing housing areas with a population the size of Redditch every year. The aim is that by 1980, no-one should have to live in a sub-standard house.

The *Evening Mail* continued, quoting the press release it had received:

> Nine general improvement areas have so far been declared in Birmingham, containing about 10,500 houses. Now the pace of tackling these areas and halting the slide into decay is to be stepped up dramatically from the present rate of 2,000 houses a year, reaching a peak embracing 11,000–12,000 houses a year by 1976.
>
> *(Op. cit.)*

The magnitude of the proposals was impressive, almost staggering in the light of past experience. A six-fold increase of improvement activity was anticipated, despite the range and intensity of problems being experienced in other aspects of housing activities. Moreover, the proposals included areas which the city council knew to have the worst housing conditions and greatest social stress.

There was little party political debate over the policy except regarding its scale. The former Conservative chairman of the housing committee warned against spending money on properties only to have them pulled down after all. The leader of the Conservative group went further: 'I feel that it is not much use bothering with these backstreet properties. Most of them should be pulled down as quickly as possible. I think the whole policy is wrong.' (*Birmingham Evening Mail*, 27 October 1972.) In this he was certainly articulating a concern shared by many Labour councillors, but while the *scale* of the policy remained in dispute, the Conservatives never went so far as to propose any alternative strategy.

From October to December, officers hurried to prepare proposals for the detailed boundaries of GIAs and IAAs or, as the latter became termed, renewal areas. A policy statement was prepared and the report of the urban renewal conference was contained in the general purposes committee's report to the city council on 2 January 1973. The report argued that Circular 50/72 'was received at the time

when the joint conference (URC) was already initiating and enquir-
ing into the needs of the city in respect of future urban renewal and
preservation . . . a detailed programme has now been formulated . . .
for implementation . . . during the next ten years'. The second phase
of the redevelopment programme would be finished and '68 GIAs
designated and twenty-six other urban localities . . . renewal areas
would be treated'. The public would be informed and leaflets
prepared for all citizens and community groups affected and other
interested bodies. The literature was despatched and the public
meeting held in the Council House solely to publicise the policy,
giving residents little opportunity to consider the proposals in
advance.

The Politics of Policy Change

For different reasons the new policy struck a chord in the hearts of
many of the city's politicians. For the Conservatives it meant most of
all an end to the growing municipalisation of the housing stock in
the central areas. To Labour councillors the key advantages were
that inner city communities could be 'kept together' and there would
be sensitive renewal and improvement of living conditions rather
than the harsh and degrading effects of mass clearance.

To both parties the new strategy suggested a new and more
sensitive role for the local authority. House improvement would
depend on sustaining public confidence, telling people what was to
happen and allowing them to participate in planning the improvement of their neighbourhoods. The Conservatives saw council
involvement diminishing, by transferring the initiative to individual
house owners for action. For Labour councillors the new policy
meant an end to the domineering bureaucracy of centralised departments controlling clearance and rebuilding from remote offices, and
the introduction of small, localised teams of officers sensitive to local
opinion.

Comprehensive redevelopment had been criticised for ignoring
the wishes of the individual house occupier and for assuming that he
wanted a better house, that he was prepared to pay more for it than
his old house, and that he was prepared to suffer years of blight,
decay and disruption whilst the slums were defined, acquired,
demolished and replaced. There was, indeed, evidence of public
dissatisfaction and protest. In his careful description of residents'
organised action against clearance in Sunderland, Dennis has argued
that the consumer of housing should have a greater say in policy

decisions (Dennis, 1970 and 1972). The 'community press' also reported residents' groups campaigning against clearance and in favour of rehabilitation. In Adamstown, Coventry, a three-year campaign by residents lifted an area from blight to the security of a general improvement area (*Community Action*, September/October 1973). In Ladybarn, Manchester, nearly 200 dwellings were saved from clearance for improvement (*Community Action*, October/November 1974) after residents' protest. In Birmingham, residents of George Arthur Road, Saltley, campaigned successfully to save their houses and for the area to be declared an HAA.

Public protest, however, is no simple indication of community wishes, as public attitudes are constrained by existing attitudes and people react against circumstances as they are and not as they might have been. Redevelopment could have been more popular had it been managed more speedily and with greater concern for its social effects. The costs it implied in individual terms could have been offset to a greater degree by increased subsidy. Improvement certainly appeared less attractive to those private tenants who expected to have to wait for years before their landlord would carry out the necessary renovations. It must be remembered that in Birmingham, as elsewhere, improvement policies were not developed solely as an *alternative* to immediate slum clearance. Following the Housing Act 1969 local authorities chose to channel resources to many of the better areas of older houses on the grounds that it would prevent slum formation in the future. To the extent that better quality housing was occupied by the (albeit marginally) more wealthy and powerful in the housing market at a time when there remained in many city centres obsolete housing without the security of GIA status and still with no firm proposals for clearance, the new policy diverted attention and money away from people and areas in greatest need, through giving first priority for action to GIAs and second status to renewal areas.

Within a framework set out by central government, then, Birmingham City Council outlined a broad and ambitious programme. The city council was exceptional in forming proposals for areas in advance of the Housing Act 1974. The council failed to consider the full implications of its proposals, both in terms of financial and manpower resources. In one sense the council was making a bid for centrally allocated resources. The Conservative Government had stated national priorities, and Labour controlled Birmingham responded quickly claiming that the city exhibited signs of stress which central government had identified as a priority for national housing expenditure.

House improvement appeared in the late 1960s and early 1970s to be an achievable policy objective when so much of central government housing strategy had failed. In Birmingham the urban renewal policy was formulated during a period when there was every indication that the city's housing problems were getting worse. Council house building had fallen and the housing waiting list had increased. The city council was finding it difficult to complete its comprehensive redevelopment programme and there was every reason to focus attention on those parts of the city where, not only was it imperative that attention be paid, but where it actually appeared possible that something could be done. Just what would be done, however, remained to be spelt out. The policy consisted of little more than an outline of proposed statutory and non-statutory area declarations, with little or no detailed knowledge of the wishes and intentions of those people then resident in such areas, and with no clear statement about the relationship between the policy and the 'normal' working of the housing market in which the city council wished to intervene.

5 The Management of Urban Renewal

Corporate Planning and Urban Renewal

Corporate planning

Local government is a popular subject for abuse in the media. Local newspapers, perhaps even more than sociologists, revel in the inadequacies of councillors and officers alike, criticise the failings of policies, love 'human interest' stories of the small man facing up to the army of bureaucrats and, last but not least, scandalise exorbitant rates and wasteful expenditure. Little wonder then, that there is at best an uneasy tension between the apparatuses of government and the proverbial man in the street.

Yet so much that local government *does* is important to people; schools, houses, welfare facilities, local roads and public transport shape the context of everyday life to a greater or lesser degree for all of us. The distance between 'authority' and people, however, has increased rather than diminished in recent years. Schemes of public participation have in some instances generated better mutual understanding, yet local government reform has created fewer and bigger units, further still from the concerns and comprehension of most ordinary citizens.

One response to the critics of local government has been the growth of more advanced techniques of management within local authorities. In particular, emphasis is now laid on the coordination of policies, of cooperation between departments and the development of a 'corporate approach' to the solution of local problems. In addition to producing more efficient management methods of defining objectives and presenting alternative ways of meeting them, this is supposed to assist councillors by providing better information and clearer policy choices. The public should benefit both through better management generally and by being given a clearer picture of the decision-making process, thus making participation more easily available.

These kinds of ideas have been advocated by a series of reports published by government committees examining local government management (Maud Report, 1967; Bains Report, 1972), the consultants' studies of 'inner areas' of Liverpool, Birmingham and Lambeth (DoE, 1977b, c, and d) and by subsequent central government initiatives on 'the inner city' (DoE, 1977e). Academic institutions, particularly the Institute for Local Government Studies at Birmingham University, have also been influential in the development of the theory of corporate management.

The development of new corporate techniques has not, however, been without its problems. Critical constraints have been imposed by the economic and social environment in which local authorities operate and over which they have little control. Market forces and the workings of private sector institutions and indeed central government can, and frequently do, upset locally developed strategies and policies. Yet the language of corporate plans often tends to assume complete control.

It is sometimes argued that 'real' corporate planning has been slow to develop as a result of the reluctance of local (and central) government departments to relinquish power to central planning units. Thus the discussion of corporate planning remains theoretical in the sense that there are few instances of local authorities which have effectively transformed traditional management structures. Corporate planning itself becomes an objective, and its very absence provides its proponents with cast-iron evidence of the need to introduce new management systems. The assumption of technical competence goes largely unquestioned, except by sociologists who rarely get through to a mass audience (for example, Dennis, 1972; Lambert *et al.*, 1978; Mellor, 1977; Bennington, 1976; Cockburn, 1977).

Even the media has mixed feelings about managerial reform in local government. Much has been written about the excesses and failures of corporate planning. The intention, though, has rarely been criticised. The objectives of corporate policy-making have been accepted, only the ability of local government to meet its newly-defined requirements has remained in doubt.

Urban renewal

The need for coordination is clearly present in any policy for the renewal of older housing. In terms of information alone the diversity and complexity of conditions in older residential areas cry out for rationalisation. After the Housing Act 1969, and in the period leading up to the Housing Act 1974, it was increasingly clear that the improvement of older housing was a complex task for local authorities. Not only did it require the involvement of many departments, but also, unlike comprehensive redevelopment where the local authority became a monopoly landlord, improvement was intended to stimulate and facilitate change within parts of the private housing market. Thus, in Birmingham, the general purposes committee of the city council had established the urban renewal conference to develop a strategy for urban renewal and coordinate departmental contributions to that strategy (see chapter 4, p. 78).

Further development of urban renewal policy was but one of a number of changes in the organisation and management of the city council. After local government reorganisation, a new committee structure was introduced and a suprimo committee established—the policy and resources committee—comprising leading members of the majority Labour Group only. In Birmingham, like Coventry (Bennington, 1976) but unlike Lambeth (Cockburn, 1977), it was the Labour Party which introduced and sponsored new management approaches. The local Conservative Party strongly opposed the appointment of a chief executive officer and the introduction of a research and intelligence section answerable to him. In Lambeth, by contrast, the Conservatives, drawing from business innovations, actually introduced corporate planning which was accepted and extended by the subsequent Labour administration (Cockburn, 1977, pp. 24–31). Attempts to develop a corporate approach to urban renewal in Birmingham took place at a time when central government was cutting public expenditure on housing. Yet, during the development of the policy and the first years of its implementation, new powers became available and a new pattern of resource allocation was established by central government in order, it was argued, to redirect attention to 'stress areas'. The tension between the management of urban renewal and the resources available for the programme will be a central theme of the rest of this chapter. But before we focus on our local study, it is useful to review some of the criticisms which have been made of corporate management, both in theory and in practice, from different viewpoints.

Critiques of corporate management

From a perspective which can be defined as 'liberal-pluralism', two major criticisms of corporate planning emerge (Howick, 1978). First, 'rational models of decision-making fail to recognise the vast scope and complexity of policy making', so in practice incrementalism becomes the order of the day. This argument also suggests that much local authority expenditure is effectively committed because of historic capital investment so that decision-making can only focus on balancing competing claims for additional resources. Annual reviews have to be carried out to evaluate the effectiveness of policy, but overall direction comes from broad established commitments which render new corporate changes impossible.

The notion of rational coordination is also regarded critically from the liberal-pluralist perspective, which believes that a public agency is a collection of diverse interests, which no grand strategy can reduce to a common denominator. Increased centralisation thus effectively gives greater weight to the values of the central organisation, which in the process loses contact with the providers of services and, ironically, the result is a less responsive form of overall policy-making. This point is amplified by Cockburn's review of the defects of corporate management in Lambeth from the council's point of view: because top-level management was divorced from implementation, it lost contact with the effects of policy (op. cit., p. 37).

These arguments, Howick points out, are similar to economic theory which focuses on decentralised decision-making and 'marginal' adjustments. This also regards comprehensive policy-making as politically objectionable 'because centralisation closes the decision-making process, and excludes from it the legitimate interests of service providers and users', making local government seem less democratic (op. cit., p. 9).

Radical criticisms of corporate management, as opposed to a liberal view of participatory democracy, make similar points, but their emphasis and interpretation contrasts starkly with the liberal-democratic position. They argue that the driving force behind corporatism in local authorities is the concern to control expenditure more closely, rather than meet 'needs' defined by socially determined criteria. Corporate management is 'really' concerned with nothing more than 'the coordinated allocation of a local authority's budget in such a way that waste and duplication are minimised and the general purposes of the authority are achieved' (Simmie, 1974, p. 5); all else is illusory. Corporate management, furthermore, removes political issues from debate, both by the production of consensus explanations 'based on homogenised data' which obscure 'underlying conflicts of interest and areas of unmet need' (Bennington,

1976, p. 181) and by removing the central decision-making body from any contact with policy implementation. Although the theory of corporate management asserts that it is an aid to participatory democracy, in Lambeth, however, Cockburn claimed that it had directly the opposite effect, as any tendency to involvement was met with the higher priority of tighter control (op. cit., p. 36).

Some radical critiques see such features of corporate management as necessary developments, and criticise the language of corporate planning for obscuring the relationship between the state and social classes in capitalist society:

> In the case of local government it is impossible to assess the effect of new management ways on the local working class without understanding much more about the function of local government, the place it has in the structure of state and its relationship with business interests.
>
> *(Cockburn, op. cit., p. 39)*

This perspective asserts that the state reflects and reproduces class interests. Thus, despite new management techniques in Coventry, 'in some respects the already better-off areas and groups within the population seem to be creaming off the main benefits' (Bennington, 1976, p. 180). Social problems should not be seen as 'malfunctions' or 'imbalances' as in corporate models, but as a product of the distribution of power in society—not the subject of debate or negotiation but class struggle (op. cit., pp. 185–6).

Bennington thus sees corporate planning as an ideology above all else; the value of rational organisation in itself is not the object of his criticism. Instead he rejects assumptions of consensus which the ideology sustains, and stresses instead the power of the state to represent the interests of dominant classes, which the ideology denies.

From theories to practice

The different critiques of corporate management described so far can be tested and evaluated only against actual examples of local authority policy-making and implementation, and Birmingham's urban renewal policy provided an excellent opportunity for doing this. The local authority set out to establish a corporate approach to policy-making in general, and the variety of issues involved in urban renewal and the diversity of departments necessitated careful coordination of policies and implementation.

Urban renewal in Birmingham, though, should not be regarded as a 'typical' or 'representative' case study of corporate management. We would be sceptical of suggestions that such a thing were possible. Rather, the study provides the opportunity to return critically to the theoretical issues posed in the introductory section to this chapter. Before we can do that, however, we need to outline the broad organisational development of urban renewal policy between 1973 and 1976, against which we can then attempt to evaluate the nature, effects and significance of corporate management.

The Organisation of Policy

The management of Birmingham's urban renewal policy was just one aspect of attempts to develop a corporate approach to policies and implementation. Its local significance lay in its novelty and in the priority given by Labour to channelling resources to inner areas. It is of general interest, though, not merely as a local story, but for its relevance to contemporary debates about the organisation and content of policies for inner city housing.

When the urban renewal policy was launched in January 1973, its implications were uncertain but potentially far reaching. The urban renewal conference had the responsibility of policy development and coordination, but no executive powers, a small budget and only one full-time officer. The implementation of policy was still vested in the various departments concerned, in particular public health and housing. An inter-departmental committee of officers was established with some delegated powers—the 'multi-disciplinary team'—but effective decision-making remained the prerogative of the existing committee and department structure. For implementation at the local level it was decided to establish six (later eight) 'multi-disciplinary' project teams located in areas affected by the policy. These teams were to be controlled by two centrally-based project team coordinators, with separate responsibility for house and area improvement.

'Teething troubles'—the classification of houses

Two major issues dominated the work of the urban renewal conference during 1973 and 1974. First, the question of the 'life' of older houses generated lengthy debate both within the city council and between the council and residents. Secondly, dependent on decisions about the life of properties, the classification and official designation of areas still had to be decided.

The areas of greatest uncertainty were the renewal areas; originally they had been scheduled for action after GIAs, but they became the subject of the first wave of house inspections to determine which houses were suitable for improvement and which should be demolished. A preliminary classification of houses was prepared by August 1973. Residents were sent either a 'white letter' indicating that the council thought the house was suitable for retention (about 9,500 dwellings) or a 'pink letter' (about 6,500 dwellings). The pink letter said:

Although no final decision has been made, it is thought that your house will need to be demolished. This is mainly because of its poor structural condition and the likelihood that repair and improvement could not be carried out at reasonable expense.

These letters set in motion a chain of objections, inspections and re-inspections. Within a month of the letters being sent out, some 400 residents had protested, requesting a full inspection, by mid-1974 some 1,600 representations had been made. Much of the time of the urban renewal conference's meetings was thus taken up with the business of 'reclassifying' properties. This was time-consuming as it involved a detailed survey by a public health inspector to assess the necessary improvements and repairs. The owner than had to undertake to do the work and the council had to be sure that it was possible to retain the house in the context of others in the same block.

The shortage of inspectors and the difficulty in extracting commitments to improve from all owners in a street block caused many delays, frustrating those who were keen to improve, but who could not go ahead until their neighbours also agreed. Absentee landlords, in particular, were rarely willing to give such a commitment. The policy was that, if the majority of owners wished to improve, then statutory action would be taken against uncooperative landlords to save 'improvable' blocks of property. The implication of this, however, was that the council would become committed to a large programme of acquisition at some later stage.

An additional cause of delay concerned standards for improvement and repair. Schedules of improvement and repair were often expensive and some of the work proposed was thought unnecessary by the owners: for example, the stipulation that otherwise satisfactory staircases be replaced by others with a less steep gradient. Such problems resulted in a series of reinspections at modified standards, and the production of cheaper schedules. The effect, though, of this process on an already overworked team of public health inspectors was to delay further the total programme of house inspection.

Where residents agreed to improve, there was no guarantee that the agreement was binding. Many who objected to the idea that their house was unfit did so to avoid clearance and improve their prospects of compensation if clearance did occur, or just to make it easier to sell; they did not necessarily intend to improve their house.

Discussions about the classification of houses, however, had implications over which the urban renewal conference had little control. Residents who accepted the council's proposal to demolish their houses contacted the estates department to negotiate voluntary sale in advance of a compulsory purchase order. Most found the department willing to negotiate, although they discovered the process was extremely protracted. It later became clear, however, that, whilst the council would acquire houses, the occupants may not be rehoused for some time. This was because of the housing department's reluctance to rehouse the occupants of 'pink letter' property immediately as there was no clear policy for the future of the properties concerned. Rehousing would create a void in a house of indeterminate life which would add to the blight already present locally. Furthermore, until a definite life could be established the housing department would not know whether to keep the house void pending clearance, to carry out necessary repairs to enable them to let it, or to instigate a full improvement scheme as part of its contribution to urban renewal policy.

Many owners felt cheated by this decision as they had been prepared to accept a lower price for their houses than they would have received if they had waited for a compulsory purchase order. They had thought that in return for this financial loss they would be moved more quickly from the area. Now this was denied and it seemed that they would be paying rent to the council in 'their own house' and could expect a long delay before rehousing.

The dilemma facing the housing department was particularly acute. The absence of firm lifing proposals until the survey and reclassification process had been completed meant that they did not know whether to improve or repair houses already in public ownership. Yet a failure to do anything—that is, holding houses void or failing to give an undertaking to tenants about their future—led to criticism that the department were not cooperating in the policy.

The classification and designation of areas was largely dependent upon the results of the lifing of properties. As such, little progress was made during 1973 and 1974. More important, the grant structure then existing in the renewal areas, meant that owners would have to pay a larger share of, generally more costly, improvements than owners in GIAs elsewhere. Particularly after the June White Paper *Better Homes the Next Priorities* (Cmnd. 5339), the city council hoped that renewal areas could be declared HAAs and larger grants thus made available. The subsequent Conservative housing bill was lost when the government fell, however, and nearly eighteen months passed before HAAs could be declared under the Housing Act 1974.

With local government reorganisation in April 1974, urban renewal policy became the responsibility of the newly formed environmental services committee, and the urban renewal conference was replaced by a new subcommittee. The multi-disciplinary team continued to meet and reported to the subcommittee. Other departmental contributions usually came in the form of 'referred minutes' and other committees sent representatives (officers and members) to the subcommittee.

For two years the problems of determining detailed house-by-house proposals dominated the approach of both councillors and officers to the urban renewal policy. Delays in making firm proposals met with public criticism as well as concern within the local authority. The criticisms which were expressed, and high priority given to the policy, however, ensured that it was one of the first policy areas subject to the scrutiny of the new performance review committee.

The review of performance
The concept of performance review is central to corporate management. This consists of an independent committee meeting to discuss the work of separate service committees or agencies within the local authority. Birmingham's performance review committee, examining the urban renewal policy, was charged:

> (a) to consider the reasonableness of the committed programme in relation to the available resources, (b) to identify specific and general problems, and (c) to make recommendations for a new structure responsible to the various committees.
> *(Report of the performance review committee to Birmingham City Council, 7 January 1975)*

The committee received submissions from most council departments as well as outside bodies. Some councillors feared that the degree of retention proposed in renewal areas was too high, and would produce an unsatisfactory 'pepper potting' of old and new dwellings, the former comparing unfavourably with the latter. Allied to this view, some officers believed that public participation (especially on the question of lifing) had created greater uncertainty, whereas with comprehensive development people had been given definite decisions. (We might add, though, that the firm commitments of comprehensive redevelopment had rarely been effected in practice.)

Despite official claims to the contrary, many members and officers were still opposed to the corporate approach implicit in the policy, whereby existing committees and departments would have to cede powers to the urban renewal subcommittee. Some critics also argued that the whole policy was too ambitious. Members representing wards affected by the policy were often in the ambiguous posture of supporting its objectives, pressing for its speedy development and operation, but fearing that the promises being made could not be fulfilled.

Reports to the committee varied substantially in perspective and opinion, as its reports to the city council emphasised:

> On one hand the urban renewal (section) representatives maintained that the programme was realistic, up-to-date and capable of being maintained so far as renewal and improvement areas were concerned, whilst at the other extreme some chief officers identified various specific delays or suggested that no programmes existed.

The considered view of the committee was that urban renewal was not, in fact, a policy at all! Rather it was:

> more of a public commitment, i.e. an undertaking to further the task of upgrading buildings and environment, without there being a defined programme analysed in terms of both time scale and resource allocation requirements, other than in relation to house inspections.
>
> *(Report of performance review committee to Birmingham City Council, 7 January 1975)*

The policy required 'tightening up' including the articulation of a detailed, tangible programme. Delays were attributed to staff shortages, central government delays in confirming CPOs (affecting redevelopment), the process of public participation and problems with outside agencies relating to environmental improvement.

One area of controversy concerned the acquisition and disposal of property, with differences being expressed about the extent to which the authority should acquire property by compulsion for the purpose of improvement. It was agreed that the principles of land and property acquisition had to be identified, but that the content of such principles was still to be determined.

No policy had been decided with regard to houses in multiple occupation, which further delayed progress. Financial aspects of the policy were discussed, but no indication given of a range of possible costs; the question of the potential cost of local authority acquisition for improvement was not dealt with.

Whilst the review had the value of sifting many problems it did not result in a reformulated policy, rather it emphasised the need for more detailed and substantial work. Uncertainty over the future of older housing, particularly in the renewal areas, remained a crucial concern. But, as the first chairman of the standing conference on urban renewal had argued shortly after the policy had been introduced: 'Let me first make it quite clear that the declaration of renewal areas has not created uncertainty—the uncertainty already existed' *(West Midlands Grass Roots 7)*.

Nothing that happened between January 1973 and January 1975 successfully confronted or reduced that uncertainty. On the other hand, the city council had responded, almost to the letter, to the central government directive that comprehensive strategies be prepared for areas of older housing. The form and content of such policies had not been specified although local authorities had been instructed to consider 'the needs and wishes of those now living in slums and older housing' (Circular 50/72). There was every reason to believe that any attempt to continue comprehensive redevelopment would have met with substantial public opposition. So, too, would any large-scale programme of compulsory improvement (which would also have had massive cost implications for the local authority). The objectives and aspirations of the urban renewal policy were rarely questioned; what remained problematic was its feasibility. The implications of any other course of action, or inaction, were never explored.

The consolidation of management and policy, 1975–6

The performance review committee had recommended few changes to the developing management structure, and the urban renewal subcommittee 'was considered to be the most effective vehicle for the production of programmes for areas, along with initial monitoring procedures'.

The officer structure which had developed was to be formalised, and the distinction clearly made between two levels of implementation: (a) multi-disciplinary team, consisting of officers delegated from appropriate departments as well as outside bodies, meeting centrally, and (b) area-based project teams.

The content of the policy had concerned the performance review committee more than its administration. The Housing Act 1974 and subsequent circulars provided the basis for the reformation of policy, and necessitated a rethink in relation to the declaration and completion of HAAs for which a five year operational period had been established.

In advance of the act the city council sought to determine a ranking of stress areas to produce a list of priority areas for HAA designation. Two problems emerged immediately: the areas already chosen as renewal areas exhibited variety in property type, degree of over-crowding, multiple occupation and social mix; the council's knowledge of housing characteristics and social composition was also extremely variable, with a much better understanding of those areas with local project teams or other agency involvement (for example the inner area study and the community development project).

Officers faced a dilemma: whether to await a survey of all areas before ranking priorities for HAA declaration or whether to act immediately and declare those areas which it knew most about and which, anyway, appeared to fit the criteria laid down in DoE Circular 14/74. Birmingham opted for the latter course although it set up a special working party of officers to find ways of ranking remaining areas in a priority list. Four HAAs were to be declared initially.

The working party adopted a set of nine criteria for determining housing stress suggested in circular 14/75. Data were selected from the 1971 census and an index created to measure the structural condition and state of repairs of properties. Each of the nine factors was given equal weight and a score for each factor was given. Scores were then added in each area so that areas could then be ranked.

Reports on the first four proposed areas were approved by the urban renewal subcommittee early in 1975. The meeting also approved the working party's report for the other HAAs—no dates were given for declaration but a further fourteen districts were ranked in order of priority. Parts of areas formerly proposed as GIAs appeared in the list as the scoring exercise had been applied to these areas as well as to the renewal areas. Some renewal areas were excluded from the HAA list, to be later 'redeclared' as GIAs. Later, three further potential HAAs were added to this list.

Both councillors and officers argued that the first four areas had been ranked highest by their statistical procedures. Some, however, doubted that this was the case, as on subjective grounds it appeared that two of the areas contained housing that was of no poorer quality than in other areas. There did not seem to be much overcrowding or multi-occupation either. Some of these doubts were confirmed by the work of the inner area study which found that, if one of Birmingham's first four HAAs was compared with nine other areas that the council was proposing to declare using measures similar to those adopted by the council, then that area did not 'score' as high as many of the others on a number of criteria. The study also reported that no amount of giving different weights to various criteria would bring the area to the fore in the ranking.

We also examined 1971 census data to test the council's ranking of areas. We selected the enumeration districts corresponding most closely with the twenty-one areas in question, and examined five crucial variables relating to overcrowding, sharing, extent of private rental, lack of amenities and level of car ownership (a proxy for income).

We found that the area examined by the inner area study came well down the list on most criteria. It was thirteenth out of the twenty-one in terms of households living at over one and a half persons per room, sixteenth in terms of households living in shared dwellings and seventeenth in terms of households living in privately rented accommodation. It had the fifteenth highest proportion of households without the exclusive use of all amenities and twelfth in the list in terms of households with no car. Another of the first four HAAs was shared last in terms of overcrowding, last in terms of sharing, it had the lowest proportion of private renting and highest incidence of separate amenities. Clearly, the council's ranking exercise owed more to expediency than technical analysis.

The council declared the first four HAAs in March 1975. The Secretary of State did not use his powers to rescind the declarations and so action could begin. The decision to declare some renewal areas as HAAs, with the rest to follow in a phased programme, however, raised a second problem of grant priorities. Increased local authority commitment in declared HAAs and preferential rate of grant, gave some areas precedence over others. Ironically those renewal areas not scheduled for immediate declaration as HAAs were to be treated less favourably than GIAs. In GIAs 60 per cent grants were available compared with 50 per cent in remaining renewal areas, yet the latter generally contained housing of poorer quality. Thus the remaining renewal areas, until they could be fitted into the HAA programme, were disadvantaged compared both to those that had been declared HAAs and also the declared GIAs. However, the rate of declaration was high, so that by the end of 1976, fourteen HAAs had been declared containing 10,500 houses.

Birmingham's areas were much larger than those being declared by other authorities and exceed the DoE suggested size range of 200–300 dwellings. Although the council's declaration reports asserted its capacity to cope with large HAAs, no attempt was made to demonstrate this. Most reports simply stated that the council had project teams working in the areas and that the various departments met together at the multi-disciplinary team; reference was also made to the council's 'agency' scheme which would expedite the house improvement process.

The urban renewal policy had not sought initially to change the 'buffer zone' approach of previous GIA declarations (see chapter 4). However, there was considerable variation between areas programmed for future GIA status, and it was difficult to see what criteria had been used to determine when areas, particularly those nearer to the city centre, should be declared.

No analysis of social stress factors had been done to determine priority—whatever policy was meant to be pursued ('worst first' or 'best first'). The Housing Act 1974 required more information from local authorities, but chief officers agreed early in 1975 that the extra work the new procedures entailed for the council should not deter them from continuing with the programme for declaration which had been already publicly announced. Indeed, every effort would be made to continue declarations since it should increase house improvement due to the preferential rate of grant that obtained in declared areas. It was not until mid 1975 that the officers began to rethink the priorities and, based on some kind of assessment of need, reranked the proposed GIA programme.

The scale of the programme was to be continued, but several changes were made to the order of priorities within the programme and to the dates of declaration. First priority was given to areas adjacent to HAAs, and some proposed GIAs were in former renewal areas which had not been included in the HAA programme. The new GIA programme scheduled nineteen 'priority' GIAs, most to be declared within two years, and also fifty 'non-priority' GIAs for treatment at a later (unspecified) time. For some areas, then, the new programme represented a reduction in priority.

Like its HAAs, Birmingham's GIAs were larger than the DoE suggested size (DoE Circular 14/75). Of thirty-six proposed and declared areas on which we extracted data from the 1971 census, only five contained less than the maximum of 300 dwellings above which the DoE considered 'management problems are likely to hamper progress' (para. 17e). Twelve areas contained over 1,000 dwellings and two areas more than 2,000.

Clearance and redevelopment in renewal areas were originally scheduled to start in 1976, as soon as clearance in redevelopment areas was completed, but mainly due to delays in acquiring slum housing it became clear that the earliest this could be achieved was 1977. The performance review committee had recommended an integration of the management of improvement policy with redevelopment policy, and this started to be effective by the end of 1975. By this time, too, a major shift in approach began to affect parts of the areas formerly scheduled for redevelopment. A number of properties which originally had been acquired for clearance would be improved rather than demolished, starting, ironically, in an area where residents had campaigned unsuccessfully for retention seven years before. This innovation was adopted by the urban renewal subcommittee after little discussion and there seemed to be no objections to extending improvement into other areas formerly planned for redevelopment. However, in other parts of the city council, both members and officers criticised these proposals. Seldom, if ever, publicly expressed, these criticisms echoed concerns about the scale of house retention under the policy generally. Councillors and officers worried that houses which had exceeded their useful life were being retained when clearance and rebuilding was a better policy in the long term interest both of the council and residents. In addition, they argued that retention in areas long scheduled for clearance was singularly inappropriate as residents had long been accustomed to the idea of clearance and rehousing. Most were now looking forward to clearance since it meant release from years of dirt, blight and dereliction.

The overall effect of changes in the urban renewal policy was to increase the amount of property included in programmes of retention and improvement. Equal priority was given to completing the redevelopment programme and pressing on with HAAs, although GIA declaration would continue. Because of public commitments already made in declared and proposed GIAs, however, in practice there was less of a shift of emphasis towards HAAs than was acknowledged.

There was, however, a substantial shift in emphasis from gradual renewal (with a combination of clearance and improvement) to an improvement-dominated programme. By the beginning of 1976 the commitment to improvement was almost absolute, and emphasised by the proposed retention of properties specifically acquired for demolition. Many officers and councillors, though, were concerned about the limited effect of the policy on the ground, and worried that improvement policy might not, after all, be an effective way of securing better housing in the inner areas.

A close look at the achievements of the policy by the middle of 1976 tended to confirm such fears. Considerable progress had been made in defining and articulating the content of a programme for action, but this had been to little effect.

The local elections of May 1976 saw the defeat of Labour and the return of a sizeable Conservative majority on the city council. Thus June 1976 was an appropriate time to review the progress of the policy which had been initiated shortly after Labour had gained control in 1972. It was essential that estimates of progress were considered carefully; distinctions had to be made between properties already up to standard, those renovated after declaration, and between tenures. In arriving at our estimates, then, we made various assumptions which, together with our methodology, are explained in appendix I. Based on this analysis, the picture at mid 1976 was bleak.

Voluntary grant aided house improvement in the first twenty-five GIAs was limited. Of 14,500 privately owned dwellings needing improvement, less than 1,000 had been completed up to the ten point standard by mid 1976. In the first four HAAs declared only 130 out of 1,500 privately-owned dwellings were improved by the end of 1976. All four areas had been subject to intense local authority action both before and after declaration, with local project teams and active residents' groups, so the slow rate of improvement was cause for some concern.

In declared GIAs, housing associations had performed very much better than the city council. About three quarters of the housing association stock was up to the ten point standard compared to only one quarter of the local authority stock.

Declared HAAs contained about 1,000 local authority owned dwellings at the end of 1976; of these, half were pre-1919 properties to be retained and improved. Clearly the speed at which the council improved its own stock was a useful indicator to private owners of the viability of investing in their own properties. In the first four HAAs, by the end of 1976 a total of forty-six council properties had been improved out of a possible 143—just under a third in nearly two years.

The performance review committee had remarked on the strategic importance of environmental improvement, but expressed concern that little was being achieved:

> The significance of the environmental works in their effect on obtaining and maintaining public confidence in these areas was particularly identified. *No evidence was submitted that the present officers involved in the renewal process are confident that these environmental works will be undertaken within the House Improvement programme.*
>
> *(Our emphasis)*

By the end of 1976, completed environmental work was minimal. Only one very small GIA was complete, and work was going on in two other areas. No significant progress had been made on permanent works outside of these areas; there had not been any progress at all in three GIAs in Handsworth which were declared *before* the urban renewal policy commenced in January 1973.

The limited progress of urban renewal was becoming clear by the end of 1976. One criticism that had frequently been voiced by Conservatives at council meetings was that the policy was 'too ambitious' and that more had been attempted than was feasible given limited power and resources. Such criticisms, though, rarely articulated the implication of a 'less ambitious' alternative nor did they indicate how their priorities would be determined for local authority action programmes. At the same time, many critics of the urban renewal policy blamed corporate management for causing more difficulties than it resolved: when the Conservatives regained power in 1976 they immediately wound down the chief executive's research and intelligence unit, dismantled the coordinating functions of the chief executive's department and made him redundant.

Others, however, blamed the lack of progress on cuts in government expenditure which, according to the editorial in *West Midlands Grass Roots* meant 'that Birmingham has no longer any real control over its urban renewal programme' (March/April 1975). The editorial reflected the continuing concern of activists that, whilst they supported the stated aims and objectives of the policy, they doubted the council's ability and commitment. Referring to the 1973 White Paper an earlier editorial in *West Midlands Grass Roots* (August 1973) had argued that the urban renewal policy should specifically seek to achieve redistributive objectives—but was sceptical of this actually happening:

> The stated objectives of the White Paper's proposals is to direct resources to those in greatest need, but this will be far from easily realised. The White Paper does not allocate new resources on a significant scale, nor does it indicate how the dead hand of departmentalism will be cast off. The commitment to the needs of the most disadvantaged will have to be total—is Birmingham, or for that matter any other West Midland authority, up to it?

Ironically, the criticisms of both conservative and radical commentators concentrated on the *limited* resources available and the problems of management involved. There the resemblance ends, the former accepting resource limitations as natural and desirable, the latter demanding more resources. Conservative critics blamed corporate management for creating problems; radicals, ironically, argued for firmer central direction but also more public participation. In order to evaluate these alternative explanations, and relate them to a more general discussion of corporate management, we must re-examine the development of urban renewal policy between 1972 and 1976, and examine what the corporate management of urban renewal meant in practice, the assumptions on which it was based, and the constraints on corporatism.

Dilemmas of Management

Responsibility for the coordination of urban renewal was vested, originally, in the ad hoc urban renewal conference and, subsequently, in a subcommittee of the environmental services committee. Neither had more than minor delegated powers, and although supporters of the policy within the city council believed that the coordinating role *should* be a powerful one, in practice it was not. Whilst many officers publicly acknowledged the importance of corporate management, frequently departments involved with the new policy continued to adhere to programmes and policies to which they were already committed. Clashes of interest and interpretation were, therefore, inevitable. Many of these differences of approach emerged during the review of performance, hence the recommendation for a more integrated corporate approach. Departmental differences, however, continued; indeed conflicts within departments were also apparent. These difficulties were particularly felt by officers working in project teams who, in their daily work, were faced with the consequences of various departments' policies for the people of the areas affected by the policy. It was at this level that apparent contradictions between policy and practice were most evident, and the limits of departmental cooperation most severely tested.

A widespread issue that exercised the minds of one project team in particular was that of 'problem families'. Put briefly, the project teams' argument was that the presence of these families in their areas was a deterrent to their neighbours' efforts to improve their housing and the surrounding area. Residents would not wish to invest their savings in their houses if they believed that their value would be reduced by the presence of 'problem families'. Many residents had some notion of what a 'problem family' was: families with noisy, unruly children, whose parents quarrelled frequently, who showed disregard for their neighbours and who did not look after their houses. Very often the housing department was blamed for their presence (Means, 1977). Residents complained that the department used the older areas as 'dumping grounds' for their worst tenants and that it did little to ensure that they behaved in a proper way. Antipathy towards the housing department was compounded by the belief that 'decent' families living locally had little chance of local rehousing.

The housing department responded that it had *city-wide* housing responsibilities which included the duty to rehouse those in need including 'problem families'. Residents could not be guaranteed local rehousing because there may be others in need elsewhere with legitimate claims to be rehoused in HAAs and GIAs.

The project teams' criticisms were not confined to housing department policy. The engineers department was criticised for delays over making firm road proposals. 'Road-widening lines' on development plan maps blighted properties which were otherwise suitable for improvement, even though the hey-day of road construction and widening was over. This was further complicated after local government reorganisation when the county council assumed responsibility for highways. Project teams, responding to residents' complaints, were concerned that the engineers department was not doing enough to persuade the county council to rescind the road lines. The estates department was criticised for being slow in carrying out valuations of properties whose owners wished to sell to the council. The treasurer's department took months over decisions on mortgages for the owner's share of improvement costs; there were also long delays before improvement grants were paid after work had been satisfactorily completed. Finally, urban renewal project teams complained that the planning department failed to produce planning briefs for their areas, did not decide on the future of industrial and commercial properties, nor on land used for housing but previously zoned for other purposes. In addition, project teams working at the local level felt constrained by their relations with the head office of the environmental department, especially criticising delays in processing grant applications.

The project teams' principal proposal for change, by mid 1975, was that the most important departments should have a representative permanently based in each project team office. This had already been done by the architects department but housing and planning had made no similar commitment.

Whilst the secondment of officers did eventually ease communications between departments, giving residents a more accessible departmental representation, most of the teams' problems reflected conflicts of policy operated by the different sections of the city council which locally based officers were in no position to alter. Furthermore, the apparent lack of commitment to the policy was a partial reflection of the departments' shortage of staff and, in a situation of restraint on local authorities' recruitment, the diversion of officers from central departments to area teams may have added to some of the problems and delays about which the teams complained.

The presence of housing officers in the area teams could not alter the housing department's view of its city-wide housing responsibility. Furthermore, planning, treasurers, estates and engineers all had other jobs as well as assisting urban renewal and could only devote part of their officers' efforts to its implementation. These were issues over which neither the urban renewal conference nor the subcommittee had any control. Chief officers and committee chairmen regularly stated their commitment to urban renewal at public meetings, but the day-to-day reality was one of frustration both for residents in the older areas and for officers of the urban renewal section of the environmental department, especially those working in neighbourhood-based project teams.

Reviewing similar issues, the Birmingham Inner Area Study stated that:

> to have one of a main service committee's subcommittee exclusively concerned with urban renewal is not an arrangement that can be recommended to other authorities. *It would have too little status and be too much asssociated with the services controlled by its parent committee.* A joint subcommittee or a subcommittee of the Policy and Resources Committee would be better, but if there is an operational corporate planning system the subcommittee's work on developing an integrated and comprehensive strategy would be best done through standard corporate planning procedures.
>
> *(1975, p. 39)*

But Birmingham never had an 'operational corporate planning system' and therefore no 'standard corporate planning procedures'. That, however, represented just as much dissension within the controlling Labour Party as between departments. A one-day conference was held in September 1974 to discuss urban renewal amongst councillors and officers. Speakers included the leader of the council, the chairman of the environmental services committee and other councillors as well as senior officers, and it was clear that many senior councillors still objected both to the idea of corporate management and to the content of the policy. The chairman of the planning committee warned against the danger of keeping up houses that were 'only going to cause problems' in the future. Underlying tensions were revealed as many councillors and officers debated the policy, though the leader of the council emphatically reaffirmed his commitment to it and stressed that departments should not consider that they had interests separate from those of the authority as a whole.

The development of the policy, and of its administration, from 1973 to 1976 were beset with numerous problems, arising from the unanticipated complexity of issues involved. Many problems came to light as the city council appreciated more fully the special difficulties of the housing market in inner areas—offering improvement grants to owners was at most necessary, but not *sufficient* to ensure voluntary improvement.

Simple assumptions about social conditions in inner areas also had to be reappraised. In January 1973 the city council had referred to the problem of 'confidence' which was lacking and had to be recreated:

> These areas contain about 75,000 dwellings frequently character-
> ised by neglect and untidyness, *which give rise to a lack of confidence* in
> the future of the area. This results in an unwillingness to invest . . .
> with a consequent acceleration of their deterioration . . .
>   The facilities and amenities of the older areas must be made
> comparable, therefore, as far as possible, to those of the newer
> areas of the city so that *once more they become desirable places* in which
> to live and where there is a sense of community.
>   *(City of Birmingham Urban Renewal Conference, 1973, p. 5;*
>   *our emphasis)*

This perspective assumed consensus over the desirability of 'improvement', and the existence of, albeit in embryo form, 'communities' living in areas to be affected by the policy. The policy also assumed official competence, implying that the city council could, admittedly within vaguely-articulated resource constraints, develop and implement programmes of action to achieve its objectives of raising housing standards, and improving the physical environment and social facilities in older housing areas.

These assumptions can be evaluated in the light of issues and problems which arose between 1973 and 1976. The question of competence can be assessed against the city council's response first to problems of the housing market and, secondly, in relation to residents' reactions and response to the policy.

Management in the market

The housing market in Birmingham's inner area was characterised by uncertainty and insecurity. We have already discussed the difficulties that owner-occupiers and prospective new purchasers faced in trying to get mortgage finance, whether for house purchase or towards improvements. The changed structure of the privately rented sector, and its rapid decline, predicated against additional capital investment by landlords. A 'valuation gap' was becoming apparent in many cases where the cost of a house plus improvement was more than its subsequent valuation for sale (Harrison, 1977). Changes in the housing function in inner areas, especially the increase in multiple occupation, as well as the existence of sizeable ethnic minorities also affected valuers' attitudes to older properties, and hence their marketability. The short lease problem further compounded all of these problems in areas affected.

Owner-occupiers were frequently put off by the intricacies and complexities which home improvement seemed to entail and found that builders of sufficient quality were not available, at least at a price they could afford. Builders, in turn, complained that it was not worthwhile doing improvement work as it took the council so long to pay out grants that they were permanently in the red.

Most crucial of all, though, as evidenced by the Birmingham Inner Area Study (1975) survey was the question of income—both level and predictability. Owner-occupiers with housing most in need of attention were typically least able to pay for the improvement—often that was precisely why they were there at all!

Determining the importance of such issues, and devising policies for them all took time, and frequently generated disagreement between committees and between junior and senior officers.

Owner-occupation

In the light of mortgage problems in inner areas, in early 1975 the council decided to aim for a near-monopoly on new lending. Also, using new legislative powers it decided to transfer existing high interest mortgages to local authority advances. More would also be done to publicise and promote the local authority scheme. However, in June 1975 local authority lending was limited to £9m (compared to £18m the previous year). The city had already committed its full allocation and was unable to grant any more mortgages until the following April.

Following the restriction on local authority lending, the DoE negotiated a new scheme with the building societies in an attempt to persuade them to lend more freely on pre-1919 property. In practice this had little impact on the contribution that building societies made towards lending on older property. The scheme agreed by the DoE and the building societies gave local authorities the power to refer applicants to building societies; this first sieve of applicants should have led to a high rate of acceptance, but by the end of 1976 the rate for older properties was still much lower than on new.

One much publicised attempt by the city council to combine low income owner-occupation with improvement work was the 'Purchase and Improvement Mortgage Scheme' (PIMS). The most serious difficulties which the scheme faced concerned the limited number of houses in council ownership which were suitable, due to short leases and the relationship between the cost of improvements and improved market value. The basic difficulty was that, if the value of an unimproved house was added to the cost of improvements and repairs (less grant), it often came to *more* than the market value of the dwelling once improvements were carried out. The fundamental problem arising from this was that neither the council nor a building society could grant a mortgage on a dwelling in excess of a surveyor's assessment of market value—particularly affecting those who required a 100 per cent loan to cover both purchase of the leasehold interest and his share of renovation expenses.

The discrepancy between cost and the post-improvement increase in market value was most marked in HAAs, ironically where it had been intended the scheme should concentrate. Renovation costs were typically higher in these areas than elsewhere and the relatively low value of surrounding unimproved dwellings had a depressing effect on the values put on the houses improved under the scheme (Bailey, 1976).

The leasehold problem seriously affected owner-occupation in some areas. In October 1975 the urban renewal subcommittee approved a policy for the short lease problem in GIAs. The strategy was to be broadly similar to that being considered for HAAs. Firstly, leaseholders would be encouraged by the council to purchase their freeholds either using the Leasehold Reform Act 1967 or by voluntary negotiation. The council would make available mortgage funds to assist purchase in suitable cases. Where negotiations failed, the council would then seek to acquire the interest themselves either by agreement or by compulsory purchase. Once the freeholds had been acquired by the council, they could either be sold to the leaseholder or a new seventy-five year lease could be granted. Either way, the property would be eligible for grant aid: indeed, the improvement of the dwelling would be a condition of the sale or lease. This marked the start of a positive approach by the council towards the problem. A leaflet was prepared on leaseholders' rights under the 1967 Act. In early 1976 a further step was taken. Where a leaseholder's interest was of insufficient length to enable him to carry out grant aided improvement works, all interests (both freehold and leasehold) would be acquired by a compulsory purchase order and then the property could be re-leased to the ex-leaseholder.

Multi-occupation
We have already mentioned the extent to which the privately rented

sector had undergone both decline and change in the period 1961–71, and concern was increasingly expressed about houses in multiple occupation (HMOs).

Very few areas of HMOs had been affected by the redevelopment programme, but by the end of 1972 it was estimated that in areas affected by the urban renewal policy, about 2,700 houses were registered in multi-occupation. Council policy had previously concentrated on limiting the spread of HMOs and, to a lesser extent, enforcing public health and housing legislation. With the introduction of improvement policies, however, a more positive approach had to be developed.

An interdepartmental working party was set up in 1974, but it took until June 1976 for the new policy to emerge. The delay was partly due to the initial hope that the threat of local authority action would stimulate conversion into self-contained flats, but this rarely ensued. More positively, there had been a rethink about the role that HMOs played in the housing market as many people relied on multi-occupied dwellings in the privately rented market as the only available source of living accommodation. In addition, multi-occupied dwellings, under the supervision of a suitable manager, provided much-needed accommodation for those discharged from mental and penal institutions.

The reluctance of many landlords to improve, however, meant that council action would have to be carefully judged. The council decided that HMOs were not suitable for family accommodation, but that families currently in unimproved HMOs, which the landlord wanted to improve, should not get higher priority for rehousing than they would otherwise get. This would slow down improvement as landlords, after being given permission to improve for use by single people or childless couples, could hardly do so while families were still in residence.

A new policy was finalised in June 1976, too late for the 'first stage' CPO in the city's first four HAAs; thus HMOs, which often contained the worst living conditions in the areas, were to be among the last properties to be treated! Having been excluded from the first stage of compulsory action, their owners were given a second chance to improve voluntarily. Failure would result in receipt of a compulsory improvement notice, possibly leading to compulsory purchase. But this whole process meant that such CPOs were unlikely to be confirmed until the spring of 1979, nearly four years after the HAAs were declared.

The absence of a policy on multi-occupation, therefore, delayed the date at which unimproved HMOs could come into council ownership. Further, local authority inaction on what were often the worst properties in physical terms within HAAs did little to engender confidence amongst other owners who were considering whether to improve their own property.

By putting off difficult decisions about priorities for rehousing, the council actually contributed to the very problems of uncertainty that the urban renewal policy was trying to resolve.

Role of housing associations

Another response to problems of the privately rented sector and the council's growing appreciation of the housing functions that the sector had previously filled, was the development of links with housing associations. Following the Housing Act 1974, it was also government policy that registered associations should be encouraged to play their role in tackling 'housing stress'. Local authorities were instructed to say how they would cooperate with housing associations in their HAA declaration documents; they should also 'zone' associations to reduce competition and consequent price inflation (DoE Circular 14/75).

The growth of association ownership in GIAs and HAAs, however, also posed problems. In some parts of the city housing associations were unpopular with residents of adjacent property who complained about standards of repair and also that, in common with the housing department, associations were 'dumping problem families' and even prostitutes, thus 'bringing the neighbourhood down'. Occasional campaigns put some pressure on associations to improve dwellings and the 'standard' of their tenants. Repair and decoration was a frequently recurring source of grievance in many areas—for tenants as well as their neighbours. Often the consequence of faulty original improvement work, low levels of subsidy prior to the 1974 Act and a lack of care both by tenant and landlord, many association dwellings started to deteriorate rapidly after a short period of use.

The result of these grievances was that some owners were more reluctant to renovate their houses and cooperate with the council on schemes for environmental improvements. They felt that it was not worth spending money if cooperation was not forthcoming from housing associations. Whilst it is by no means clear that the housing department or all private landlords would have carried out the work of renovation and finding tenants in a way that was more to their satisfaction, the grievance remained: the associations could negate effort to improve.

Getting the work done

Little attention had been given to the availability of builders for house rehabilitation before the introduction of large-scale improvement policies. When owners approached the council about grant-aided work they were given a long list of builders who operated in their area. No specific recommendations were made, and owners were left to select their own builders and enter into contracts. Many owners had difficulty choosing a builder and often complained that firms on the council's list were not willing to do improvement work, failed to turn up after verbal agreements, or even had gone out of business many years before.

An implicit assumption of the urban renewal policy was that there existed, within the city, an adequate reservoir of small building firms ready and able to do house improvement work of the scale anticipated in the policy. This, we should recall, involved a *six-fold increase* in grant-aided improvement activity. In practice residents encountered many difficulties finding builders who were prepared to undertake grant-aided work, and frequent complaints were made to voluntary housing advisers as well as council officers.

Our research was constrained by time and personnel from undertaking an extensive analysis of the structure of the local building industry. But our discussions with voluntary agencies, council officers and residents' organisations highlighted the critical importance of the delays and frustrations caused by the general lack of builders willing and able to do improvement work. Given the low level of interest generally, it is extremely unlikely that the local building industry could have been geared up to doing the physical work necessarily envisaged in Birmingham's urban renewal policy.

In response to residents' complaints and difficulties, the council established the 'urban renewal agency' in January 1975. The idea was that owners would enter into a contract with the council which, on receipt of the necessary forms and a fee, would act on behalf of the owner to get the work done.

The agency also aimed to enable several owners to act together. The council would draw up a contract with a group of owners in an area and then find a single builder to carry out work to all the dwellings in the contract and also, possibly, to do environmental works. It was hoped that not only would this reduce costs, because of the economies of scale yielded by the size of the operation, but that it would also attract larger firms into the improvement business.

For the resident the operation seemed simple, but from the viewpoint of the council the new scheme was very complex, involving many processes and a high level of interdepartmental cooperation. Three departments were most heavily involved: building finance (quantity surveyors), architects and environmental. The housing department would be affected if a contract also involved local authority dwellings or when decanting was required. Moreover, officers of different levels within each departmental hierarchy were involved. Each project team would have an agency officer under an agency coordinator based in the central environmental department offices. The flow of work was long and complex, involving over twenty administrative processes.

In mid 1975 eight owners agreed to participate in the first scheme. Contracts were signed and negotiations were under way with a group of another seventeen owners. Progress, however, was very poor, and few houses were improved by mid 1976. The first problem concerned builders; most of the size tendering for agency contracts had little experience of improvement work, and that was limited to work on void houses. Principally they had worked on inter-war dwellings owned by the housing department. They were not prepared to carry out work while the resident was still living in the house, and residents' 'interference' became a source of discontent to workmen and supervisors.

Local project teams also faced difficulty in finding enough owners to participate to make schemes viable. This task became more difficult when the first owners involved expressed their dissatisfaction with the scheme to their neighbours. The main problem expressed by residents was the slow rate of progress. For, whilst the locally based agency officers and architects responded very quickly to an owner's request for information and an initial survey, long delays frequently occurred once initial details had been sent to the building finance department, which soon proved unable to process the work quickly and dissatisfaction grew as the delays lengthened.

Two further factors contributed to residents' apathy. Firstly, many objected to having to pay the 10 per cent fee; some thought that they should not pay anything while others simply thought the fee was too high. Second, there were discrepancies of up to 20 to 30 per cent between the estimated cost when properties were inspected and the actual cost once work had been carried out (Bailey, 1976). Owners claimed that they were 'duped' into using the agency on the basis of false information.

A further major problem was that, by the middle of 1976, it was argued that it was too expensive to run. The council was incurring expenditure which was not covered by the 10 per cent fee charged to owners. The council costed its inputs in relation to the service, including the agency officers, the quantity surveyors and architects. In principle each of these activities received a fixed proportion of the 10 per cent fee, in practice the expenditure incurred, particularly by the architects was in excess of the income produced from the charge to owners. This was exacerbated at first as costing including development work done establishing the scheme. The agency service was discontinued in mid 1976 by the incoming Conservative council, ostensibly on grounds of its cost.

Housing costs and incomes
Although the cost of improvement was a critical deterrent to many owners (see Birmingham Inner Area Study, 1975), the council had little control over owners' ability to pay their share or the subsequent valuation of improved properties. Generous interpretation of the rules was possible, but grant levels were widely considered too low to act as the necessary stimulus, even if all other things had been equal. Both the leader of the council and his senior officers made representations to central government, but there was to be no increase in available grants until towards the end of 1977, by which time inflation in building costs had dramatically increased the real amounts that owners would have to meet themselves (Paris, 1977).

With regard to problems of valuation, the council was almost entirely powerless. Its own purchase and improvement scheme, too, was affected by the same problem. There were, however, also suggestions of dissent between departments within the authority, with the city council's own valuers being criticised for undervaluing property whether improved or not.

The management of confidence
The extent to which residents' confidence in their neighbourhood could be heightened by improvement policy was never made clear. Rapid increase, especially during the 1960s, of multiple occupation, the clear deterioration of the general physical environment, the accumulation of litter, closure of well established shops, in some

areas blatant prostitution, as well as rapid population turnover, have all had profound effects on residents' perceptions and aspirations.* These feelings were probably most marked in the older, white residents, who frequently saw their new Asian neighbours as evidence of the neighbourhood's decline.

Ironically, many of their complaints were precisely the concerns of Asian newcomers, who were particularly distressed by the blatant prostitution. For many of this group, though, as the inner area study report has emphasised, areas like Small Heath presented opportunities as well as constraints. There was a pool of accessible, relatively cheap housing for owner-occupation, low-cost premises for commercial and religious purposes and access to available job opportunities. The private market enabled relatives and friends to live in proximity to each other, so that community ties could be sustained and strengthened. Critically, though, few Asians could afford to undertake full improvement of their housing, though many wished to repair and improve incrementally.

There existed a diversity of attitudes towards the urban renewal policy, manifest in different ethnic evaluations of present housing conditions and in the racial hostility, albeit rarely openly expressed, of many white residents. Whilst there were various 'communities', these did not exist in a simple geographically expressed fashion, rather they were communities of interest and belief which crisscrossed any lines on maps or bureaucratically defined areas. All that was shared was spatial location and position in the housing market.

The latter, however, was also complicated by differences of interest, however marginal in broader class terms, which seemed significant to individuals involved. For instance, tenants of a private landlord who did not improve, but used all available tactics to delay compulsory purchase, often thought that they would benefit more from council acquisition for clearance and subsequent rehousing.

Many owner-occupiers, especially the elderly, expected their homes to 'last them' without additional expense for the rest of their lives—they neither wanted to be disturbed by slum clearance nor by rehabilitation. Other owner-occupiers welcomed the new policy because it gave them the chance to sell their property and move out, whereas clearance would have reduced the marketability of their

*Particularly in the inner part of the Middle Ring: Aston, Balsall Heath, Sparkbrook, Sparkhill, Small Heath, Saltley, Handsworth, Soho and Rotton Park. These areas contain virtually the whole of the HAA programme, as well as approximately half of the GIA programme.

house and may have forced them into becoming dependent on the council for rehousing.

What most residents shared, however, was scepticism about the council's intentions and ability. Many voiced disbelief that clearance would not affect them, albeit a disbelief largely tempered with relief! Whatever the optimistic scenario painted by councillors and officers at public meetings, for residents it could only be evaluated against knowledge of their own and others' experiences of other council policies, particularly comprehensive redevelopment. The latter had been an experience of delays, disruption and, at the very time the new policy was introduced, everyday encounters with vast cleared sites dotted with odd derelict houses which were to have been redeveloped many years ago. This did not inspire an attitude of confidence; the order of the day was 'wait and see'. Others, with less knowledge of redevelopment, shared their caution and distrust. Other promises had been made and broken, why not these? Recent black immigrants, used to bureaucratic indifference and hostility, often just wanted to be left alone.

In response councillors and officers argued that they were trying to 'keep communities together' which improvement policy could achieve better than redevelopment. Improvement, they claimed, benefited everyone, even landlords could sell their properties to the council or housing associations which would then improve them for the benefit of existing tenants. Such suggestions, however, tended to confirm residents' suspicions that the council failed to understand their problems, fears and aspirations. White residents often feared and disliked their relatively recent black neighbours, and the latter knew only too well the realities of constant discrimination.

Where the council could have given a lead, as for example through programmes of environmental improvement or the speedy modernisation of its acquired older housing, there were few encouraging signs. Environmental work was minimal or non-existent and the council's stock, apart from a few isolated cases, was showing few signs of setting the pace.

Many owner-occupiers also feared that little was being done to influence others, particularly private landlords, to improve. The urban renewal subcommittee favoured either voluntary improvement or compulsory purchase in the HAAs rather than seeking to use powers to compel owners (whether landlords or owner-occupiers) to improve. However, there were disagreements about the nature, scale and timing of compulsory acquisition, so much so that when the first set of CPOs were made in HAAs no clear policy had been decided and many properties were excluded even though they needed improvement or repair. The HMO policy was still under discussion, and various other properties had to be excluded (those where improvement caused 'hardship', for example elderly owner-occupiers) and those above the rateable value limit for improvement grant aid.

Residents were not made aware of problems of policy coordination and departmental conflict. Such things, indeed, were carefully avoided by speakers at the platform in public meetings. What was communicated in practice was a series of delays and difficulties which again confirmed the sceptics and troubled the optimists.

The onus for involving residents and convincing them of the viability of improvement policy was increasingly placed on the neighbourhood-based project teams. These, however, were effectively low-tier implementation agencies, faced with dilemmas of responsibility and departmental conflicts above their heads. The Birmingham Inner Area Study (1975, p. 33) reported reluctance amongst senior officers in housing, planning and social services departments to second their officers to area teams 'because they felt the urban renewal section did not really understand the professional roles of the planner, social worker or housing manager'. The local area teams also came to experience the difficulties of 'communicating' with the public acutely as public participation exercises developed (see chapter 6). For them, more than other officers, the assumptions of both consensus and competence came to be tested and questioned.

Powers and Resources

The review of performance and the Housing Act 1974 provided the framework for further development of the urban renewal policy. The Act itself, however, also gave rise to difficulties, and was followed by a series of measures designed to restrain local authority expenditures. In combination these added up to constitute a severe constraint on the viability of the policy of urban renewal, partly in terms of the sheer amount of officers' and councillors' time that was consumed in making constant readjustments to policies and programmes of action.

Problems with the Housing Act 1974

Partly as a response to 'gentrification' the Act required owner-occupiers not to sell their houses for five years after receiving a grant. Landlords had to keep the dwelling available for letting for the same period (seven years in HAAs). If an owner breached these conditions of a grant, for example by selling his house, a local authority could require him to repay the grant, at compound interest. These restrictions doubtless deterred some owners from seeking grant aid. Although the council decided to implement the penalties flexibly it made little effort to publicise this decision.

Another part of the Act imposed a restriction on local authorities approving a grant to an owner-occupier whose house was in a GIA, HAA or priority neighbourhood and which had been tenanted during the previous twelve months. This was designed to prevent landlords from engaging in the often profitable exercise of selling unimproved, formerly tenanted properties, with vacant possession to owner-occupiers who will improve.

A further difficulty associated with the Housing Act 1974 was that, in HAAs, there was no equivalent to the government grant for environmental improvements that existed in GIAs. The Act provided government money for 'environmental works' of 50 per cent of expenditure up to £50 per dwelling, but this was restricted to work on the exterior of dwellings and on land within the curtilage of dwellings. Thus the council could do only limited work to improve the 'environment' and could, therefore, do little to create the right 'atmosphere' for house improvement. The council's dismal record on environmental work in GIAs, however, suggested that this constraint was not in itself likely to be critical!

Cuts in public expenditure 1974–6. Rateable value limit
Section 62 of the Housing Act 1974, gave the Secretary of State the power to specify a 'rateable value limit' on owner-occupied properties eligible for improvement grants—houses above the specified limit would have applications refused. In November 1974 a Statutory Instrument (SI 1974, No. 1931) was issued declaring that the limit would be £175 per annum (£300 in Greater London). Birmingham's programme probably suffered more than that of any other authority, as many dwellings in both its declared and proposed GIAs and HAAs were over the £175 limit.

The aim of the limit was to effect a general reduction in improvement expenditure, but crucially in Birmingham it often affected those very properties most in need. In one area, formerly a renewal area and later an HAA, 24 per cent of dwellings were owner-occupied and had rateable values over £175, representing some 60 per cent of all owner-occupied houses in the area. In another area, still a renewal area, as many as 32 per cent of dwellings were owner-occupied and over the limit.

The council made vigorous representations to the DoE about the new limit. The urban renewal officer prepared a document spelling out the council's difficulties and it was sent to the Minister for Housing, Reg Freeson, immediately prior to his visit to the city in April 1975. The officer argued that the limit discriminated against those in most need of assistance because many owners would not be able to carry out improvement work unaided. He claimed that HAA policy had been jeopardised by the restriction. Some months later a fuller representation brought the racial dimension to the fore, arguing that in one HAA in particular the restriction severely affected the housing opportunities of Asians, who owned large, ill-repaired houses.

However, no change was made to the limit until a further instrument (SI 1976, No. 526) came into operation in April 1976, raising the limit for owner-occupied houses that are to be converted into flats to £350 (£600 in Greater London). This instrument reprieved most large multi-occupied houses with resident landlords, as the owner-occupied part of the dwellings could get grants as rateable values rarely exceeded £350. However, until late in 1977 the £175 limit still applied to houses whose owners wished to improve them for single family use.

'Section 105' allocations and council mortgages
Section 105 of the Housing Act 1974 required local authorities to get the permission of the Secretary of State for the Environment for their proposed expenditure on improvement and conversion of houses in their ownership. Prior to the beginning of the financial year 1975/6 local authorities thus sent 'bids' to central government for planned expenditure on this work. Birmingham requested permission to spend £10.4 million but was only allocated £5 million. This meant that the improvement of older purpose-built council housing as well as acquired older housing would have to be severely cut back. Representations to ministers brought no positive response. As contracts had already been made for the improvement of inter-war housing little of the £5 million could be diverted to older acquired housing.

Mounting pressure from local authorities had the effect of getting an extra allocation for improvement to council stock. This, however, was only allowed at the expense of local authority mortgages; authorities could only borrow half of the amount they had borrowed during the previous year for lending to owners. By June, when the circular was issued, Birmingham had already exceeded the 50 per cent limit and thus further advances were not possible.

Whilst the effects of the freeze on council mortgages had no *direct* impact on house improvement, officers and councillors feared that it would produce adverse indirect consequences for the policy as a whole. In practice, mortgages were tightly rationed and many vendors were unable to sell, lowering confidence even further in urban renewal policy precisely in those areas where the council sought to stimulate improvement.

Further cuts introduced during 1975 had an immediate, albeit shortlived, effect on urban renewal. In June, Circular 64/75 restricted the scope for local authority acquisitions. Generally this did not affect HAAs and GIAs, but it did mean that owner-occupied and tenanted housing outside declared areas could not be acquired by negotiation. The consequence of this was to slow down the improvement drive in areas where owners wanted to sell to the council in advance of statutory declaration.

The cuts in perspective

By the spring of 1976 there was some relaxation of central government financial control. Mortgage lending still had to be rationed, but the section 105 allocation was increased to £10 million (including £1 million for the relief of unemployment). By this time, too, council policy was aimed at directing available funds to inner areas. This did not necessarily entail diverting resources specifically to areas affected by the urban renewal policy; but it was hoped, for example, that most mortgage applicants for pre-1919 dwellings would want to buy in those areas. A ceiling above which mortgages would not be granted was imposed aiming to channel funds to cheaper housing in the worst areas.

Cuts in public expenditure alone were not the cause of the urban renewal policy's failure. Conflicts within the city council, public scepticism, the cost of improvement relative of its benefits, institutional lending policies and, as in the case of environmental work and HMO policy, the council's failure to move ahead, all contributed to the dismal record. So too did the sheer complexity of market relations within which the council sought to intervene.

But the cuts in expenditure were important by contributing to the prevailing atmosphere of seemingly inevitable delays and uncertainty. Whilst many public expenditure cuts did not immediately affect the urban renewal policy, and others only affected various parts of the policy, their effects in *combination* were important. Emerging policies on particular issues had to be abandoned, delayed or reorganised. Component parts of the policy seemed to be in a perpetual state of flux and uncertainty.

The effect of the rateable value limit can never be certain, because it is difficult to estimate how many owners would have improved if the restriction had not been imposed. It was likely that owners of large, dilapidated houses which would have been expensive to improve even with grant aid would not have sought grants even if they were available. Similarly, no real disincentive was placed on landlords of multi-occupied properties, as there was little prospect of either capital or revenue gain from improvement work.

Even the cut-back on local authority mortgages did not have an immediate impact on the older areas, because in the period up to the cut-back, when mortgages were available, relatively few advances had been made in these areas. The government's cut in council mortgage finance did not so much cause a mortgage famine, as stem the trickle which had been slowly flowing in preceding years. But the cut did critically affect the plans which were just being developed in Birmingham to redirect its own mortgage finance towards the inner areas.

This mood was communicated from councillors and officers to the public, not as an overt political issue, but as an unavoidable and distasteful fact of life, regretted but inevitable. Ministers could be lobbied and the DoE cajoled but, crucially, the city council had no control over the outcome of such attempts to influence decisions, taken elsewhere, which restructured the framework of its own operations.

The Management of Crisis?

The complexity of issues, attitudes and interests involved in just one policy of one local authority amongst many in modern Britain may seem overwhelming. But an understanding of diversity and its accurate representation, are necessary prerequisites to attempts at understanding relationships, the nature, effects and significance of which we have described in such detail.

Without any doubt, sincere efforts were made by many councillors and officers to develop a corporate approach to urban renewal.

What that meant, however, needs to be reviewed in order to separate out special features of the local situation from more general considerations of corporate management. The effects of the urban renewal policy must also be put into the context of the way in which corporate management coped with the particular circumstances of nationally determined powers and resources which were applied to the special features of inner city housing markets.

The nature of corporatism in Birmingham's urban renewal policy

The coordination of urban renewal policy represented an attempt to bring together the work of existing departments to focus on area-based programmes of action requiring the integrated involvement of different groups of officers. It sought to reduce departmentalism, avoid duplication of effort and conflict between the activities of various sections within the authority. Disregarding for a moment the aims and content of the policy concerned, these are commonsense and unobjectionable maxims of management. The policy itself hoped to effect an improvement to the housing conditions and residential environment for those citizens living in the oldest housing and poorest environments. This broad objective was shared by the major political parties, voluntary organisations and the residents of Birmingham's older housing.

The development of a corporate approach, however, was limited for reasons which were both more, and less easily avoidable by the city council. Neither the urban renewal conference nor the urban renewal subcommittee had significant executive powers. The former was a specially constituted body with no executive function and the latter was subordinate to the environmental services committee, which itself had less standing than other committees, particularly the central policy and resources committee, but also the prestigious education and housing committees. The post of urban renewal officer was not of chief officer status, and many officers operating at grass-roots level were seconded from other departments on a temporary or part-time basis. The council's commitment to the policy and its implementation thus never amounted to its elevation as a programme area to which departmental interests were subservient. Indeed, it was the other way round: management of the policy was charged with persuading, negotiating and bargaining with senior committees and senior officers in what remained a departmental structure of policy-making and administration.

Between the establishment of the urban renewal conference and the policy review the complexity of issues raised problems of approach, knowledge, and coordination. In responding to central government instruction to prepare a programme for older housing, the council was confronted by complicated legislative powers and a potentially massive commitment of resources. The assumptions on which policy development were based, and which in turn guided the organisation of policy, proved to be less than adequate to this task.

The imposition of resource constraint underlined weaknesses of the council's assumption of competence. In the face of market conditions antagonistic to the improvement of older housing to the proposed standards, neither the powers nor resources were available to the local authority. The extent to which the council could develop policies considered appropriate to the local situation was severely limited, despite central government advocacy of such policies.

A crucial assumption, namely that of the viability of coordination, perhaps existed more as an objective than an expectation. Many Labour councillors wished to break down the strength of the biggest departments within the authority and achieve a situation in which officers were more clearly answerable to elected representatives. The Labour Party thus set out both to achieve political objectives and demonstrate its managerial capability. But departments which had gained strength over many years did not relinquish power so easily, particularly in face of coordinating agencies of relatively weak status. Many proposals considered important to the progress of urban renewal policy were met with conflicting priorities and practices of service departments, and these were resolved by higher tiers of decision-making which could not satisfy inherently different objectives. The existence of diverse views regarding the content of the policy itself, held by councillors as well as officers, predicated against the rapid development of the policy and, in turn, presented the public with a series of uncertainties, delays, and changes of direction. This reinforced an atmosphere of confusion and scepticism confirming existing doubts about the council's sincerity and ability.

A further assumption upon which the policy was based was that of symmetry between the council and residents regarding the objectives of the policy. This broke down in the face both of residents' distrust and the realisation that consensus was based on different interpretations of what 'improvement' meant, as well as conflicts of interest structured around market processes and the bureaucratic distribution of resources.

Effects

Between the spring of 1972 and summer of 1976 the corporate management of Birmingham's urban renewal policy was concerned with the development rather than the implementation of policy. A long walk through Birmingham's inner areas revealed few changes that could be directly attributable to the endless series of public meetings, the lengthy meetings of councillors and officers, or the tremendous work behind the scenes both within the urban renewal section and on the task of coordinating departmental inputs. The councillors most involved had very few evenings at home, officers frequently worked ten- or twelve-hour days only to be rudely received by residents' associations and community activists.

If so little happened on the ground, though, does this not suggest that the policy had equally little effect, whether measured according to physical change or people's understanding of local authority policy? Residents, certainly, had few insights into the ways in which the policy was organised; nor, on the whole, was it important to them. The atmosphere of activity and concern, however, generated at public meetings and in locality-based offices of the urban renewal section, as well as the sincerity of the chairmen of the urban renewal conference and subcommittee, created a strong impression amongst residents. Hope, indeed, springs eternal: something was clearly happening, or, more accurately, *about to happen*. The future remained uncertain and hypothetical, but even the sceptics usually conceded that the council was trying to understand their problems, even if they subsequently decided that councillors and officers 'really' did not care or understand.

The corporate approach was relevant so long as the intention of coordination and the potential implications of coherent housing policies in the older areas offered inspiration to politicians and the hope of a better future for residents.

Past problems were attributed to difficulties of coordination and communication, not the limited autonomy of a local authority constrained by central government and market forces. The conception of corporate management provided a logical solution to limited powers and resources and problems of coordination. This was infinitely preferable to attempting to transform the attitudes and activities of the existing departmental structure (whilst in fact retaining the same structure) or challenging the imperatives of the economic and political system.

The significance of management

The complexity of issues that the council faced raised difficulties, but there was no reason to suppose that organisation, overtly structured around departments, could have better confronted this. Professional interests remained deeply rooted, and many problems of attempted coordination derived from different departmental views and power. The evidence, indeed, underlines the need for better coordination. One response might be to give the responsibility for urban renewal to one major committee, especially a housing committee, having full-time specialists from different backgrounds combining within its department to coordinate policy. This would have strengthened the policy in Birmingham, but could not in itself resolve the question of conflicts between departments. Moreover, what was basically a *housing* renewal policy, was but one of many major local authority programmes. The critical consideration must be the very context of local authority management more than its form. A corporate approach to policy at the local authority level could neither affect the powers and resources available to that authority nor, therfore, could it alone affect the scope and limits of local authority involvement in housing.

We found little evidence to substantiate the argument that corporate management of policy resulted in a reduction of democratic involvement in policy-making. That is, however, because the base from which such a view could be taken was itself questionable. Residents in Birmingham's inner areas had not participated at all during previous programmes of comprehensive redevelopment, whereas the urban renewal policy sought residents' participation and involvement. At a meeting for officers and councillors in the Council House in September 1974 the chairman of the urban renewal subcommittee tried to get more ward councillors involved in the policy. Birmingham's Labour Party, whilst more open internally than the Conservative Party, has long had a tradition of powerful leaders and a strong inner caucus (Newton, 1976). To suggest that corporate management was an anti-democratic tendency, in this context at least, would be to erect an argument based upon a myth of a participatory past which never existed.

Did corporate management, finally, serve as a means of financial restraint? Again, there is no evidence to indicate that this was a necessary feature of corporate management, as budgetary control can be exercised within any management structure. Our experience of urban renewal in Birmingham was that budgetary constraint was imposed in spite of a corporate approach, certainly not because of it, and that the admittedly embryonic overall corporate process was not more likely to obscure and mystify cuts in public expenditure than any other framework of administration.

The corporate approach to urban renewal management was a guiding principle which was never achieved. It provided new 'technical' substance to political inspiration; this had the effect of continuing to present the appearance of competence despite the realities of departmentalism and external constraints. Whilst the assumptions of consensus on which the policy was based proved tenuous an atmosphere of action and concern was generated, despite manifest delays and minimal progress on the ground.

It is useful, then, to reflect whether the management of renewal from 1972–6 amounted to the management of physical change to ageing houses and their environs, or whether it amounted to the management of people living in them. If it was substantially the latter, then the notion of 'crisis management' might assume an attraction. That is, the role of management was to define problems in technical, apolitical terms and, despite physical deterioration during a period of economic recession, hold out the prospect of a better future.

There was no evidence of organised popular dissent before the policy was conceived. There was no 'crisis' in the everyday sense of houses falling down or street violence. But the policy *had* originated in concerns that comprehensive redevelopment was failing to match the rate of housing decay and also causing social problems. Improvement policy was thus based on calculations about the probability of deteriorating housing conditions and social relations in inner areas, and sought to avoid this prospect. Thus we can usefully think of 'crisis management' as attempts to *avoid* crises of whatever magnitude. The more efficient the management, so much the better; but policies which are unable to confront the causes of crisis remain dependent on other interventions. If more powers and resources had been available to Birmingham City Council then the urban renewal story 1972–6 might have been very different. The hard fact that they were not available, therefore, means that we cannot explain what *actually* happened merely by reference to their absence. The local authority, following central government directions, sought to develop a policy within the framework of existing powers and political assumptions, at a time when resources were being limited. The production of a more 'comprehensive' policy obscured the concurrent period of central government withdrawal and the problems inherent in the council's attempts to grapple with the conflicts and uncertainties of the inner city housing market.

6 Public Participation

Public Participation in Urban Planning

The practice of citizen involvement in public affairs has its roots deep in human history. The forms of involvement, however, have been as varied as the multitude of different societies within which some or all members have had differential influence over the development and implementation of collective activities. As such, the concept of 'public participation' can refer to quite different kinds of relationships, existing in diverse social contexts. Additionally, whilst different commentators might agree to use the term public participation to describe a particular observable relationship, they may disagree profoundly about its genesis, meaning and significance. Such disagreements derive from assumptions that different analysts make about the role of the state (and hence the relationships between individuals and formal political institutions), and, secondly, the nature and desirability of social change.

Two opposing views are typically taken regarding the growth of the demand for participation in public decision-making. One argues that public participation is the spontaneous product of growing public disenchantment with government. Whether this is orchestrated through middle class pressure groups or community action by inner city residents, public participation is seen as a demand which has produced concessions from government (Hain, 1977). The other interpretation sees public participation, not as a consequence of public dissatisfaction, but as a device initiated and sustained by government to provide legitimation for actions that it already intends to take, particularly when that action may otherwise meet public opposition (Cockburn, 1977). Such debates, however, cannot be settled in the abstract—we have to examine specific instances of public participation to judge whether either explanation holds. We also have to accept that both versions could be true in particular instances, and that local studies must therefore be related back to broader theoretical concerns.

The most popular context for studies of public participation in Britain has been in the field of urban planning. More often than not studies have criticised the 'failure' of planners to participate positively with working class residents (Dennis, 1972; Davies, 1972). The same thing can be said about a study of the diversity of opinions which influence planners' (and the public's) view on the practicality of involving the public in the preparation of plans (Drake *et al.*, 1975). Moreover, the need for a theoretical framework to comprehend the almost bewildering complexity of views, opinions, interpretations and evaluations of public participation has been ably demonstrated by Andrew Thornley (1977) in a recent essay.

But the location of public participation within its broader political context, and an examination of a particular participatory effort in this light, can generate insights into this broader structure of political relations which are lost to those whose concern is with public participation itself, particularly when their major focus is on the narrowly defined statutory obligations of local authorities. As such we are not seeking to criticise those works already cited, indeed they are all essential contributions to the subject.

Rather, we can focus on public participation in order to explore questions about the relations between legitimate authority and democracy, between the state and citizens. Public participation is not new to the extent that citizens participate in the process of government, as classical theorists of representative democracy will readily affirm (Fagence, 1977, Chaps. 1 and 2). But when normal rules of behaviour are substantially modified, as has been the case during the last ten years with state-sponsored participation in planning (Town and Country Planning Act, 1968; 'Skeffington Report', 1969), then outcomes that are either unanticipated or unwelcome to the state may result; thus there has to be a constant process of redefinition and reinterpretation of the new rules. So the *form* of participation becomes crucial, as do the expectations of participants in the modified political context.

In so much as public participation has introduced innovatory features into public life, then it provides a valuable research setting for investigating established political problems and their resistance to change. In particular, where central government has placed a statutory obligation on local authorities to participate in urban planning, it is the duty of the latter to administer the process and take account of views made (as in the case of public participation in structure planning). The extent to which Birmingham City Council sought to involve residents in urban renewal policy, albeit poorly defined initially, was a major *local* initiative. In part designed to avoid mistakes that had been made in previous policies, public participation in urban renewal raised important contradictory features of the local authority's claim to legitimacy.

Such contradictions emerged during attempts by residents and their organisations to affect the development of policies. They critically affected those local government officers involved in the process of mediating between the city council and residents. They were inextricably linked to the claims of representative democracy and local autonomy. The rest of this chapter is concerned, first, to introduce the specific circumstances under which public participation came to play a part in Birmingham's urban renewal policy, then, second, to examine in some detail what actually happened. Finally we reconsider the political effects of public participation in Birmingham.

Urban Renewal in Birmingham: Public Participation as the Incorporation of Protest?

Neighbourhood-based participation exercises have been the subject of numerous studies and we have previously discussed one such instance where 'participation' came to mean 'technical co-operation' along parameters worked out by local government officials (Lambert *et al.*, 1978). So long as small-scale, piecemeal participation exercises remained the order of the day, then some neighbourhoods, perhaps containing a more articulate neighbourhood association or with better access to the local press, could claim disproportionate amounts of locally-determined resources. 'Participation' could mean little more than competition between neighbourhoods for priority of allocation; city-wide processes of policy formulation and implementation remaining unaffected.

The occasion of Birmingham's new urban renewal policy introduced a different dimension to the situation. Public participation was proposed both as a means of developing the policy *and* as an objective of the policy in its own right. One of the first tasks of the Urban Renewal Conference had been to 'encourage public participation' (Millar, 1972, p. 203) whilst the council's explanatory booklet on the policy announced that the conference was 'anxious that the local communities join with them to ensure the success of the urban renewal policy' and that local residents were to be 'invited to contribute their knowledge of the problems and needs of their area by becoming involved in the early stages prior to the design of the environmental improvement' (City of Birmingham Urban Renewal Conference, 1973, p. 12). The city council could argue that its objectives were identical to those of residents of older areas: namely, that money should be injected into those areas in order that physical conditions and confidence in the area's future were raised.

It has been argued elsewhere that government uses techniques of public participation in order to define the interests of residents as congruent to its own. In this way local groups which set out to oppose public policies may be 'incorporated' by public participation exercises which redefine the situation and modify the aims and aspirations of such groups in line with local authority policy (Bonnier, 1972; Mason, 1977). The aims of the organised community become redefined as the same as those of the local authority and the activities of the former thereby emasculated (see also Cockburn, 1977).

This perspective describes public participation as a process whereby the potential anger and frustration of communities affected by planning is diffused, so that concerted action to challenge the existing order of things is diverted into 'useful' and 'constructive' discussions with each other and with representatives of the local authority concerned. In these circumstances, residents' committees and federations become crucial parts of the process of incorporation as they take on the role of representing a notional constituency in interaction with the local authority, but in practice have no influence on that authority.

This approach views the interests of the local authority, as an agency of the state, as structurally in conflict with those of organised residents and thus any apparent similarity in the expressed goals of the two must represent a success on the part of the former in incorporating the latter.

But, as we argued in chapter 4 the similarity of interest between large sections of the population in the inner areas, and some of the elements within the local authority, cannot wholly be explained in these terms. There was a substantial, albeit in practice short-lived, concurrence which can not be explained in terms of some conspiratorial attempt by local government to quieten revolt; rather, the aims of the new policy and the enthusiastic manner of its presentation found agreement among many of those who would be affected by it. Whilst many would have welcomed house improvement itself, what the new policy meant for others was a halt to the bulldozer and the hint that at least they would be left alone.

So the popular response was initially one mainly of acquiescence with the broad objectives of the new policy. Most people living in areas to be affected, of course, only came to be aware of the policy gradually, and so it would be misleading to suggest that there was any spontaneous response or reception at all, whether enthusiastic or oppositional.

The major impetus towards the development of participation came from within the city council. When the policy was introduced there was still considerable disagreement both within the Labour and Conservative groups on the city council and between senior officers in different departments. The disagreements within the Labour group were resolved through debate and resolutions confirmed authoritatively at council meetings. Many members were suspicious that the city council might be raising hopes which it could not fulfil, as what was politically desirable appeared to conflict with what they believed to be technically feasible. Bound by majority decision and strong leadership, their enthusiastic support had to be won, and an appeal to the widest constituency possible—the community as a whole—was one means of ensuring it.

The 'competence' of a local authority in terms of technical ability and resource availability, however, is largely circumscribed by factors outside of its control (Lambert *et al.*, 1978; above chapter 5). The contradiction which was raised over participation was not one of the problems of incorporating antagonistic community demands, instead it was the problem of the autonomy of the local authority in relation to central government and in the context of formidable market forces both within areas of older housing and the economy as a whole. One source of protest which was incorporated was that of those Labour councillors and local government officials who spoke against the policy in private—usually on technical, not political grounds—but whose voices were muted by the whip in the Council Chamber and the rules of bureaucratic conduct in public.

Any theoretical critique of public participation which assumes a monolithic state misses the essential contradiction which is as much present in the local as central state, which is that the state reflects and corresponds to the class structure of society as a whole, and that, within any local authority's area, there are class divisions and interests which are also the basis for divisions within the city council (see also Pickvance, 1977b). Thus, when Birmingham's newly elected Labour council sought to involve residents in its new policy, it was not trying to get them to act against their own interests—quite the reverse—it sought to establish and reinforce its own political strength through policies intended to benefit those of its supporters in the worst housing conditions. Whilst we have pointed out weaknesses in the analysis upon which it was based, Birmingham's urban renewal policy was in intention a real attempt at positive redistribution. However, the new policy represented a considerable shift away from the previous approach to urban renewal, namely comprehensive redevelopment. Many councillors within the Labour group, reinforced by some senior officers, were opposed to the introduction of a large-scale programme of house and area improvement. Public support was thus essential to win such opponents over to the new policy; clearly there was mounting opposition to an extension of the clearance programme, and vociferous community action groups claiming to represent popular opinion were demanding more public participation. What remained to be determined, however, were the rules of the game.

In practice the contradictory nature of participation has more clearly been revealed, critically in terms of the very competence which was held in question. Many issues have been encountered, as the appeal to the public inevitably created new relationships which questioned established channels of authority and competence. The role of the locally elected councillor came to be examined, as did the question of who could legitimately participate from 'the community'. The social heterogeneity which characterised older areas was a factor totally ignored in the city council's quest to 'keep communities together'. New stresses, in many cases unanticipated, were placed upon those junior local government officers who actually met and 'participated' with the public. The extent and influence of participation, ill-defined and loosely conceived initially, came to be a central problem for those officers who were seeking to develop and implement Birmingham's urban renewal policy.

Public Participation in Practice

One of the most striking and novel features about public participation in Birmingham's urban renewal policy was the creation of two levels of participation. From the introduction of the policy it was intended that not only should the public be involved with planning at the local level, but also there should be participation at a city-wide level. This would be through a representative committee which would hold regular meetings with councillors and officers at which issues and matters of general policy were to be discussed. The two levels were in practice overlapping, with many of the principal participants active at both levels; the different practices involved, however, and the issues raised, merit separate descriptive treatment before attempting any overall evaluation in terms of the political and theoretical issues involved.

Participation at a local level

Public meetings. Before the urban renewal policy was launched, the council's former public health committee had embarked on one form of public participation. In each GIA there had been a public meeting at which people were told of the council's intentions and were asked for their reactions to plans for environmental improvements.

The pattern of major public meetings continued through the early development of the policy. The chairmen of the urban renewal conference, usually accompanied by major committee chairmen and senior officers, embarked on a campaign of public meetings in all areas where action of some kind was proposed. Those meetings often turned out to be stormy affairs, where the speakers on the platform were received with scepticism and complaint from the floor of the hall.

In part, undoubtedly, these meetings were keenly anticipated by various project-based community workers or self-styled activists who took the opportunity to seek a public confrontation with councillors and officers. But many in the audience, whilst in agreement with the need to improve their areas, took the opportunity to air misgivings and scepticism about the sincerity of the new proposals. For many older residents, the 'real' problems of their neighbourhood concerned the type of people who had recently moved in. Frequently referring to some time in the past when their area had been a 'nice place to live', in recent years things had changed through the arrival of coloured immigrants and 'problem families'. These had led to the 'deterioration' of the district and no amount of environmental improvement would reverse this trend. Further complexity was introduced by the profound difference of opinion typically expressed between owner-occupiers and tenants. The latter, particularly in poorer privately rented accommodation, often saw 'improvement' as an obstacle to their gaining access to council housing. Instead of the move that would have been their right under comprehensive redevelopment, they feared that they would now remain in unimproved, deteriorating older property.

The problems raised were often defined by council representatives as problems of *communication*. Sure, it was argued, residents were right to be sceptical about the new policy (councillors and officers were only too aware of vacant sites on which the city council was unable to build and the blighted terraces emptily awaiting demolition). But once the policy was fully explained, then the potential benefits should be clear to all.

Project teams. The task of communication through detailed local negotiations with residents fell to the neighbourhood-based project teams. They were expected to encourage the formation of local residents' organisations, starting at the lowest level with 'street committees' concerned with environmental work in GIAs. Subsequently, often with the enthusiastic assistance of project teams, more permanently based residents' associations were established in GIAs and HAAs with a wider concern for all issues affecting their area.

Some project teams proved to be particularly successful in establishing residents' groups in their area. Sometimes they were assisted by the efforts of community workers employed by a variety of non-statutory agencies in the city. Often, though, groups were set up unaided by this form of 'outside' help and many of the largest, most active residents' associations were run entirely by local residents.

The degree of involvement by project teams with local residents varied greatly. The first teams to be established within neighbourhoods affected by the policy were led by enthusiastic and able young officers, mainly from public health backgrounds with the notable exception of an architect in one area. Other factors were important, particularly the enthusiasm of local residents, but the extent of activity largely reflected the views of different team leaders about the importance of public participation. Some welcomed the chance to attend residents' meetings to answer questions and discuss progress, seeing this as one of the most important parts of their job. Others attended meetings but would be unhappy to do too many and would not regard participation as the most significant of their various roles. Some worked hard to help establish broadly based residents' associations whilst others were more content to liaise with groups which simply wished to discuss environmental improvements.

In some areas close relations were established between project teams and the leaders of residents' associations. Residents would regard the team leaders, unlike the rest of the council, as allies. This close working led to some conflict between the teams and the central urban renewal section, with senior officers arguing that team leaders were going too far in their attempts to foster public involvement.

The tension in the team leaders' dual role as community developer and local government officer was illustrated in a confidential memorandum issued by the urban renewal officer, 'leaked' to a local community journal. The officer wanted to make it clear that he approved of the teams' assistance to local residents' associations in the production of reports and minutes, but that council officers must be sure that their names did not appear on any documents which were critical of the city council or its councillors. The memorandum went on to say that: 'Team leaders must do their utmost to placate residents and make them fully aware of the action which is being taken on their behalf by members and officers of the Council' (*West Midlands Grass Roots*, No. 19, November/December 1975). Thus the problem for project teams was not just one of 'communication', rather, even at this level, important differences had to be resolved, and the role of the project team a contradictory one.

Residents' associations. Many residents of Birmingham's older housing areas thought that ideas of 'improvement' were a diversion from their real problems. This had often been articulated at large public meetings, so it was not until smaller groups of the less sceptical, more cooperative residents formed special committees to meet the project teams that details were discussed and firm proposals made.

Even amongst these groups, however, there was great variety in the kind of association that became established. Some were nominal associations—a small committee of activists claiming a membership defined as all those living within a particular area. Others were properly constituted bodies with official records of membership and a membership fee. Some claimed to be 'representative' of their area, holding regular public meetings and annual elections for officers. Many simply comprised an informal grouping of residents in a particular street who met to discuss problems and interests. Those groups which progressed beyond the stage of holding street meetings to discuss environmental improvements to forming a residents' association inevitably became involved in other issues. They held meetings with a wider group of officers than those simply concerned with the urban renewal policy and sometimes also with the police over problems of prostitution and crime.

The issue of the 'representativeness' of residents' associations is frequently raised in discussions about public participation. Thus, the fairness of local government officers' finding out what people want simply by approaching residents who are part of an organised group could be questioned. The officers' response to this challenge was that they had other ways of discovering the views of residents: meetings in the areas and questionnaire surveys of each household asking people to record their ideas about their area. Alternatively, they would argue that all meetings and associations were open to anyone in the area and, if some did not join in, that was their decision and the opinions of the active section of the population would prevail; if an 'unrepresentative' plan emerged, it was through people choosing not to participate rather than because they were being prevented from doing so.

Few would claim that most residents' associations were 'representative' of their area's population, however that term is defined. Whilst there were notable exceptions, it was the experience of most team leaders and community workers that most associations consisted of disproportionate numbers of owner-occupiers rather than tenants, white residents rather than black, and the elderly rather than the young. The characteristics of the leadership exhibited an even more marked tendency in these directions.

The unrepresentativeness of some groups was, in part, a reflection of the business that associations were first set up to handle—improvements to the environment and area planning. These, for many people, were, at best, marginal considerations. Put simply, those living in poor accommodation, who were under threat of eviction, who wanted to move from the area or who were unemployed had other things to worry about than whether trees were to be planted along the edge of their road or whether a parcel of land should be used for playspace. Some groups, though, remained hostile to particular sections of the community, notably 'problem families', and it was not surprising that those sections failed to join in with meetings and activities. In some areas, hostile feelings were extended to almost all council tenants; complaints were also directed against tenants and landlords of multi-occupied houses. Hostility against black people was also expressed, usually in a very muted form when they were present, but there existed among a large section of the white population a very virulent form of racism which came out during 'private' discussions.

The style that most groups adopted was that of discussion with the council and the exchange of letters and telephone calls with officers and members. Few took more aggressive action although this was sometimes threatened: rates should be withheld, the Council House should be occupied. Generally, the style was that of reasonable negotiation—and in most areas this produced what the policy required—a plan for future action, that was, partly at least, a product of the efforts of local people.

The area plans. The advent of HAAs made new demands on the council's efforts at securing residents' involvement. In these areas, as we discussed in the last chapter, there were to be area plans for land use, the life of properties and additional amenities and improvements. In the HAAs project teams encouraged the formation of residents' planning committees, sometimes as an adjunct to a residents' association, whose sole task was to discuss planning proposals.

The actual programme for residents' involvement followed a fairly regular pattern in both GIAs and HAAs. Soon after declaration, a public meeting was held to inform people what a GIA or HAA meant and announce the council's intention to involve the residents. Project teams then encouraged some form of residents' grouping to discuss the council's planning and improvement proposals. After agreement had been reached proposals were circulated to the appropriate departments and, where necessary, to the county council and water authority for amendment. A final public meeting was then held to announce the joint council/residents' planning committee proposals and the agreement of residents sought. The plans then went on the round of relevant council committees for comment and approval and, at this late stage, further amendments could be made. In practice, although each project team was beginning to produce area plans or schemes for environmental improvement, this was not achieved without a great deal of difficulty in many areas.

One fundamental problem, from many residents' viewpoints, was the *relevance* of what was being put forward. Whilst the teams would emphasise that the plans and designs they had drawn up prior to the meetings with residents were only *suggestions* about what could happen, the actual range of alternatives open were extremely limited.

This was particularly so for environmental improvements in GIAs where, because of cost limitations and frequent lack of vacant land, improvements were to be small in scope. Often little could be done to provide new social facilities and only the smaller of the intrusive industries could be removed, otherwise all of the environmental grant would be used up.

Profound difficulties were raised by suggestions about improvement on private land. Proposals for 'back access' parking schemes, involving the use of a strip of rear gardens, only needed one objection to fail; this was almost always forthcoming, on the grounds that intruders might take advantage, or simply that people did not want to reduce the size of their gardens.

During the preparation of the first HAA area plans further problems arose. As with other parts of the policy's implementation, conflicts occurred both between the residents and the council and, critically, between various elements within the city council itself. One such area provides an interesting example.

The HAA in question had formerly been part of a redevelopment area designated for total clearance. Elderly households predominated, the local school was likely to be closed and shopkeepers were leaving the area. The residents' main objective was to bring new life into their area, and they were happy to forego open space proposals suggested by the city council in favour of new housing development on a vacant site in their area. Although they were supported in this by the project team and the environmental department, the planning department held firm in its objection to new housing on that particular site.

The urban renewal subcommittee approved the residents' plan including the controversial proposal in January 1976, but it then started on a cycle of the other relevant committees. However, the planning committee subsequently refused to support any decision on the site until there had been an 'on site' inspection. After the inspection, the judgement of the planners held sway and the proposal to use the site for housing was dropped.

Our intention of including this story in our account is not to question the planners' judgement about the suitability of the site, but to illustrate what was, from the residents' viewpoint, a conflict between the promises made about public participation and its outcome in practice. They had been assured, both by councillors and officers, that the days of the council deciding matters and informing residents later were over—now the new urban renewal policy actually involved residents in decision-making and the residents' judgement should be critical. But, in spite of the widespread acceptance of the residents' views among officers and councillors, the objections of one department had triumphed. Residents saw that it was not, therefore, simply a case of them versus the council, but more that various elements of the local authority were in conflict with each other and the final outcome reflected the power position of the different committees and departments involved.

Participation at the city-wide level

The background. The idea of setting up a federation of residents' associations originated from the first chairman of the urban renewal conference. In addition to continued public participation at the local level, he envisaged the formation of a small group of residents' association representatives who would meet officers and councillors to discuss general issues and problems that affected all areas throughout the programme (*West Midlands Grass Roots*, April 1973). He stressed, however, that the new group 'should consist primarily of ordinary residents'. Of the eight or so members proposed only two should be 'professionals' (by which he meant community workers and various self-styled residents' representatives).

In May 1973, Community Planning Associates, a voluntary 'planning aid' group, called an open meeting of residents' association representatives, advice centre and community workers to discuss the chairman's proposals. There was some hostility from left wingers who suggested that the council wanted a token committee through which it could blame residents if things went wrong. Would the group not form some sort of buffer which would deflect residents' anger about lack of progress in the policy? After much debate, dominated by the 'professionals' rather than the 'ordinary residents', it was agreed that the chairman's proposal be followed up.

Before any small meetings with the urban renewal conference, however, the residents' organisations decided to form a federation to which all community organisations in areas affected by the policy would be invited. This was to be the 'community forum' which would discuss issues and problems raised by individual organisations. From those present at community forum meetings a smaller 'liaison group' of about eight people would be elected to meet representatives of the city council.

Thus the delegation would be responsible to a wider group of people—taking to the council only those issues which had previously been raised at a community forum meeting and reporting back on what happened in discussion. This had not been part of the chairman's suggestion. The consensus of the May meeting, however, was that this would have to be an essential part of this new form of public participation: otherwise the delegation would not be responsible to anyone.

The meeting raised, but did not resolve, the dilemma about the relationship between 'professionals' and 'ordinary residents'. Among the former group were a variety of community workers, students and planning lecturers who, it was felt, may have had different ideas about what should happen compared with the majority of 'ordinary residents'. If this group should dominate then the liaison group would hardly be 'representative' of the people in the renewal and general improvement areas. On the other hand, as it was pointed out at the meeting, 'professionals' could provide a certain amount of knowledge and expertise that may be useful to residents' groups especially if there were issues over which they were in conflict with the council. Theirs could be an alternative source of information to that provided by the officers. Ironically, at this meeting and indeed at subsequent meetings of community forum, it was the 'professionals' themselves who were worried that there was a danger that they would dominate proceedings—the 'ordinary residents' usually welcomed their interest and saw them as a source of help rather than a hindrance.

The first eighteen months. The first meeting of community forum took place in June 1973 and monthly thereafter in various parts of the city. A chairman, who was an 'ordinary resident', was elected and members of community planning associates provided secretarial support. The first delegation went to meet some of the members of the urban renewal conference and their officers in July and thereafter more or less every two months.

Many issues were discussed at community forum meetings and taken to the liaison meetings. In particular, residents were concerned that slow progress was being made in deciding which houses could be given a 'thirty-year life'. We discussed the 'reclassification' of properties in chapter 5, so for present purposes we should note that the urban renewal conference was trying to integrate residents' wishes, however poorly defined, in the decision about property retention.

The 'professionals' on community forum raised the question of compensation for people losing their homes through local authority action, and the need to publicise recent changes in legislation (the Land Compensation Act 1973). After discussions at the liaison group meeting it was agreed that the city estates department would arrange for the leaflets to be printed. However, nothing was done and, despite much pestering, no leaflets were published until about twelve months had elapsed from the preparation of drafts by forum members.

Many residents' groups complained that private landlords were hindering the improvement drive through a failure to give undertakings to renovate their houses. In particular, where those whose dwellings adjoined owner-occupied houses, their reluctance to act often prevented the reclassification of dwellings for retention. The council's response was that every effort would be made to encourage voluntary improvement but, where this failed, compulsory measures would be adopted.

One last issue concerned the operations of the city treasurer's department, which was notoriously slow in informing people whether they were eligible for loans towards their share of improvement costs. The department was also very slow in paying once work was completed. Officers in the department argued that staff shortages had led to delays, which had been made worse by a great increase of work brought about by a recent housing committee decision to start a mortgage scheme particularly aimed at providing up to 100 per cent loans for first-time buyers. However, efforts were being made to process applications more quickly and the target for approval and payment was set at within a month of application and completion, respectively. Community forum members continued, in spite of the officers' assurance, to hear of complaints of long delays and, in fact, there was *no* noticeable speeding up of the department's operation until its volume of work was greatly diminished following the mid-1975 cut in mortgage lending.

The major complaint voiced at community forum and in the liaison group meetings was that relatively little seemed to be happening; much had been promised but little was being done to fulfil those promises. Landlords were not being forced to improve, the council was not improving its houses, the process of reclassification was slow, former owners were not being compensated for loss of their dwellings, council tenants were not being rehoused in spite of assurances that they would be, very little work had been done in the way of short term amenity works in the renewal areas and it appeared that the money allocated for such work was not being spent.

There was a feeling too that, whilst the meetings with councillors and officers were serving some purpose, the response from the council side was patchy. Many officers from the environmental department were considered particularly helpful but the response from other departments was curt and guarded and, frequently, there was no one present at meetings from some of the departments central to the policy.

The 'walk-out' and reorganisation of participation. Matters came to a head at a liaison group meeting late in 1974. Two officers' reports which had been commissioned at previous meetings failed to materialise. One was supposed to examine the possibility of speeding mortgage approval and payment and the other was to deal with ways that road sweeping and rodent control could be improved. No officer from the treasurer's or the relevant section of the environmental department was present although a brief letter had been sent on both topics. One simply confirmed that the system of mortgage approval was being speeded up. The other stated that the level of road cleansing and rodent control was adequate except at holiday times.

The chairman of the forum pointed out that neither of these replies was adequate, particularly the latter because there *was* a need for improvement to the services and he easily found support for his suggestion to the other members of the liaison group that they should 'walk-out' as a protest at the lack of the council's efforts. The twelve-strong delegation agreed unanimously and left saying that they would attend a further meeting when satisfactory reports were available. Thus the meeting closed with some six other agenda items left undiscussed.

The 'walk-out' caused something of a flurry in the environmental department and, following a story in the local press, a meeting was held between officers and members of the community forum in an attempt to smooth things over. Meanwhile action was taken at the political level—the chairman of the urban renewal subcommittee sympathised with the views of the liaison group and wanted to find ways of making the liaison process more effective.

After several months a new participatory structure was established. A community forum delegation would meet the whole of the urban renewal subcommittee and supporting officers at special informal meetings every two months. At these meetings officers could be requested to prepare reports and take action on issues raised by community forum.

Reports *were* produced and on some issues it was clear that the new meetings were 'plugged into' the local authority structure in that items were referred on for thrashing out in officers' meetings. The response among officers and members was varied, however. Some officers were prepared to meet community forum, to provide information and discuss policy, whilst others were clearly hostile, resenting the incursion of the meetings on their time. The latter tended to present the minimum of information required and stated rather than discussed council policy. The response from councillors was even less encouraging from the community forum viewpoint. On average only a quarter of the full urban renewal subcommittee membership attended any one meeting and, of those who did, most said very little or nothing at all and often seemed unable to contribute much to the proceedings. Discussions were dominated, on the council side, by officers, the chairman of the subcommittee and the Conservative 'shadow' chairman.

On occasions the community forum representative found some of the Labour councillors arguing on their side over a particular issue and against the officers. On other occasions many community forum delegates found themselves agreeing with much of what the Labour councillors were saying and disagreeing with what the Conservative opposition said ought to happen. In practice, therefore, the exercise in city-wide participation came at times to take on a 'political' dimension which it had frequently been denied.

Participation in Perspective
Residents' involvement and the politics of participation
We should not exaggerate the scale or intensity of the participatory effort involved in Birmingham's urban renewal experience. Public meetings varied tremendously in attendance, with an audience as large as two or three hundred on rare occasions but usually with little more than fifty folk. The majority of residents' associations were glad to get thirty people along to meetings and street meetings often consisted of no more than half a dozen people. Moreover, the largest meetings were more for the presentation of information than any two-way dialogue. Community forum meetings attracted between twenty and fifty people, with attendance usually consisting of a core of six to ten 'professionals', a variety of interested students

and residents drawn mainly, although not exclusively, from the neighbourhood in which the meeting's venue happened to be sited.

For some councillors and officers, however, this generated an enormous amount of work. The three successive chairmen involved and the urban renewal officer in particular attended between them literally hundreds of meetings of all sizes and composition. They were in no doubt that residents in áreas affected by the policy did have views that they were willing to express, however contradictory these may have been. Project team members, in daily contact with the public as well as in more formal meetings, also engaged in constant dialogue with people living in Birmingham's inner areas.

The extent of the commitment of residents involved was as diverse as the scale of activity. Many residents were no more than passive spectators, hoping to find out what the council proposed to do to their homes. Others joined enthusiastically, particularly at the local level, and became committed to the preparation of plans for their own neighbourhood. The leading members of community forum devoted many evenings to meeting local groups, preparing reports and liaising with the city council.

With a regular attendance of between ten and twenty residents' representatives at liaison meetings with the urban renewal sub-committee, and the wide network of contacts thus represented, it was impossible for the city council to ignore the strength of feeling and arguments put forward.

In order to explore the political significance of these events we should remember that participation was encouraged and facilitated by the city council. This was an innovatory departure from previous practice, particularly from the total non-involvement of the public (except as subjects) in the process of comprehensive redevelopment. Further, the broad objectives of the city council and the vast majority of residents who actually became involved were congruent. Both wanted to see improvement in the fortunes of the inner areas. In that sense public participation was non-political. The party political debates within the council chamber concerned the means of achieving those objectives and the pace with which action should proceed.

At the city-wide level there were some important abstentions from community forum. The leaders of one large neighbourhood federation, representing numerous smaller street and area groups, refused to attend on the grounds that community forum was 'too political' or 'too left-wing'. Others did not attend simply because their own association activities took up most of their time and no further evenings could be devoted to any additional meetings.

The charge that community forum was left-wing was certainly an accurate description of some of its leaders at various times in its history. Some were members of the Labour Party, often well to the left within the party. This was one reason why many council officers were distrustful of the forum and argued that it was not representative of the majority of people living in areas affected by the urban renewal policy.

The feeling of almost all of those who attended community forum meetings, certainly of most residents rather than community workers was that residents' associations should be '*non-political*': the proper concern of their organisations was to represent the views of their constituents and not to show favour to particular parties. Concern was sometimes expressed about the developing involvement with local trade unions although, on several occasions, motions were · carried out to continue the links developed between the leadership of community forum and the union movement. These links took two forms. First, discussions were held between officers of community forum and UCATT shop stewards over the viability of extending council direct labour activities into urban renewal, especially during a threat of lay-offs following the 'Section 105 cuts' (see chapter 5). As the threat of redundancy receded, however, the dialogue folded up. Leaders of community forum were also active in the Birmingham Campaign Against the Cuts, with various meetings and a city centre march. Attendance at the march was, however, minimal from residents involved in community forum and their respective associations.

However 'non-political' forum meetings were to be, this did not stop members becoming agitated about what was, or rather and more usually, was not happening. When it was aroused, residents' anger was more often than not about *failures* in achievement, the slowness of action and details of implementation. This is not to say that conflicts between the council and the associations were insignificant—far from it—for most, and in some instances, all of the residents' hostility was directed against the council. But, critically, this was over the inability or failure of the latter to deliver what had been promised, rather than the promises themselves. This last point needs emphasising. Most associations and most of those coming to community forum meetings saw *the council* as their principal point of contact for information and action, and as their adversary when things were going wrong. Thus, most of the time, the objective of the organisations was to liaise with, badger and complain to the council in an attempt to get the improvement drive off the ground. The function of community forum, for most who came, was to assist local associations in their efforts to affect the council and its policies.

Many residents appreciated the reasons underlying the failures. All those coming to community forum meetings knew of the cuts in public social expenditure and many grasped the fact that the improvement drive did little to change basic property and economic relations. Relatively prosperous owners who could afford their share of improvement costs renovated their homes first, while the rest did theirs later or not at all whilst the intransigent freeholder or landlord could, at least temporarily, effectively deny their tenants any potential benefits from improvement.

Throughout our involvement with the forum and residents' associations we did not, however, observe the emergence of any radical consciousness from residents' awareness of failure and injustice. The question is raised as to whether the absence of a radical consciousness was itself a product of the participatory involvement. One thesis which we examined at the outset of this chapter suggested that public participation in planning urban change was a way in which the state sought to incorporate the interests of local residents and thereby quieten any potential revolt. To develop this thesis further, such incorporation would be achieved through the involvement of residents in decision taking and this would give the *appearance* at least of power over circumstances affecting their lives.

By a series of bargains and truces drawn up by both sides, residents could be given the impression that they were making incremental progress towards achieving their goals. All the time, however, the state would be determining the parameters of the dialogue and keeping the most important decisions within itself. A consequence of the involvement of residents in discussions with officers and members of an authority would be a greater awareness of the 'problems' of local government making it easier for delays and difficulties to be accepted by residents as an inevitable part of the system.

The process of incorporation could be further facilitated by the involvement of community 'professionals' whose reasoned and responsible approach in negotiations with the local authority would channel people's anger and frustration into useful and constructive avenues and thereby further de-radicalise the residents' perspective.

The arguments set out above are more a pastiche of a theoretical approach to the problem of participation than a coherent theoretical account. There were, however, critics at the time of forum's creation who argued along very similar lines and urged the creation of an independent body of residents dedicated to social change by direct action rather than involvement and negotiation with the authority. Whatever version of the incorporation thesis is adopted there are, in the light of our experience, difficulties which make it hard to sustain wholly.

By whatever means the incorporation of citizens' groups is achieved, the effect of the process is the bringing about of a congruence between the goals of community groups and those of the state, thereby smothering protest (Bonnier, 1972). The question is raised as to whether incorporation is an *inevitable* process. Our experience in Birmingham suggests that incorporation of independent associations is not, in all circumstances, a consequence of participation with the local state. We would question the extent to which participation could have quietened revolt since the evidence of revolt in the inner areas of Birmingham seemed scarcely to be present before participation was introduced. In the implementation of housing policy, apart from occasional sparks of protest against the clearance process and the airing of individual grievances, the atmosphere was generally that of quiet compliance or resignation to that which was going on. At times, the process of participation seemed more to engender hostility, albeit in a muted form. This was because residents had at least been given the chance to express their views and, more important, had been told that they could exert some influence over what was to happen. To the extent that little or nothing happened or that residents exercised little real power, this provided one condition for the organised expression of protest: the promise of power had first been given and subsequently denied, thus falsely raising expectations.

We found no evidence to sustain the view that 'professionals' exerted a conservative influence over residents' association activities. Generally more liberal and in some cases more radical than many of the residents they sought to assist, some community workers found themselves at odds with residents over particular issues and tried, where possible, to steer discussion and action on less contentious lines. The issues of difference varied but probably the most important were those of race, 'problem families' and tinkers, and the solutions to these problems. At least one residents' group sacked its 'professional' assistant and the fundamental issue underlying the dispute was a deep ideological rift.

Any approach to the thesis of incorporation needs to take account of other, and probably more powerful, influences on people's consciousness than those stemming from participatory exercises. Elsewhere, for example, we have described a process whereby the way the distribution of urban resources is managed *individualises* the perspective of those depending on local authority services. The effect of such a process is to de-politicise the circumstances surrounding state provision. The general and overriding requirement for more and better housing becomes perceived through, for example, the operation of a housing waiting list as a series of individual needs. From the perspective of individuals requiring a dwelling, needs are not to be met by organised, collective action but rather through special pleading and the seeking of favours from those with resources to distribute (Lambert *et al.*, 1978).

Clearly, the effects of both material and ideological factors on the development of radical consciousness are important. Indeed, rather than stress the independent effects of particular organisations and relationships on working class consciousness, we would regard the failure of any radical perspective to emerge as a product of deeper elements within working class consciousness of which racism is one notorious example. Furthermore, the interest of class became obscured through apparently significant differences in housing tenure, in house conditions and through popularly held notions of what constitute respectable and unrespectable styles of life.

The essential problem here lies in the processes involved in the transition between what Pickvance (1977b) has called a 'social base' and a 'social force'. The former term refers to a population group affected by a given issue and the latter a mobilisation of group members into a coherent and organised collectivity 'for itself'. For Pickvance, critical factors affecting the transition between social base and social force lie not only in the demographic nature of the former but in elements of the social structure and value orientations of those involved. Thus class and ethnic divisions and differences in subjective perceptions of what ought to happen may be important differentiating factors within a social base and hinder the formation of protest movements.

The point we wish to make is not that the participation of residents in decision-making was irrelevant to the process of de-politicisation, but that it was only one possible factor which influenced the way protest was or was not articulated. We would suggest that the process of incorporation is not inevitable and depends in part on the extent to which those involved in participatory exercises, on both sides, choose to define their role and strategy. We would cite the example of the 'walk-out' from the formal meeting as evidence that those involved in the participatory exercise were aware of the need to avoid incorporation and to maintain an independent, critical perspective. Moreover, it would be wrong to consider 'the other side'—the local authority—as a monolithic whole which is at all times opposed to the interests of those affected by its policies. There were, in particular, members of the council in Birmingham who were involved in developing the renewal policy who genuinely believed that there was a need to allow residents to have a say and indeed to ensure that their views had an effect on policy outcomes. Those most enthusiastic were probably to the left in political terms whilst members and officers who could be regarded as on the right in political terms tended to be more guarded in their reception of residents' involvement and some even saw it as an intrusion on their right to take decisions.

These differences in perspective cannot be carried too far in our analysis since the thesis of incorporation critically rests on the *effects* of participation rather than the subjective intentions of those who set up the new procedures. Thus, whatever radical activists or authority members may have intended, the results could have meant in certain circumstances the stifling of a radical consciousness. In any context of public participation this could be an objective consequence. However, in the particular context in which we studied and worked, the case that it was participation which led to incorporation was not proven.

Participation and the local authority

Residents, councillors and officers of the city council shared a normative definition of public participation: it was 'non-political'. Such a definition, however, was predicated upon mutual comprehension of the rules which define the proper concern of 'politics'. As such, certain questions do not get asked, issues are never raised. We would suggest, however, that participation brings into question some of those very assumptions, particularly the nature of representative democracy and the ability of citizens to determine their own lives.

How much could public participation have been an alternative to established forms of representation? Undoubtedly this was the fear of many councillors, hence their eager affirmation of the non-political nature of public participation. Similarly, the insistence that 'ordinary residents' should predominate in the liaison meetings reflected concern that 'professionals' might exploit the situation to discredit the city council and thus undermine their councillors' claim to legitimacy. Whilst the extent of popular involvement was, in one form or other, fairly significant, all participants accepted that theirs was an additional input to policy-making, not an alternative. The role of councillor as the sole legitimate representative may have been questioned by some of the leaders of community forum, but most residents involved looked to councillors for information, assistance and leadership.

The effect on officers was more problematic. Senior officers found themselves exposed to public criticism at public meetings and almost invariably sought to make general statements about policy and then to turn general issues into individual cases to be dealt with 'after the meeting'. Usually those complainants at public meetings were pleased to receive individual attention, even if the promise 'to look into your case' subsequently yielded very little. For junior officers, particularly those working in neighbourhood project teams, there were more fundamental problems to cope with.

They became placed in a novel relationship with residents on the one hand and the local authority on the other. Previously, they had been responsible to senior officers and, where policy decisions were

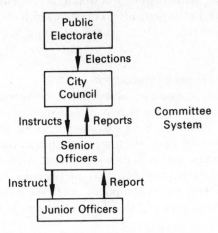

Fig. 6.1 Formal responsibilities in local government

needed, writing reports which were subsequently modified or approved and presented to committee as the report of the department concerned. Contact with residents was specific and took the form of meeting individual cases to be dealt with routinely and separately (for example, housing visits, housing allocation, inspections of house conditions). We can locate them graphically in diagrammatical form illustrating the conventional pattern of relationships between the public (as electors), the council and its officers (Fig. 6.1).

By involving junior officers directly with local residents, assisting them in the formation of associations and preparation of plans, a new structure emerged.* Junior officers, in particular project team leaders, became answerable *both* to residents and senior officers. Normal practice had obscured much of the working of policies from the public eye, the new structure had the opposite effect.

One issue illustrates well the dilemma facing local officers. Some pieces of land containing housing were required by the planning department for the purposes of future school extension. Often, during comprehensive redevelopment, unfit properties had been acquired and land thus easily obtained. However, in this particular HAA, the properties were, as far as the project team leader was concerned, capable of improvement. He was, however, under pressure not to classify them as suitable for improvement as they would then have been retained. The council owned some and the tenants wanted to stay in them after improvement. Others, which were owner-occupied, were denied grant assistance. On grounds of house condition and residents' desires, the houses should be 'reclassified' yet the project team leader was constrained by senior officers in his own and other departments.

His position, and that of other officers involved at the grass roots level, contained tensions absent in the previous, more formal situation. Again, using a diagrammatic presentation, we can illustrate the new structure of relationships with the dual responsibility of the project team officer (Fig. 6.2).

Clearly, this is an oversimplification of complex processes of interaction; the effect, nonetheless, was important. Some project team officers specifically came to interpret their job as mediation, seeking to be neutral; others took a more pro-resident stance, whilst

---

*We are grateful to Charles Adams for suggesting the diagrammatic illustration of the changed relationship.

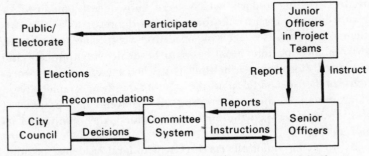

Fig. 6.2 Reformulated structure of relationships in participation

others sought to be little more than mouth-pieces for the official departmental explanation of the world. At least one project team leader resigned out of frustration and the feeling that he had responsibility without power: he could not fully 'participate' as he had no influence over the critical areas of decision-making and resource allocation for his area of responsibility.

Political effects of participation
The shift away from comprehensive redevelopment towards improvement took place during the same period that state-sponsored public participation was being encouraged. The town planning profession, in particular, became obsessed with the concept of public participation, but other sections of central and local government also sought to develop community involvement—particularly in the social services, education and health.

The effects of state sponsored participation exercises on the political structure now need to be considered. We have referred to the widely held notion that participation by residents' groups was to take place on non-political lines. For most, this meant that groups would not show favour to any particular political party and would work with councillors on either side of the political spectrum. The question is raised as to the extent to which this 'independence' of residents' associations from the political structure posed a threat to the existing political system. In relation to grass roots community initiatives, Peter Hain has argued that 'the community action movement has challenged local government, swept aside the pontification of politicians, and provided new hope to the poor, the dispossessed and the powerless' (1977, p. 9).

Whilst there was perhaps evidence that new hope had been

engendered in the hearts of some as a result of the urban renewal policy and its participatory drive, there was little evidence that the community groups initiated by the council had come to pose any serious challenge to its authority. Neither could it be said that residents' activities had swept aside politicians' rhetoric or the need for political debate. As far as inner city Birmingham is concerned, Hain's statement bears no relationship to the activities of what were frequently small and sometimes unrepresentative groups of residents whose main aim was to get the maximum amount out of the existing political system rather than set up an alternative structure to it.

Most groups were concerned with small geographical areas, a narrow set of issues and with seeking to extract from existing agencies the maximum possible amount of resources to benefit their constituents. For the most part, the focus of their attention was on the local authority and on its powers and responsibilities and not the wider political and economic framework within which it was located. This is not to say that many residents were unaware that public sector spending restraint and the workings of the market and fundamental property relations all influenced, often deleteriously, the operation of the urban renewal policy. What did not emerge was any serious political challenge to the wider framework which was taken as 'given' and beyond their influence. Our analysis is similar to that of Hindess' study of working class politics. He noted that, within a context of political inactivity and acquiescence, there was a growing involvement of working class people in tenants' groups, squatters' organisations and community associations which were outside the sphere of conventional politics. Hindess concluded that such extra-political activity was ultimately ineffectual because it remained encapsulated within a concern for specific objectives or demands and not with wider social change. It posed few threats precisely because 'many of those involved tend to accept current definitions of politics and therefore tend to view their own action as being non-political, as being concerned with only one issue' (Hindess, 1971, p. 154).

The participatory effort did very little to change the overriding influences on the council's urban renewal policy. Nor did it raise residents' consciousness to a level that would lead them to challenge these influences. Four years on from the declaration of the policy most houses were still unimproved and many were likely to remain that way for several years yet. In those areas that had seen some comprehensive house and environmental improvements, physical conditions were still inferior to those of the middle class suburbs. The streets were still dirtier, the houses still more cramped, the gardens still smaller and the people still poorer. Neither the policy, nor the participatory effort that was part of it has or could have done much to affect these realities.

7 Improvement Policy, the Problem of Control

State housing policy is likely to remain the subject of political debate long after the local incidents described in this book have been forgotten. But the issues with which we have been concerned are still central to discussions about older housing and the role of the state in improving or replacing existing dwellings. In this chapter we shall reflect on our experiences in Birmingham in the light of contemporary debates about housing policy and the inner city and we conclude with some consideration of alternative policies.

Our first chapter argued the case for attempting a theoretical analysis of urban renewal, not merely as an academic exercise, but as the basis for better understanding of processes and relationships which in turn inform political debate and action. The extent to which better policies may subsequently be developed, however, depends on the perspective of the commentator, for it is facile to expect politically neutral, technical solutions to questions of resource distribution and redistribution in an unequal society.

The issues that we have addressed range greatly in scope and detail. The common concern has been older housing, in particular improvement policy, but in order to say anything of wider meaning we have had to examine the context within which policy has been developed and implemented. The relationship between central government and local government has had to be a central theme, for improvement policy was developed during a particular phase of the history of state housing policy (chapter 2), initiated at both levels of government (chapter 4) and crucially affected by relationships of statutory authority and resource allocation between the two (chapter 5).

We have not yet sought to answer the question of why the state is so heavily involved in the housing question, though it was essential to locate the development of improvement policy within a broader history of state housing policies. Traditionally, state interventions have sought to raise the quality of housing as well as increase the quantity of provision; but this has involved contradictory elements. Whilst the Left has campaigned for state intervention to remove market inequalities, state action has never sought to abolish market relations altogether. Indeed, improvement policy was developed during a period of political convergence in many aspects of state housing policy, particularly support for owner-occupation.

Improvement policy was developed initially as one way of dealing with older houses in conjunction with slum clearance, but has now largely replaced clearance, which is seen merely as a 'mopping up' exercise to deal with small areas of older housing. A new consensus of owner-occupation and improvement has come to typify state housing policies for what is now called 'the inner city'. Yet the capacity of the local state to effect the changes which, it is claimed, improvement can bring, remains to be demonstrated on any significant scale, either in Birmingham or elsewhere.

A second theme has been that of the relationship between the state and market forces. This relationship is crucial from the macro-level, in terms of structuring financial policies which shape strategies to allocate resources for state interventions (chapter 2), right down to the micro-level, for example the effects of 'fringe' lenders or building society 'redlining' on local policies for improvement (chapter 3). Assumptions about the techniques of state-initiated 'voluntary' improvement, critically over the significance of grants as an adequate and sufficient financial incentive, were shown to be faulty by the evidence in our third and fifth chapters.

State housing policies have been instrumental in effecting changes in the structure of the housing market, but it should be remembered that private market institutions have not sat passively by without themselves exerting an influence. House construction and improvement rely almost wholly on the private house-building industry, whose investment decisions and willingness to enter into public sector contract work are determined by the profit motive rather than any desire to meet social needs. Finance for owner-occupation is predominantly controlled by the building societies, whose main interests lie in a steady and safe return on investment funds rather than the provision of good housing for working people.

Additionally, we must consider what happens to housing, as a commodity, as it ages. The effect of general inflation and the relationship between supply and demand influence the price at which any particular commodity changes hands. In the case of older housing they have had crucial effects in maintaining relatively high prices despite dilapidation. At the local level it was clearly in the interests of dealers, 'merchant professionals' and others to maintain a 'healthy market' in older property. The cost of improvement though, even with the aid of a grant, was often more than residents could afford, or even thought worthwhile.

The internal organisation of a local authority—the local state—and its ability to 'manage' is a theme which has been vigorously debated over the last few years (Pahl, 1975; Bennington, 1976; Cockburn, 1977). In Birmingham organisational changes were introduced, albeit slowly, to confront a policy area the complexity of which was not initially grasped. Conflicting opinions both between and within political parties, however, and the strong vested interests of different council departments, retarded the development of an integrated approach to urban renewal (chapters 4 and 5). Corporate management, when applied to urban renewal, was concerned more with the production and management of a *policy* than with changes to the environment—whether the latter was conceived in social, economic or simply physical terms. For all the lines on maps, the public expressions of intent, innumerable meetings between hosts of people, bureaucratic organisation and reorganisation, pressure group lobbying and sheer hard work, there was precious little improvement.

There was all the difference in the world between having a policy and actually doing anything. The gap was usually explained by reference to problems—unforeseen complexities, insufficient public confidence in the policy, cuts in central government allocations, the need to streamline service provision, 'political interference' with officers and 'irresponsible' community activists making life difficult for well-meaning politicians and officers. Little local problems? We believe not; rather such 'problems' raise a fundamental question about the nature of a policy which cannot cope with them. What *is* a policy: an aspiration, a statement of intent, a course of action, or some combination of all of these? Birmingham's performance review committee commented at one stage that the urban renewal policy had been 'more of a public commitment' than a clearly defined programme of action informed by resource availability. Even the subsequently reorganised policy, however, took as its starting point the powers and resources available to local government rather than any clear conception of the real-world phenomena that it purported to affect. It had institutional and symbolic existence and significance, but remained remotely distant from the forces structuring housing access and affecting property decay in inner Birmingham.

The connection between ordinary citizens and the political system provided a fourth theme. Despite the council's stated intention of involving residents in decision-making, what was actually offered was a limited form of participation (chapter 6). There was involvement of a kind at the city-wide level, but the liaison group was responding to policy change rather than initiating action. It had no authoritative claim to represent a wide constituency and so its legitimacy could easily be denied by antagonistic councillors or officers. Even so, it was an important feature in the council's claim to be a participatory authority and a potentially active force of opposition and complaint should the participatory nexus be broken. Neighbourhood groups were encouraged by the council but the response to their demands was limited by the need to pursue city-wide rather than local policy objectives and by resource constraints. Some local councillors feared the development of alternative sources of legitimacy and sought to control group activities. Others, however, sought to become involved in their activities by offering close cooperation and support, sensing no doubt a pay-off in terms of electoral support.

Local government officers found themselves torn by conflicting loyalties, particularly when residents' definitions of their own interests clashed with those of different departments in the council as a whole. The diversity of interests often worked against the emergence of consensual 'community' views on anything other than the most basic and obvious matters and so the scope for change was limited.

Improvement Policy and the Inner City—Critique and Convergence

The context of debate about improvement policy has shifted substantially between 1969 and 1978. It is useful to examine three components of those debates before turning to the major theoretical conclusions of this book. First, there has been growing criticism of improvement policy. The political Left has regarded improvement as a way of lowering standards for working class housing, subsidising private landlords and encouraging owner-occupation at the expense of public sector renting. Criticism has also been articulated by professional interests, in particular the Environmental Health

Officers' Association. In their submission to the DoE's housing policy review, they argued strongly that improvement policy has gone too far and that the clearance rate should be stepped up (Environmental Health Officers' Association, 1977).

Simultaneously, however, government has come to proffer a new explanation of, and policy for, the decline of the inner city. Finally, with the publication of the *Housing Policy Review* (DoE, 1977a), a new conventional wisdom has been established about housing policy, crucially about 'desirable' and 'natural' forms of tenure and state subsidies to housing (Harloe, 1978a). Whilst this does not by any means mark the end of party political debate over housing, at the time of writing there is a remarkable consensus between the Labour and Conservative Party leaderships over many aspects of housing policy. There remain important differences of emphasis and rhetoric, but the centre has undoubtedly moved to the right, so that the encouragement of owner-occupation and relegation of council housing to an inferior form of tenure is the almost inevitable effect of developments based on this consensus.

These three issues are of critical importance for any fundamental review of improvement policy in Birmingham during the period of our study. Crucially, they define the context within which any consideration of alternative approaches to housing policy must be located.

Growing criticism of improvement policy

In our study of Birmingham we have noted the scale of the local policy as well as its initiation in part before statutory powers and associated resources became available. After the Housing Act 1974 most authorities, particularly in metropolitan areas, embarked on major policies of improvement. By the end of 1977 in England 240 HAAs were in operation in seventy local authorities, and over a thousand GIAs were in existence. In London alone there were sixty HAAs and a hundred GIAs.

But by mid 1978 doubts were being raised about the impact of this policy, beginning to confirm the predictions of those like Fred Berry, one of the most consistently constructive critics of housing policy over the years, who had argued that:

I could write a little more enthusiastically about HAAs did I not recall going over much the same ground in 1964 and again in 1969. It is difficult to avoid the conclusion that the HAA concept is just another manifestation of the failure to face up to the fact that sooner or later a house wears out.

(Berry, 1976)

A polemical pamphlet, produced by the Community Development Project Political Economy Collective (1977), argued on evidence from eight projects that the great improvement drive had become the great improvement fiasco. *The Poverty of Improvement* made three central points about the improvement programme. 'The most prominent feature of the improvement programme', it claimed, was the use of diversionary devices which obscured 'a continued cutback in the resources necessary to make the programme successful.' The pamphlet also argued that the context of improvement policies was misleading, as the choice usually presented was between life in a slum or in an improved house—the option of 'a new house on a council estate with adequate community facilities' was never offered. Finally, a choice was set out. Either policy could continue in a piecemeal way, discriminating '*against* those in poorest housing conditions', or a new policy could be forged, with a sufficient level of resources and more comprehensive powers available to local authorities. The report concluded that the Housing Act 1974 had two crucial weaknesses, lack of powers and lack of resources, reflecting that 'with hindsight, it seems laughable that anyone assumed even inadequate resources would be available'.

In September 1977 Shelter published a response to the *Housing Policy Review*. According to Frances Kelly and Jim Wintour, the authors of *The Housing Crisis Nationwide*, 'in no area of government activity is the gap between rhetoric and performance more marked than in the field of home improvement' (1977, p. xvi). They took issue with the claim in the review that present trends indicated substantial progress being made in dealing with the backlog of bad housing conditions. On the contrary, they argued:

> In fact, if present trends continue there will be *no* further progress in dealing with bad housing conditions, because there is at present *no* net improvement taking place in England's housing stock.
>
> *(op cit.)*

They showed that, since 1975, the rate at which houses were deteriorating into unfitness or gross disrepair was only just equalled by the rate of improvement; there was no net gain. It was their contention, by reference to the government's own statistics, that it

would be necessary to increase the average national rate of improvement *threefold*, sustained over the next ten years, to eradicate the
backlog and compensate for houses becoming unfit during the same
period.

The Lambeth Inner Area Study (DoE, 1977b, p. 148) suggested
that there was a danger that the shift from comprehensive redevelopment to improvement 'could go too far'. The study's consultants
argued, first, that large-scale slum clearance and redevelopment had
become substantially inappropriate. They suggested that such
schemes 'were unduly expensive and socially disruptive . . . often
involved the destruction of adequate houses and their replacement
by dwellings which were poorer value for money. Their main
justification was to produce "housing gain" which . . . is better
achieved outside Inner London altogether' (pp. 148–9). However,
they also argued that an 'area approach' to improvement by means
of GIAs and HAAs was inefficient in management terms, failed to
discriminate selectively in favour of the worst properties, and
inhibited a mixed approach of improvement and redevelopment.
Their case, essentially, was for a different kind of improvement,
which was more 'flexible' in approach and encouraged 'maximum
investment by owner-occupiers in a framework in which the future
of their property is secure . . .' (p. 183).

This is reminiscent of the idea of 'gradual renewal' suggested by
McKie (1970) and substantially incorporated into DoE Circular
13/75. It appears an attractive alternative approach to wholesale
improvement or clearance although it would require an extremely
sensitive form of management and adequate resources to ensure that
property scheduled for retention is improved and that property
scheduled for clearance was demolished and replaced within a
reasonable period of time.

The debate about the merits of improvement policy thus continue.
The issues concern whether the scale of retention of dwellings for
improvement is wrong, whether there should be a return to more
clearance or whether, given existing levels of house retention, a
different approach should be adopted to getting the stock upgraded.

The inner city
In the summer of 1977 the Labour Government published the White
Paper *Policy for the Inner Cities* (Cmnd. 6845). This followed growing
public concern that inner urban areas in Britain were beginning to
display similar characteristics of decline and stagnation to inner city

areas in the United States of America. The *Sunday Times* had sponsored a conference on the theme of 'Save our Cities' and, at this conference and subsequently, Peter Shore, Secretary of State for the Environment, advocated a new priority for government policy—an inner city focus for action and expenditure.

The White Paper responded to many government-sponsored studies and experiments carried out during the previous ten years, in particular to the inner areas studies, one of which we have just mentioned. These were three projects, focusing on parts of inner London, Liverpool and Birmingham, and conducted by private firms of planning and architectural consultants (DoE, 1977 b, c and d).

One feature of the new policy initiative towards the inner city was the explanation of the cause of the inner city problem:

> Since the Second World War, much has been done to improve the conditions of life in the inner parts of our cities . . . While the achievement has been real, too little attention has been paid to the economic well-being and community life of the inner areas, and the physical fabric in some parts is badly neglected or decayed. The extent and the changed character of the inner area problems are only now becoming fully understood.
>
> *(Cmnd. 6845, p. 1)*

The implication of this statement is that, if policies had been different and had fully understood changes that were 'naturally' taking place, then the inner city problem might not have arisen. Whilst emphasising that important variations existed within and between different cities, the White Paper described four major components of the inner city problem.

First, economic decline was explained as the product of jobs lost through redevelopment and, more important, through the removal or closure of manufacturing industry. Inner areas, secondly, were described as exhibiting signs of increasing physical decay, with substantial areas of poor housing, cleared sites vacant and derelict, empty factories, docks and warehouses all awaiting an uncertain future and receiving little upkeep. The populations of inner areas, the White Paper went on, suffered social disadvantage. High unemployment, low incomes and poor educational achievement went side by side with 'a pervasive sense of decay and neglect which affects the whole area, through the decline of community spirit, through an often low standard of neighbourhood facilities, and through greater exposure to crime and vandalism' (p. 4). Finally, attention was drawn to the concentration of ethnic minorities in inner areas. The White Paper did not say why this was a problem, but asserted that minorities' 'particular needs' will be 'fully taken into account in the planning and implementation of policies . . . and allocation of resources . . .'

Inner areas were seen to be in decline in a more-or-less 'natural' way; the government defined its task as 'the need to arrest decline'. Without specific government involvement and action, a bleak future was forecast:

> The inner parts of our cities ought not to be left to decay. It would mean leaving large numbers of people to face a future of declining job opportunities, a squalid environment, deteriorating housing and declining public services. But without effective action, that could be the future for those who live in inner areas, bringing with it mounting social bitterness and an increasing sense of alienation. The hearts of our cities would suffer as the surrounding inner areas went further downhill.
>
> *(p. 5)*

The value of this analysis lies in its appreciation that housing decay is but one manifestation of more widespread processes of urban and regional change. Thus, by implication, housing was not an independent variable amenable to improvement by housing policy alone.

The strength of this point, however, was offset by considerable weaknesses in other parts of the argument in the White Paper which, in combination, outweigh the merit of taking a broader view of the context of urban renewal. First, the notion that decline is 'natural' omits discussion of the structural causes of decline. Over the last hundred and fifty years' growth, expansion and decline of industry has been an *uneven* process, both in spatial and non-spatial terms, so that there have been marked changes between and within regions in terms of investment and prosperity. That process has not been 'natural' except as far as developments in private commerce and industry, with inevitable effects on spatial patterns of economic growth and decline, are taken for granted. Since the Second World War British metropolitan regions have been substantially restructured (see, in particular, Hall *et al.*, 1973) and the processes of change have had effects on older urban areas, whilst their causes have been external to such areas. So it is sensible to think of inner urban areas—which contain much of the housing supposed to be affected by improvement policies—as *residual* areas manifesting features unlike those in other locations.

It was not, however, only areas of pre-1914 housing and industry which contained the poor and the powerless. Unemployment and bad housing were also widespread within vast sections of municipal housing, and the worst incidences of malaise were frequently in scattered pockets in 'yesterday's' problem areas—the 'depressed regions'.

The notion of an inner area problem implies an inner area cause and, for the government's policy, inner area solutions. It is a curious kind of 'spatial fetishism' which explains the nature of phenomena in terms of their locational distribution. The correct view is surely to view the plight of the inner areas as a product of uneven development and an inevitable consequence of a private market economy largely unchecked by positive state intervention.

Another criticism concerns the White Paper's cautious reference to ethnic minorities. Concentrated into inner areas by their position in the labour market and consequent low incomes, as well as the limited availability of accessible housing elsewhere, immigrants remain systematically disadvantaged in Britain. Moreover:

> The persistence of racial discrimination has had two consequences which have led to a sharp deterioration in race relations. On the one hand, it has encouraged an upsurge of crude racialism and the growth of organised racist groups. On the other, it has provoked the activity of those West Indian extremists who feel so deeply resentful and hostile that they see only a future of conflict.
>
> *(Select Committee on Race Relations and Immigration, 1976/7, p. 30)*

Thus an important feature of the inner areas was the concentration of easily identifiable ethnic minorities experiencing severe social and economic problems. Neo-fascist political parties had gained in electoral support, though since 1977 there was a growing campaign by broadly-based organisations against the National Front and racism in general. Even so, a speech on race and immigration in 1978 by the opposition leader, Margaret Thatcher, brought an immediate improvement in the Conservatives' popularity according to opinion polls.

It is probable that the White Paper deliberately underemphasised the issue of race for sincere liberal reasons, but there can be little doubt that the potential for civil disorder on a racial basis has continued to be taken seriously by the government. But such fears, as well as concern generally for conditions in inner metropolitan areas, came up against a more fundamental concern, briefly referred to in the White Paper (p. 5):

> Some of the changes which have taken place are due to social and economic forces which could be reversed only with great difficulty or at unacceptable cost.

At the time of writing the new policy for the inner city was focused on seeking to revitalise 'inner city economies'. Central government was making specific grants to local authorities with inner city problems and new 'partnership schemes' were being developed whereby central government representatives would collaborate with local authority councillors and officers in the development of local strategies.

Housing policy was envisaged as being much the same as in recent years, with a continued emphasis on improvement policy. The White Paper recognised some of the criticisms of improvement policy which were made during 1976 and 1977, but only responded in terms of a limited return to clearance, with a clear commitment to improvement as the main plank for inner city housing policy.

Housing policy—the new consensus?
We have already referred briefly to the convergence of attitudes towards housing policy which had hardened by 1977. The roots of this convergence lie in the 1950s, both in the Conservative government's acceptance of the need for a certain kind of council housing, but also, and more significant, in its successful encouragement of owner-occupation. Both Labour and Conservative governments witnessed a continued decline of the private rented sector despite various Conservative attempts to revive the private landlord. The continued growth of owner-occupation has meant that the Labour Party has come to fear alienating owner-occupiers, many of whom have traditionally voted Labour.

Fundamental to this convergence is a view of the housing problem as well on the way to being solved. Clearly, house conditions for the vast majority of the population are immeasurably better today than a hundred or even fifty years ago. Some suggest that this is mainly an effect of public policy, so that critics of the few, isolated problems that remain should be patient or, better still, silent:

> Those who decry this achievement because it has not yet covered

100 per cent of the population appear to yearn for a Utopian existence.

(Nevitt, 1978)

Della Nevitt's own analysis of housing issues, however, also acknowledged that much of the improvement in housing conditions had been a product of economic growth. Whether public policy has benignly reduced *relative* deprivation, however, remains assumed rather than investigated (Townsend, 1976 edn.). The extent to which intervention in housing is redistributive is therefore problematic. It is also difficult to demonstrate the changes that state intervention has introduced compared with what would have happened had the state remained uninvolved in housing production and distribution. In particular, it cannot be known what forms of work- or community-based demands and organisation would have developed had there not been direct state intervention; nor can we do more than speculate about the sorts of housing provision which might have arisen as a result.

Let us, however, consider the dimensions of the claim that there has been a consistent bettering of the housing situation in recent years. The most lucid discussion of recent statistics was Christine Whitehead's paper in the *CES Review 1* (1977). She was fascinated by the apparent contradiction between claims that housing problems were being systematically reduced and counter-claims to the contrary. For example, she referred to Peter Shore, Secretary of State for the Environment, who believed that 'our programmes have meant a vast improvement in the quantity and quality of the stock' (November 1976). On the other hand, Timothy Raison, Conservative spokesman on housing, had argued that, despite a growing surplus of housing over households, 'our housing problems seem to be getting worse' (April 1976). Most emphatic was Shelter, which had said in September 1975:

> It is widely accepted that a civilised community should ensure that every family has a decent, secure home at a cost they can afford. Yet despite all the promises and hopes, this country today has blatantly failed to satisfy those aims . . . policies designed to alleviate housing need have directly harmed the homeless and badly housed.

Whitehead set out to quantify changes in the housing situation, specifically in order to determine who had gained and who had lost as a result. In terms of the net gain in terms of quality and numbers she noted, first, that the rate of overall betterment was 'clearly slowing down'. In addition:

> . . . policy changes, such as the switch from rebuilding to rehabilitation, have worked to bring about a different distribution of housing services than that which would have prevailed under the policies of the 1960s. In particular, more of the gain has gone to better quality dwellings and to *existing* owner-occupiers and local authority tenants, while less has been available to help those in the private rental sector.
>
> *(p. 46, our emphasis)*

Her general conclusions also indicate the need to treat the thesis of overall improvement in conditions critically. She indicated the continued need for large-scale rehabilitation and improvement. Access into owner-occupation had become more difficult for poorer households; fewer re-lets and increased demand 'have added to the difficulties faced by local authorities in meeting housing need'. Vacancy levels had increased, as landlords continued to seek to disinvest (pp. 52–3). Her final conclusion was uncompromising:

> The declining rate of addition to housing together with its changing distribution has meant that certain groups' expectations are not being fulfilled. This must result in increased dissatisfaction with the current situation.
>
> *(op. cit.)*

Whitehead's careful technical critique of the new conventional wisdom, then, provides a sound basis for a sociological interpretation of claims and counter-claims about housing policy.

One final piece of evidence, however, remains to be introduced. Whitehead had referred to the 1971 House Condition Survey, and suggested that its estimate of improvement was over-optimistic. The results of the 1976 House Condition Survey reinforce this view; additionally, there is clear evidence of increasing dilapidation in much of the older housing stock. As yet, this is measured in terms of an escalating need for repairs, rather than a growing proportion of unfit property (DoE, 1978). The significance of this trend is great: there are signs of a substantial potential increase in decay and dereliction of this older housing. This was precisely what improvement policy was supposed to prevent, but has so far barely influenced. Is the implication for a wider distribution of the same level of resources for 'repairs', suggested in the Housing Policy Review? Or does this not raise much more fundamental considerations of policy for and the politics of housing in Britain into the 1980s?

State Housing Policy

We have already demonstrated in this chapter that what happened in Birmingham was not unique, but an example of practices and problems to be found generally in metropolitan Britain. Detailed variations, of course, existed, but the broad parameters were the same: (a) the failure of improvement policy to achieve substantial changes in housing conditions, (b) the definition of a peculiarly inner-city problem of jobs and housing and, (c) political convergence in many policy areas, crucially the support of owner-occupation, and rehabilitation rather than replacement of older housing.

In this and later sections we refer both to our local study and to discussions of the broader context already outlined. Thus we are not simply presenting conclusions from the local study; rather, we shall draw on specific features of the empirical work in order to explore a theoretical critique of improvement policy which is directly concerned to make the connections between the local and the general.

Over the last four or five years there has been a resurgence of critical research and theorising on the subjects of housing and housing policy. Much has been exploratory and most debates have yet to be resolved (for a good review of recent work, see Hooper, 1978). A central concern has been to establish the nature of housing as a distinctive kind of commodity, and the ways in which state policies affect the production, exchange and use of that commodity (see Political Economy of Housing Workshop of the Conference of Socialist Economists, 1975 and 1976; Community Development Project, 1976a and 1976b; Pickvance, 1976 and 1977).

Housing is a peculiar commodity, being an essential requirement for life as well as a source of profit for capitalist investment, but also very expensive in relation to occupiers' incomes so that it must be paid for over long periods of time, either in terms of direct loan repayments or through rent. However, even given the gradual nature of payment for housing provision, it is generally accepted that the burden of cost should not fall wholly on the occupier and the present system shares costs through various state subsidies.

As an essential but costly requirement, housing is inevitably the subject of demands by organised labour. Whilst these demands have frequently been opposed by interests concerned with housing, it has been in the interest of most employers to keep down the price of housing, as this in turn reduced the probability of increased wage demands. There has thus been some support for minimising workers' housing costs through subsidies, and also for providing an adequate supply and quality to ensure the maintenance of a healthy work force. The increasing cost of providing council housing has, however, meant that there has been growing interest in reducing state housing expenditure and passing the cost of workers' housing directly onto workers themselves.

Housing, as the subject of different class interests, has figured prominently in political debates and state practices. Opposed interests enter the political arena through political parties which, in Britain, represent constituencies defined loosely in class terms. Policies which emerge as a result of political decision thus represent institutionalised compromises between conflicting interests containing a balance of some kind. What may be viewed as a gain in terms of some increase in social provision wrested from the economically dominant class by workers may, at the same time, be claimed as the result of an enlightened piece of liberal reform carried out by a benevolent ruling class. 'Concessions', or 'liberal reforms' may thus, objectively, refer to *the same compromise*.

One major class compromise was the welfare state, in which a particular balance was struck between the interests of capital and labour and within which the state assumed responsibility for the provision of certain minimum levels of essential facilities, including health care, education, income and housing. In practice, however, the distribution of such facilities has been critically determined by class (Westergaard and Resler, 1976)). This is not to say that state action has not directly benefited workers through the enhancement of social facilities. Rather, whether this improves the poor's position *relative to* the rich is problematic, because it depends on the extent to which other changes in the environment counteract redistributive mechanisms. What is also difficult to determine is the extent to which state action serves working class interests at the expense of the dominant class. In that the means of production, distribution and exchange are still substantially privately owned, the demand for goods and commodities by state services thus serves the interest of those who benefit through profit, interest or rent.

State strategies are thus a product of the development of class forces within particular societies, with welfare states themselves representing a compromise between capital and organised labour which assures the continuation of the capitalist mode of production and, at the same time, carries a guarantee against the excesses of unconstrained capitalist accumulation (Harloe, 1978b).

The history of housing policy has never been that of smooth progression towards universally accepted goals, but rather the arena for class struggle both within and outside parliament. Hence there have been concessions to labour (building of council housing to minimum standards, rent control, subsidies to council tenants, rent rebates) and, at the same time, maintenace of capitalist relations of ownership and production (the private ownership of land and the building industry). The emphasis of state intervention has fluctuated through a series of shifts more or less in favour of either capital or labour, so no static theory could cope with the complicated developments over time.

Let us examine some recent changes in housing policy to illustrate this point. The financial crisis of the late 1960s, at a time when it was becoming clear that housing conditions were still deteriorating in many areas, required a reduction in public sector construction but also some recognition of the continuing problem of decay. The failure of comprehensive redevelopment adequately to solve problems of decay and shortage, combined with growing dissatisfaction over new public sector dwellings from users, and concern over the escalating cost of public sector building, necessitated new state strategies of intervention. The economic justification for improvement was that incremental addition of investment in the older housing stock could avoid the need for massive periodic investment in clearance and new building. The Housing Act 1969 thus deliberately sought to encourage improvement in areas which were not yet considered bad enough for clearance—the stated aim was to reduce the rate of decay.

During the early 1970s, however, the rapid slump in new building, and the limited effect of improvement ensured a worsening of conditions in many inner areas. In addition, slum clearance was grinding to a halt as local authorities with large tracts of cleared land were held back from building by a Conservative central government which failed to adjust the housing cost yardstick in line with increased costs. The government meanwhile sought to reduce council house subsidies, to increase tenants' rents, encourage the sale of council housing and private sector new building, whilst doing little about property speculation and the effects of gentrification.

The Labour Party was elected to government in 1974 pledged to revitalise the public sector, facilitate council building and make more powers and resources available for improvement. Party political differences appeared marked, especially with a temporary rent freeze and repeal of the Conservative Housing Finance Act 1972.

Many of the radical measures promised by the Labour Party during the election campaigns of 1974, however, failed to materialise. The government faced the worst economic crisis in Britain since the 1930s, with an escalating balance of payments deficit, raging inflation and rapidly increasing unemployment. The response has been a reorientation of strategy away from welfare state policies by means of what Miller (1978) has described as 'the recapitalisation of capital'. Miller argues that in the United States and the United Kingdom distinctive features of contemporary state strategies are:

(1) contracting the public sector, reducing taxation on corporations and the well-to-do, and expanding the private sector;
(2) increasing the role of manufacturing, especially exported goods, within the private sector.

(Miller, 1978, pp. 202–3)

Miller continues by suggesting that this recapitalisation strategy, as one of numerous possible responses to crisis, need not inevitably win the day. However:

In the ideological hegemonic sense, the recapitalisation has already clearly worked. Left-liberal ideas are on the defensive.

(pp. 207–8)

The consequences of recapitalisation for housing consisted of both state withdrawal from areas of direct intervention, for example slum clearance, and the introduction of cuts in expenditure. These, together, mark a tendency for the state to release control on housing leaving a greater level of responsibility both in financial and managerial terms to private individuals and organisations.

The long-awaited Housing Policy Review (DoE, 1977a) emphasised an increase in owner-occupation and improvement. The probable effects on the public sector were clear. The reduction in slum clearance and the expansion of owner-occupation to meet general needs marked a step towards a distinctive welfare role for the public rented sector which would concentrate on meeting only those needs where private provision remained unprofitable.

A recurring theme amongst contemporary Marxist reviews of housing issues has been the argument that state policies, particularly by supporting owner-occupation, deliberately fragment working class interests in housing (Clarke and Ginsberg, 1975; Community Development Project, 1976a and b; Castells, 1977). In a recent review of both Weberian and Marxist discussions of housing, Peter Saunders (1978) argued that a theory of state initiated 'fragmentation' would have to be abandoned or at least modified in the light of consideration of important contemporary changes in the British class structure. Crucially, he claims, we should view owner-occupation as an indicator of the strength of 'the new middle class' (after Carchedi, 1975). The main significance of owner-occupation, according to Saunders, is the capacity that owner-occupiers have to benefit in financial terms through their tenure position. He identified three sources of wealth accumulation via owner-occupation: 'the disproportionately high rate of house price inflation, the level of interest rates in times of inflation, and government subsidies' (pp. 245–6). The major political conclusion that Saunders draws from his discussion of owner-occupation, in agreement with an earlier argument put forward by R. E. Pahl (1975), was that there is a critical difference of interest perceived by owners and non-owners of property, which limits the scope for *joint* political action. This was certainly our experience in Birmingham over issues of redevelopment (see Lambert *et al.*, 1978). Saunders, however, attempts to argue against the thesis that state policies directly fragment working class interests, arguing instead that the 'new middle class' (owner-occupiers), stands in an intermediate position between labour and capital. His concluding argument stresses a 'necessary non-correspondence' between economic classes and political action because, following Hirst (1977), he considers that the political arena has an important degree of autonomy from economic forces so there cannot, therefore, be a simple relationship between economic relations, class action and political institutions.

He fails, however, to distinguish differences among owner-occupiers, inferring greater unanimity than his evidence can support. Additionally, we consider that support for owner-occupation is only one way in which class interests in housing are fragmented. For example, rent levels vary considerably between local authorities and between council housing and properties owned by housing associations. Crucially, within the public sector, which is itself highly differentiated in terms of quality, price and location, the practices of local authority housing management individualise collective issues through processes of allocating dwellings. The management of public sector housing and access to it, as we had seen earlier in Birmingham, is perhaps the most important fragmentary influence, especially because:

> It is not an overtly repressive mode of management but one which maintained systematic inequalities. Its ability to control the terms, the forms and the content of local political debate and action removed from local politics important issues about the unequal distribution of scarce resources and successfully redefined public issues as private troubles and political issues as technical concerns.
>
> *(Lambert* et al., *1978, pp. 169–70)*

The fragmentary effects of improvement policy, apart from those caused by differences between statutorily defined areas for action and levels of grant entitlement, lie in a substantial withdrawal by the state from direct intervention in housing provision. The result is the retention of individualised property ownership and therefore differences in tenure groupings in areas of housing affected by state policy.

In theoretical terms, fragmentation should be considered more as an *effect* of state intervention than as a specific *aim* of such interventions. Also, the extent to which owner-occupiers, especially those at the margin, actually benefit financially is often very difficult to determine.

The notion of the impartiality of the state wrestles with the unquestioned imperatives of private capital accumulation. Thus, whilst improvement policy provided an apparently technical response to problems of older housing, it also represented a respecification of the housing question which facilitated reduction in expenditure. Further, during the 1970s, with the emergence of a generalised recapitalisation strategy, improvement policy reinforced the contraction of the public sector by maintaining an active private sector involvement in older housing.

At this stage in our analysis we wish to stress two points. The first is that state policies are not class neutral and that any specific policy may represent compromises or truces between conflicting interests. Secondly, we would wish to stress the importance of the recapitalisation strategy with critical effects on housing policy and, of particular concern to us, the treatment of older housing.

The Management of Policy

Improvement policies have depended to a greater extent than clear-ance on private institutions and market forces. The stated intention was that, by providing an improved environment and subsidies to the individual owner, houses would be improved and become a more attractive proposition in the market place. Building societies, estate agents and private builders would be essential ingredients in this process. It remained the difficult task of the local authority to elicit the cooperation of these organisations and to provide a background of intervention to maintain the confidence of both owners and private institutions to ensure the success of improvement schemes. The task of the local authority was, therefore, to manage the processes affect-ing house and area renewal.

The ability of the local authority to manage is of vital concern both for the analysis of particular policies and the development of more general concepts and interpretations. Before seeking to develop such generalisations we briefly summarise the conclusions of earlier chapters dealing with urban renewal in Birmingham.

The third chapter concluded that the interaction of state inter-ventions and market processes during the 1960s and early 1970s had important effects on the structure of inner city housing markets. In particular, areas could be broadly identified which were significantly different from dominant types of residential neighbourhoods, con-taining 'a large stock of dwellings which by the 1960s was rapidly wearing out and which, following years of neglect, urgently required attention' (p. 65). The city council assumed, implicitly, that a policy of improvement, meaning private improvement stimulated by grants, loans and some public works, first 'would be welcomed by those concerned with property exchange as making sound economic sense, and second, that a modernised house was a good investment' (p. 66). Neither assumption, however, was entirely valid in the light of our analysis of the operations of the local housing market. Major institutions, particularly building societies, considered that improvement policy did not make economic sense, and that even modernised older housing was not a good investment in some areas.

The capacity of the local building industry to cope with the potentially massive amount of work that improvement would bring was never assessed at the policy's outset. It rapidly became apparent that the industry was completely unable to respond: the work involved often being too small in scale for the larger firms but attractive to the smaller concerns whose standard of workmanship proved sometimes to be appalling (chapter 5).

The question of the authority's ability to control also turned on the relationship between local and central government. Our fourth chapter set out to examine the relationship between national policy changes and the development of a local policy, so we were concerned with the question of the relative autonomy of local politics and policy making. There was little evidence of peculiarly local debates or initiatives, though improvement policy represented an apparently acceptable compromise between different local political responses to past intervention. Birmingham City Council responded directly to central government initiatives, though earlier and with more enthusiasm than most local authorities. An ambitious programme of area declaration was outlined hurriedly in response to DoE Circular 50/72. Crucially, the urban renewal policy was formulated by an incoming Labour-controlled council, when improvement appeared to be 'an achievable policy objective when so much of central government housing strategy had failed' and 'during a period when there was every indication that the city's housing problems were getting worse' (p. 86). But the policy, however ambitious, at first consisted of little more than lines on maps and statements of public intent. Little was known of the wishes and aspirations of residents in the areas to be selected, nor of the operations of the housing market within those areas. Both the details of the policy and the manner of its administration were uncertain in January 1973.

The efficacy of the local policy initiative in Birmingham was, to a large extent, determined by the level of resources and powers made available by central government. Chapter 5 described how cuts in spending caused a slowing down in the programme. More critical in their effects on the policy's operation, however, were the legal framework within which house and area improvement were situated and the organisation of the housing market in inner areas. The level of grant, the kind of work which was grant-aidable, the restrictions placed on the use of compulsory improvement powers, the slowness of their operation and the complexities surrounding the procedures for environmental improvements were all determined by legal and administrative processes. Whilst Birmingham, like many other authorities, used the maximum possible leeway within this frame-work, the sanction of law was ultimately critical.

Chapter 5 also discussed how Birmingham first declared a new policy which affected its older housing stock and then subsequently sought to develop an administrative structure and procedures through which this policy was to be implemented. The distinction between policy and administration is an important one. Offe has distinguished between the content and form of state activity:

> For what the state does if it works on a problem is a *dual* process: it organises certain activities and measures directed toward the *environment* and it adopts for *itself* a certain organisational procedure from which the production and implementation of policies emerge. Every time a state deals with a problem in its environment, it deals with a problem itself, that is, its internal mode of operation.
>
> *(Offe, 1975, p. 135)*

Policies generally contain statements about objectives which can be expressed in hierarchical terms. Often quite unexceptionable, the highest objectives in the hierarchy are statements such as 'the improvement of living conditions' or 'the provision of greater choice in the housing market'. The achievement of these broad objectives, however, subsequently requires the establishment of a series of sub-objectives. These often involve political choices and are therefore surrounded by a greater level of controversy. In Birmingham, as we have argued, it was not the broad policy objectives which were contentious but the method by which these were translated into practice. More precisely, it was the failure to reach goals and to honour promises which excited most opposition from the residents affected. The powers and ability of the local authority to grapple with the problems of improvement were under test particularly in those areas where public participation exercises were most developed. Things had been promised at public meetings for a long time so that, given the establishment of local project teams and an overall administrative framework, the task became one of delivering the goods. Many residents looked to the council for the resolution of their environmental problems. Thus noisy neighbours, strangers' cars parked outside their homes, unruly youngsters in the street and prostitutes plying for trade on the street corner were all seen as problems for the council to solve. And when council officers frequently explained that they had no powers with which to tackle these problems, the response was: 'who does have the powers then?', or, 'how may they be gained?' Residents, therefore, expected the local authority to be competent and to be able to control the environment in which their policies operate.

Earlier in the book we analysed the development of corporate management techniques. These techniques were an essential part of the authority's approach to problem solving and the urban renewal policy provided an early and severe testing ground for the implementation of corporate techniques following their official introduction in 1974. We have identified two kinds of failure. First, whilst lip service was paid to the need for corporate cooperation, departmental interests and allegiances hindered its progress. Second, and more important, the corporate approach to urban renewal was dogged by endemic problems which seem to hinder any attempt to manage policy—a badly organised programme, false assumptions about the environment of the policy, and inadequate resources.

The central issue which concerns us, both in theoretical terms and from a desire to see practical effect, is the competence of the local state, specifically its ability to manage a programme and the outside influences which shape it. Our conclusion is that the problems of management are more difficult for improvement policies than for slum clearance. The reason for this is that so much of the implementation is mediated by private individuals and agencies which are outside direct public control.

Improvement policy requires new entrepreneurial forms of intervention, persuading and cajoling owners of old houses to spend their own money, plus variable grant assistance, to bring that housing up to a better standard. Local government officers and elected councillors designate areas as eligible for certain subsidies, liaise with owners and tenants, inspect houses, supervise elements of rehabilitation work, strive to coordinate state activities—acquisiton and improvement of council owned houses and environmental works—and hope that something will happen to fulfil their aspirations and promises. Meanwhile local political differences frequently emerge, conflicts of interest erupt in the communities that improvement policy aims to 'keep together' and profit guides the actions of entrepreneurs and professionals involved in the 'messy' end of the private sector.

State Action in the Housing Market
A low rate of profit has taken mainstream private investment out of older housing in general and rented housing in particular. What private investment has remained in the older areas is largely carried out by owner-occupiers to their own homes and the problem has been that the rate of this investment, and its volume, have been inadequate to keep pace with decaying structures and rising

standards. The task of improvement policy has been to speed up and increase the volume of investment through state subsidy. But successful improvement cannot rely wholly on state action. There was a need to engender the confidence of residents, to generate a healthy market with plenty of buyers and to ensure rising, or at least stable, property values through sustained improvements to dwellings and the environment. An essential ingredient to all this was a stable supply of loan finance both for improvement work and, crucially, for property exchange. We found that building societies, the dominant lenders in the housing market, were frequently unwilling to lend on property which was, or was to be, the subject of improvement schemes. Many found improvement policies irrelevant to their operation. Those who would lend imposed stronger restrictions on borrowers than they would elsewhere; moreover, when mortgage finance became scarce, lending in the older areas would be abandoned first.

It is important to remember that the approach of the building societies, and the surveyors who advised them, was a rational response for organisations running a business on commercial lines. Indeed, building societies are *required* to carry out their financial affairs in a responsible and prudent way—their prime responsibility being to their investors and not would-be purchasers or improvers. Building society attitudes reflected the dominant economic logic which had caused the decline of older housing areas. These areas represented poor opportunities for profit and therefore were bad areas in which to invest.

The decline of mainstream investment in older housing produced, in a situation of shortage, distinctive consequences. The profit motive, expressed through a desire to seek new lucrative ventures as other avenues declined, led to a variety of distinctive kinds of investors and users of property in the older areas. This variety was described in chapter 3 and included the marginal owner-occupier, the tenant with little choice in the housing market, the new immigrant and the poor as users; investors included the landlord of multi-occupied property, 'dealers' (both in bricks and mortar and freeholds), fringe lenders and quasi-social landlords such as housing associations.

The question must be raised whether the inner, older areas exhibited processes which were fundamentally different from those elsewhere. This can be answered in two stages. First, and most obvious, these areas were affected by basic property relations and the dominant drives of a private market economy which pervaded the whole of society and therefore every spatial unit. Second, however, the specific local response to adverse market circumstances was a distinctive set of market relations , investors and users which are fundamentally different from much of the rest of the housing market. For this reason the notion of sub-markets and the idea of inner areas as being residual takes on significance.

Chapter 3 discussed the valuation of properties and the way this was carried out. The notion of a dwelling's value raises fundamental theoretical and practical questions which concern, in particular, the older part of the housing stock. To consider the theoretical questions first: every dwelling is of use to the household which occupies it, satisfying their need for shelter—in other words it has a use value. It is, however, also worth something in the market place, and for the owner who may also be the occupier, a dwelling has an exchange value. As houses grow older and wear out, use values are consumed without further additions of either labour or capital. In a similar way, the price at which older housing changes hands in the market might be expected to fall.

Many factors, however, have countered this. First, particularly during the 1960s and 1970s, there have been continuous increases in *all* property prices. Second, continued overall shortages, particularly in major urban areas, have provided an excess of would-be purchasers over the supply of many of even the worst properties. This, undoubtedly, has been influenced by the need for immigrants, faced by lack of alternatives, to buy their own housing. Third, continued state support for owner-occupation has reinforced the first two factors, since part of the cost of a house can be discounted on the assumption of tax relief on mortgage interest. Finally, the widely-held ideology concerning the benefits of owner-occupation sustains the belief that *all* housing is a good investment, irrespective almost of age or condition. The knowledge of shortages, poor quality, lack of mobility and a future of inevitably increasing rent in the public sector all add fuel to the hope that 'a home of my own' will give security in old age and freedom from bureaucratic regulation.

Essentially, therefore, there is now a gap between the use value of deteriorating property and its exchange value. The latter has not declined in response to changes in the former. The consequence of this, therefore, is that older dwellings may be over-priced compared with newer property in the suburbs.

Problems of value concern different notions of present and future exchange values. In practical terms the crucial difference in Birmingham was to be seen in the expectations of the prospective purchaser of older housing that exchange values would increase, or at least be sustained through the life of the mortgage, and those of the professional valuer who thought values may decline. Practically, therefore, the problem was that, whilst shortage and other factors might have forced prices up, the professional valuer felt that this would not continue in the future and that the differential would be reduced. The result was an unwillingness to recommend lending.

We would stress the importance of two critical features in the older housing areas. First, the areas have become increasingly unprofitable for mainstream private investment. Secondly, they have become more homogenised in terms of class and income. It is for these reasons that state action has been necessary to remove the decay. Traditionally, slum clearance and redevelopment constituted the scenario for action and, with all its faults, this process led to comprehensive enhancement in the social infrastructure. In part, market forces in housing were circumvented by an authoritative mode of control and allocation of resources. Land and buildings were municipally acquired, dwellings were cleared and redeveloped on a comprehensive basis and, irrespective of the market position of house occupiers in both job and housing markets, those displaced were re-accommodated. We are *not* saying that this process was achieved without problems; indeed we have referred to the difficulties that have been encountered. What we are saying, however, is that the state had the capacity and powers to achieve, using slum clearance, an improvement in living conditions, albeit over a protracted timescale. The statutory powers and resources may have been weak and imperfect but at least they were within an authority's grasp.

Improvement policy relies on a *far less developed* base of power and resources. Its procedures are far more tied up with economic forces and property relations than are those of clearance. We would stress three elements in this. Firstly, the extent of improvement has largely depended on an owner's income and therefore on his place in the labour market. Secondly, the physical task of improvement rested in the main with private builders who, not being in contract with the local authority, were only loosely supervised and controlled. Unlike clearance, the state could therefore exercise only limited control over the technical process of housing investment. Thirdly, because improvement policy assumed that most property would remain in private ownership, the role of private institutions in housing finance and exchange remained crucial.

Public Participation

The involvement of the public in programme implementation was a key feature of Birmingham's urban renewal policy. Liaison between residents, council members and officials at a central level through the community forum was possibly unique in Birmingham. But the effects of the participatory efforts both on the authority's management structure and in terms of concrete changes to the environment must not be overstated. At the local level most participation concerned details of environmental improvement; whilst some innovations resulted from residents' involvement, many changes were self-evidently necessary. Irrespective of the presence of residents these would probably have been introduced by the council in any case.

At the central level in Birmingham the forum may have produced some changes but its main function was to reveal both problems and shortcomings in corporate cooperation and the flaws in the policy which were created by the context in which it operated. Thus, the complaints of forum members that little or nothing was happening highlighted not only difficulties internal to the form of management adopted but pointed to underlying constraints imposed by the class structure, inequality of wealth, market forces and central government political, financial and administrative control.

From the viewpoint of many within the authority, public participation worked. At the local level, in spite of many hours of discussion and hard slog, area plans and schemes for environmental works emerged. At the central level, whilst tangible results were harder to demonstrate, residents and community workers proved themselves capable of making relevant comments on and constructive criticisms of the policy and its implementation. Whilst some in the local authority regarded the need to participate as a necessary chore or even an unwelcome incursion on their time, many genuinely believed it was a good thing, and was fulfilling the purpose defined at the policy's inception. It is worth contrasting the comparative success of participation in the urban renewal policy (defined in terms of tangible results for the local authority) with the other major initiative in public participation to be launched in the early 1970s in Birmingham—citizens' involvement in the preparation of the structure plan. This involvement could be described at best as minimal, and at worst as a dismal failure. Attendances at public meetings were poor and there was a very low level of response to written communications seeking the public's opinion. One senior official commented privately on the exercise that in a city of a million people perhaps only two or three relevant and useful comments had emerged.

The differences between the two participation exercises were of course those of scale and relevance to the ordinary person. Unlike structure plan issues and the context in which they were discussed, participation in renewal policy took place at area and street level and concerned immediate problems, the importance of which most residents could grasp and talk about in a meaningful way. The solutions proposed were to be implemented (or at least were supposed to be) within a matter of months rather than, as with the structure plan, years or even decades.

In chapter 6 we rejected the notion that there was some conspiratorial attempt to incorporate residents' action groups. We argued that the local state cannot be seen as a monolithic whole, a point which those who engaged in public participation rapidly appreciated. They both witnessed and even became involved in the feuds and alliances accompanying local authority decision-making. The participatory process itself created a new form of division and contention within the local authority and, as we have described earlier, it set up new dilemmas of allegiance and responsibility for junior and middle level officers.

The immediate concern of much participatory activity was with the technical issues of implementation. This activity was, however, firmly set within a political context and raised questions about the distribution of resources and the legitimacy of those who claimed to represent the community's aspirations. Many residents realised that the task was not simply trying to persuade the council to plant trees in one area or to clear up another. The achievement of these limited objectives raised fundamental questions about the authority's resources and ability to control. Whilst much of the participatory exercise could be described as 'technical cooperation' (Lambert *et al.*, 1978) there was a growing awareness of the political framework and, at the forum level, emerging links with trade unions. Whilst, however, the awareness of the wider issues and the uncovering of the critical constraints of the policy were clearly present, what failed to emerge was any serious challenge to the economic and political structure which imposed those constraints.

Reflections on Improvement Policy

Improvement policy has been a way of resolving, albeit temporarily, structural contradictions arising out of previous state interventions in housing. Increased costs of slum clearance and council housing, combined with state support for owner-occupation, were associated with a respecification of the nature of housing problems which facilitated reductions in state expenditures whilst maintaining the appearance of progressive intervention. The form of state intervention changed at the level of the local state, because improvement policy required, for the first time ever, that the local state become actively involved in attempts to reinvigorate parts of the *private* housing market.

Comprehensive redevelopment accelerated a process of restructuring the British housing system after the Second World War. But the proper redevelopment of inner areas was vitiated by central government delays and restricted financial allocations as well as by the sheer enormity of the slum problems facing urban authorities. The accumulation of changes to the overall structure of the British housing system, however, meant that the state necessarily had to find new ways of intervention. The sustained legitimacy of the state and institutional politics depended in part at least on claims that the housing problem *could* be solved, and successive governments pledged new and radical approaches to its solution. State intervention over forty years had changed assumptions about the role of the state, created expectations of future state actions, and affected the reorganisation of the housing market. By the late 1960s improvement was an ideologically acceptable alternative to redevelopment, not least because it was based on assumptions acceptable to the Labour Government—continued intervention but reduced state expenditure.

If we compare improvement policy with redevelopment, however, we can see that the former is in practice no easier to accomplish than the latter. Certainly, the powers and resources were constrained, but with comprehensive redevelopment the local state was allocating resources within an environment which became predictable and, to a large extent, internally stable. That cannot be so with improvement policy unless the state assumes total control of all housing within specified areas or within defined categories.

The central contradiction of improvement policy is that it is a market-oriented form of intervention, specifically seeking to stimulate market processes, yet at the same time not controlling crucial market relations which are precisely the cause of housing decay. Thus there remains a need for intervention in order to sustain particular commodity forms and relations, or the promise of improvement is belied by failure to effect changes in house conditions. Then, either there has to be increased intervention, possibly of a different sort (municipalisation and improvement) which would run counter to current tendencies (sponsorship of owner-occupation and voluntary improvement), or policies would have to be abandoned in favour of some other strategy of state intervention.

Moreover, because improvement policy itself only contains the appearance of a technical-rational approach to 'problems' of older housing, but is in fact a specific compromise arising from quite different forces, the powers and resources available to the local state have fluctuated in response to structural imperatives of recapitalisation and recommodification. The problems affecting the development and implementation of Birmingham's policy were not separate from that policy—they were part of it, part of the very essence of 'policy'. The search for legitimation through 'participation' inevitably failed to reconcile the underlying conflicts arising from class fragmentation and market exploitation.

So we end with a view of improvement policy which rejects a separation between the claims and actions of the state and the complex environment of its operations. First, 'a hierarchical structure of "neutral" officials is simply insufficient to absorb the decision load that is implied by productive state activities' (Offe, 1975, p. 136). Second, in capitalist states, the primary functions of state activity are fundamentally in contradiction: policy has to obey contradictory laws, fluctuating between the interests of capital accumulation and social cohesion. Incompetence is thus built into the organisation of policy-making and implementation; rational class-neutral planning is intrinsically impossible.

'Policy' is hence an ideological term for specific instances of state involvement in the class struggle; it is a function of the compromise between classes, structured by the struggle between capital and labour within capitalist societies. It is not something separate, distinct from 'the market', or internal to the state. It is both things at all times, and irretrievably so.

Alternatives?

We do not see that it is our prime task to suggest alternative policies. We have been concerned mainly to analyse the current nature and consequences of a given set of powers, resources and strategies.

Nevertheless, we should discuss alternative strategies for dealing with older housing, particularly in such ways as to benefit working people.

We must first deal with the allegation, often made, that Birmingham's urban renewal policy ran into difficulties because it was too large in scale. It was argued that it attempted to do too much too soon. This was an easy criticism to make but it ignored both the sheer scale of the problem of substandard housing in Birmingham and also the exhortation given to local authorities in DoE Circular 50/72 to prepare plans for dealing with unsatisfactory housing by 1980 if not before. Whilst officers within the authority realised at the time of the circular that it would not be possible to have dealt with each individual dwelling by clearance or improvement in that time scale, it was intended that at least a programme of area action would be under way to ensure that the vast majority of the substandard stock would be programmed for action whether by clearance, by general improvement or as renewal areas. There was also expected to be a substantial amount of renovation and clearance actually completed by the end of the decade. The task was massive. At the announcement of the policy in January 1973 perhaps around 60,000–70,000* dwellings had to be cleared or improved. And within the time scale envisaged by the government circular this meant that around 8,500–10,000 dwellings a year would have to be treated by clearance or improvement. A key theme of this book has been that, whatever the council's commitment to the achievement of the policy, the base in terms of resources was inadequate. This resource base must be seen in its widest sense as comprising financial resources both of the individual householder and the local authority, legislative powers, council personnel and capital and labour resources of the building industry.

In our approach to policy reform three important features need to be borne in mind. First, we have referred to the growth in owner-occupation, both to date and as a goal of future policy. This growing privatisation of the housing stock has consequences for the level of government control over future investment in house improvement. As owner-occupation grows the greater the level of necessary investment initiated by the individual. Unless new subsidy structures are devised, the level of such investment will vary according to many factors outside the direct control of public policy: the level of

---

*Authors' estimate based on numbers of dwellings in general improvement and housing action areas less those already at the 10 point standard.

earnings, the savings/consumption ratio and so on. Second, Britain has an ageing population structure. This has implications for the housing market, particularly given the growth of owner-occupation, as there will be increasing numbers of elderly householders living in privately owned dwellings suffering from growing obsolescence and disrepair. The problem is more than the simple observation that the elderly tend to be relatively poor and therefore unable to meet their share of renovation costs, but that the stock in which many of them will live will be unsuitable for their needs in terms of size, internal layout and location. Even if they could afford to improve, the dwelling which would result from such work would be unsuitable for them and traditionally many have turned to the public sector for a small flat or bungalow. Third, housing decay is a continuous process and has to be dealt with through continuous measures of improvement or clearance. Since comprehensive redevelopment went out of fashion there has been a dramatic fall in the level of slum clearance in England and Wales from nearly 350,000 demolitions or closures in the five year period 1968–72 to around 255,000 in the period 1973–7. Most of these dwellings would have been in, or acquired from, the private sector. This fall in the rate of clearance or closure of some 95,000 dwellings has not been matched by an increase in grant-aided house improvement in the private sector. In the same periods the rate of improvement grant approvals to private owners increased only by around 6,000 from under 607,000 in the period 1968–72 to just over 613,000 in 1973–7. Moreover, this relates to grant *approvals* rather than actual payments for work completed and the true rate of improvement is therefore lower. The efforts to get private houses improved over the period 1973–7 have yielded only limited results, therefore, and on the two fronts of clearance and improvement there was a considerable shortfall in the level of activity in the second five year period compared with the first. These 'lost years' of relatively low levels of housing activity will have to be made up in the very near future.

Since the housing acts of 1969 and 1974 there have been many suggestions for reforming policies towards the older housing stock. The government has made its own position clear on the need for change in its Green Paper on Housing Policy (DoE, 1977a). The Green Paper stated that the primary objective of renovation policy is to be the improvement of a larger number of dwellings than hitherto to a decent basic standard rather than the improvement of a smaller number of houses to a higher standard. There is, therefore, to be a 'more flexible' approach to improvement grants to ensure that this change of emphasis takes place. Grants for 'repairs only' are to be made available on a wider basis, the process for the compulsory improvement of dwellings is to be simplified and consideration will be given to raising the cost and rateable value limits on improvement grants. The government has also announced its intention of examining the possibility of allowing tenants of privately rented dwellings to apply for renovation grants for work on the houses they occupy. This approach, whatever its potential merits, is at best only tinkering with a system which has proven incapable of tackling the problem of large-scale renovation.

The most fundamental issue to be grasped in the debate about the future of the housing stock is the question of the balance between clearance and improvement. There is a growing feeling, and it is an opinion which we endorse, that the trend towards improvement has gone too far and that the rate of clearance has fallen far below the level necessary to ensure that the current volume of housing replacement takes place. The debates about improvement *versus* clearance frequently turn on questions of comparative cost and the social disbenefits of clearance. There are, however, social factors which argue *against* improvement in certain communities and the debate about cost is far from proven. Perhaps the most concise and sound approach to the problem of alternatives is found in the response of the Environmental Health Officers' Association to the Green Paper and it is worth quoting from it at some length:

> Clearance must be considered not only in the context of the condition of the total housing stock and of the social consequences but also have regard to the acceptability of houses by the public.
>
> Even if it were possible to bring all the unfit houses into a state of fitness by repair and modernisation, it is not necessarily the best policy. There are many houses which are physically incapable of satisfactory improvement and others on which it would be sheer folly to spend large sums of money . . . Many local authorities have found in their municipalisation programmes that the cost of repairing and modernising a house which is already sixty or more years old is not very much less than the cost of building a new one. The parable about putting new wine in old bottles is still as valid today as when it was first said.
>
> In the most successful years of clearance national performance averaged 60,000 houses. When we consider the total housing stock of 18 million, we see that on that policy it would mean that each house will have to last 300 years. Any prudent organiser allows for

a planned replacement of his stock. Can it reasonably be argued that the replacement of 60,000 houses per year is too rapid a rate? On the contrary it would seem that the 'improve at all costs' policy will put a millstone around the necks of our children and our grandchildren.

(Environmental Health Officers' Association, 1977, pp. 33–4)

In the most pragmatic sense, then, there is a need to set higher targets for the clearance and replacement of the housing stock. The task of dealing with obsolete dwellings cannot, however, be handled all at once so a programme would have to be spread over several years. This idea is of course not new; it is embodied in the current Department of the Environment's concept of 'gradual renewal' and was advocated in some detail in the Denington Report (Central Housing Advisory Committee, 1966). This approach, however, has its own problems, since the act of deciding that a dwelling would be required for clearance at some stage in the future has the effect of increasing blight, adversely affecting its saleability and mortgage-ability. Furthermore, conferring a short life on a dwelling deters owners from carrying out repairs and improvement. These consequences are, however, not unknown and indeed they are familiar points made in criticism of post-war slum clearance programmes. Given the need to develop a long term programme of action they are problems which will continue to face us and which must be confronted.

The problems of saleability and mortgageability are difficulties which could be reduced by the adoption of firm programmes with sustained levels of resources with which they are to be implemented. This would reduce uncertainty but, given the likely resistance on the part of commercial lenders to mortgaging properties with lives of less than twenty-five to thirty years, an increased role for municipal mortgage lending would be required. This would require a stable level of resources and flexible lending policies, including a willingness to advance for the full length of a dwelling's life. Even these measures would probably fail to overcome problems of selling short-life properties on the open market so that automatic and straight-forward arrangements would, therefore, need to be made for local authorities to acquire them.

The problems of decay brought about by the unwillingness of owner-occupiers to invest in properties facing demolition would need to be tackled both through enforcement of the public health and housing acts and by encouragement through a more generous and flexible system of grant aid. This may well require shortening the required life of a dwelling before grants are considered, as well as making greater contributions towards repair costs. The environmental health officers have specifically urged the government to reduce the minimum life for 'intermediate grants' towards standard amenities and repairs from fifteen to eight years.

As far as house improvement is concerned, the question of enforcement of housing standards is a crucial one. Whilst agreeing with the Green Paper that the voluntary approach to house improvement should be attempted first, we think that an effective and simple enforcement procedure is clearly required for those who do not respond to voluntary measures. This particularly applies to dwellings owned by private landlords. We do not believe that there will be any major upswing of improvement activity either as a result of the Green Paper's suggestions for providing for grants to tenants or as a result of the often-heard call for the freeing of rents from artificial restraint. Outside specific geographical areas and sectors of the market the private landlord is in rapid decline and any freeing of market forces is unlikely to reverse this process. It failed to happen after the Rent Act 1957 and today, as then, there are more fruitful (and easier) ways of getting a return on investment.

The task of improving the private sector stock must be simplified and shortened. The approach we suggest would provide an alternative to the complex and time consuming compulsory improvement arrangements. At the start of a programme for improvement, whether area based or not, landlords of improvable dwellings would be offered grant aid. Failure to avail themselves of this, given the willingness of the tenant to have his house improved, would set in motion a binding arrangement which would force the owner to sell his house either to the tenant (with an obligation on the latter to improve) or to the local authority, and an authority will be duty-bound to carry out renovations within a specified period after purchase.

The approach to owner-occupiers must in some ways be different from that to the landlord, although the local authority clearly should have a duty to ensure that the stock is maintained and replaced irrespective of tenure. Whilst more generous grants and less inflexible grant arrangements may improve uptake, there are still likely to be owners who will resist improvement, however generous the subsidy they receive. One approach which is worthy of consideration is providing local authorities with new powers for carrying out improvement and repair schemes in default of an owner who has failed to respond to the offer of grant aid. The costs to the authority, less grant aid, could then be recovered, either by voluntary payment by the owner or by making the costs a charge on the property to be recovered when it is sold. In this way the owner would be freed from the complicated task of completing grant forms and, what is probably more onerous, finding a builder and raising his share of the cost. Owners simply wishing to be left alone, for example the elderly, need only be troubled on public health grounds.

The problems of implementation are wider than those of persuading or forcing owners to carry out improvements. As we pointed out in chapter 5 many owners were unable to find suitable builders to carry out the work and indeed the capacity of the building industry was a major constraint on the urban renewal policy. As we see it there is no alternative to the expansion of direct labour operation. Already in some areas council house renovations are carried out by tradesmen employed by the local authority and are under the authority's direct control. A pool of labour experienced in the specialist task of house renovation would be established and an expanded role for direct labour could then provide a viable alternative to the private builder in the sphere of improvements to privately owned dwellings. Such an arrangement ought to ensure a better and more consistent standard of workmanship through direct supervision of the contract by the authority's technical staff.

The measures that we suggest would require a greater level of resource allocation by government and, perhaps more important, a re-emergence of state control and influence in areas of the housing market. We have pointed to the failure of improvement policies and attributed much of the blame to a lack of control of key processes and decisions by the state. Unless there is a reversal of the withdrawal of control which improvement policies have traditionally represented, we see no sustained improvement taking place in the areas of poorer housing.

In conclusion, we must emphasise our own view that the continued support for owner-occupation, together with the present system of housing finance and subsidies and the continued domination by private capital of house production and housing markets will, even given the moderate proposals we have made, prove insurmountable obstacles to real improvement. Reforms of policy, unless they are part of a radical restructuring of the economy and of society, will never succeed in eradicating the housing problem.

Appendix I
A Note on Research Methods

The findings presented in this book have been derived from a variety of research methods, the particular approach chosen depending on the kind of data we wished to reveal.

The objective was to discover in some detail what changes had taken and were taking place both within local areas and the local authority as a result of a major policy initiative in housing. In particular we wished to examine the relationship between the stated objectives of policy and their actual effects both on the ground in the streets and neighbourhoods of inner-city Birmingham and on the assumptions and activities of key private sector agencies.

This kind of data required some fairly long term and close involvement in particular localities. Both as local residents in areas affected by the policy and as persons with some knowledge of housing, we were allowed privileged access to a number of community associations and a city-wide forum of residents' groups. In our dealings with local residents we were seen not so much as researchers but as fellow activists and our task was as much to contribute our time, knowledge and ideas to the activities of the associations and the forum as to take away information and experience for the purpose of the research project.

We have called this approach 'research-action' and in our book with John Lambert we have discussed its merits and difficulties in some detail (Lambert *et al.*, 1978). The success of this approach to research obviously depends on access to the organisations one wishes to study and it was by virtue of our personal links with local people and groups that a privileged vantage point was secured. Any other researcher new to the area and coming in from outside simply to study and not participate may have found it difficult to gain acceptance.

Research-action was only one method which we have adopted in our work and much data was gathered using more conventional techniques, for example unstructured interviews, document searches and manipulation of published quantitative data such as census material. As well as at formal interviews, information and opinions were also obtained by a variety of informal discussions with officers and councillors.

The interviews with representatives from building societies and estate agents were guided around a check-list of points—no set questionnaire was used. No interviewees objected to the discussions being tape-recorded and after each interview a transcript was prepared.

We could summarise the main areas of our empirical work and research techniques used as follows:

Data Area	Principal Research Technique
Development of the policy	Unstructured interviews with members and former members of the council and senior local authority officers.
	Searches of committee reports and council documents released by members of the council.
Older housing market in Birmingham	Unstructured interviews with building society branch managers, surveyors and officers of housing associations.
	Work on census and other published material.
Management of the policy	Research-action.
	Searches of council documents released by members of the council.
	Informal discussions with members of the council, local government officers and community workers.
Public participation	Research-action.

A Note on Calculating the Rate of House Improvement

In chapter 5 we demonstrated the extent of progress in house improvement in GIAs and HAAs. The information was derived from records kept by the urban renewal section of the environmental department. The figures on grant take-up and completed work should be straightforward. However, data on the dwellings in the area, their tenure and condition at declaration is more problematic since this relies on the extent of the project team's research work that was carried out prior to declaration. In arriving at the estimate for privately owned dwellings which were in need of improvement we have deducted the following from the urban renewal section's figures for total dwellings in the GIAs and HAAs: (a) dwellings scheduled for clearance (where appropriate); (b) dwellings owned by housing associations and the council, and (c) dwellings up to the ten point standard at the time of declaration. These elements were shown as discrete totals in the council's analysis for monitoring progress but it is clear that there may be some double-counting between (b) and (c). Some dwellings owned by housing associations and the council may have been up to standard at declaration. Our analysis assumes, because of an absence of evidence to the contrary, that there is no double-counting. If there were any we consider that its influence would be slight and would not greatly affect the results. If double-counting could be identified and were to be eliminated, it would, of course, increase the estimates of privately owned dwellings in the GIAs and HAAs; and grant aided renovation, expressed as a proportion of all private, improvable dwellings would appear even lower than we have shown in our analysis.

Appendix II
A Note on Developments
since 1976

Our empirical work stopped in the summer of 1976 and we wrote most of the first draft of this book throughout the rest of the summer and autumn. Since then, certain policy changes have taken place. These, whilst reflecting the philosophy of the new ruling Conservative group on the council, do not materially affect the urban renewal policy's assumptions and strategy and do not alter the validity of what we have argued so far in this book.

The Conservatives took control of the council after the May 1976 elections. Very soon after taking office the research and intelligence unit of the chief executive's department was closed down and later the chief executive himself was made redundant. Further efforts to 'decorporatise' the council's management system included the decision to abandon the urban renewal multi-disciplinary team. This was replaced by smaller working parties which, although consisting of representatives of the different departments, were unlike the multi-disciplinary team in that they were chaired permanently by an officer from the urban renewal section. The new council continued to declare areas for HAA and GIA treatment although there was some deceleration in the rate of declaration. A number of existing HAAs were made into 'specimen areas' in which progress was to be made at a fairly rapid pace. These areas were to demonstrate to the council, the private sector and the public in general what urban renewal could achieve. It was claimed that the acceleration of progress in these areas would not hinder work elsewhere.

As we discussed in chapter 5, the Urban Renewal Agency Service had proved to be too costly. It was replaced by a new house improvement service which would provide, for a fee, an owner with a list of approved builders who had agreed to carry out grant aided improvement schemes at a negotiated rate. The new package the council offered, therefore, was a reputable builder, a fair price and supervision of the work whilst it was under way. Unlike the old Agency Service the council was not a party to the contract and was not itself involved in design work.

Whatever the changes that were brought about during the later half of 1976 and during 1977, they had little effect on what had always been a fundamental problem—the low rate of take-up of renovation grants, particularly in the HAAs. By April 1978 out of a total of 12,500 dwellings which were scheduled to be retained in the declared HAAs, only 600 had been improved with grant aid in the private sector. In the first four areas there was less than two years to run of the statutory HAA period.

The solution which had been envisaged since the formation of the policy had been the municipalisation of unimproved property after owners had had a reasonable chance to cooperate. Indeed, compulsory purchase procedures were already under way in the first four HAAs. Any further substantial acquisition programme would, however, be unacceptable on political grounds and would be extremely costly.

The scheme which emerged to solve the problem was one which involved the increase of public funds for the improvement of housing, whilst retaining dwellings in private ownership. The plan was to use central government finance from the special fund established to stimulate the construction industry, and later from the Inner City Partnership Scheme, to carry out renovation to the structure and curtilage of private homes with the owners' consent. Work would be limited to the outside of a dwelling and it would then be up to the owner to apply for a renovation grant towards the rest of the improvement work that was required. In this way the necessary contribution from the owner would be much reduced and, at the same time, expenditure from public funds would be far lower than it would have been had the dwellings been acquired and wholly improved by the local authority.

In chapter 5 we recounted a dismal story about progress on environmental improvements in GIAs. Since 1976, some progress has been made in these areas and in some HAAs. Most work had been done on private land, for example improvements to boundary walls and rear access alleys. Improvements on the highways has progressed very slowly and in many areas no work has been started.

We can summarise the changes that have taken place over the last two years. There have been changes in the authority's management structure. Novel approaches have been adopted to tackle the fundamental problem of the low incidence of private house improvement. Limited progress has been made on environmental works. In most areas, however, the position was much the same in 1978 as it had been in 1976. Indeed, often further physical deterioration had taken place particularly in house conditions.

The DoE Circular 50/72, which triggered the preparation of Birmingham's Urban Renewal Policy, envisaged the elimination of slum and substandard properties by 1980. This cannot be achieved; there has, after all, been very little improvement . . .

Bibliography

Bailey, N. J. (1976) 'Urban Renewal and Institutional Change: A Case Study of Public Action in Little Green, Birmingham', M. Soc. Sci. thesis, Centre for Urban and Regional Studies, University of Birmingham.

Bennington, J. (1976) *Local Government Becomes Big Business* (2nd edition), London, Community Development Project Information and Intelligence Unit.

Berry, F. (1976) 'Housing Action Areas', *Municipal Journal*, May 1976.

Birmingham Inner Area Study (1975) *The Management of Urban Renewal*, draft of IAS/B/10, London, DoE.

Boddy, M. (1976) 'The Structure of Mortgage Finance: Building Societies and the British Social Formation', *Transactions Institute of British Geographers*, NS 1.

Bonnier, F. (1972) '*Les Pratiques des Associations de Quartier et les Processes de "Recuperation"'*, *Espaces et Sociétés*, nos. 6–7.

Bowley, M. (1945) *Housing and the State 1919–1944*, London, George Allen and Unwin.

Burney, E. (1967) *Housing on Trial*, Oxford University Press.

Carchedi, G. (1975) 'On the Economic Identification of the New Middle Class', *Economy and Society*, 4.

Castells, M. (1977 edition) *The Urban Question*, London, Edward Arnold.

Central Housing Advisory Committee (1966) *Our Older Homes: a Call for Action*, London, HMSO.

Central Housing Advisory Committee (1969) *Council Housing Purposes, Procedures and Priorities*, London, HMSO.

City of Birmingham (1973) *City of Birmingham Structure Plan, Report of Survey: Housing*, City of Birmingham.

City of Birmingham Urban Renewal Conference (1973) *Urban Renewal Policy: General Improvement Areas and Renewal Areas*, City of Birmingham.

Clarke, C. and Ginsberg, N. (1975) 'The Political Economy of Housing', in Political Economy of Housing Workshop of the Conference of Socialist Economists.

Coates, D. (1975) *The Labour Party and the Struggle for Socialism*, Cambridge University Press.

Cockburn, C. (1977) *The Local State*, London, Pluto Press.

Community Development Project (1976a) *Whatever Happened to Council Housing?*, London, CDP.

Community Development Project (1976b) *Profits against Houses: an Alternative Guide to Housing Finance*, London, CDP.

Community Development Project, Political Economy Collective (1977) *The Poverty of Improvement*, London, CDP Political Economy Collective.

Counter Information Services (1973) *The Recurrent Crisis of London*, CIS.

Crossman, R. H. S. (1975) *Diaries of a Cabinet Minister, Vol. 1, Minister of Housing, 1964–66*, London, Hamish Hamilton.

Cullingworth, J. B. (1966) *Housing and Local Government*, London, George Allen and Unwin.

Cullingworth, J. B. (1973) *Problems of an Urban Society, Vol. 2*, London, George Allen and Unwin.

Davies, J. G. (1972) *The Evangelistic Bureaucrat*, London, Tavistock.

Dennis, N. (1970) *People and Planning*, London, Faber.

Dennis, N. (1972) *Public Participation and Planners' Blight*, London, Faber.

Dickens, P. (1976) 'Class Conflict and the Gift of Housing', paper at International Conference on the Sociology of Regional and Urban Development, Messina–Reggio, April 1976.

DoE (1977a) *Housing Policy: a Consultative Document*, Cmnd. 6851, London, HMSO.

DoE (1977b) *Inner London: Policies for Dispersal and Balance—Final Report of the Lambeth Inner Area Study*, London, HMSO.

DoE (1977c) *Unequal City—Final Report of the Birmingham Inner Area Study*, London, HMSO.

DoE (1977d) *Change or Decay—Final Report of the Liverpool Inner Area Study*, London, HMSO.

DoE (1977e) *Policies for the Inner Cities*, Cmnd. 6845, London, HMSO.

DoE (1978) *House Condition Survey 1976*, London, HMSO.

DoE Circular 50/72, *Slums and Older Housing: an Overall Strategy*, London, HMSO.

DoE Circular 13/75, *Housing Act 1974: Renewal Strategies*, London, HMSO.

DoE Circular 14/75, *Housing Act 1974: Housing Action Areas, Priority Neighbourhoods and General Improvement Areas*, London, HMSO.

DoE Circular 64/75, *Housing Expenditure Changes*, London, HMSO.

Donnison, D. (1967) *The Government of Housing*, Harmondsworth, Penguin.

Drake, M. *et al.* (1975) 'Aspects of Structure Planning in Britain', Research Paper no. 20, Centre for Environmental Studies.

Duncan, T. L. C. (1974) 'Housing Improvement Policies in England and Wales', Research Memorandum no. 28, Centre for Urban and Regional Studies, University of Birmingham.

Duncan, S. S. (1977) 'The Housing Question and the Structure of the Housing Market', *Journal of Social Policy*, 6.

Eddison, T. (1975) *Local Government: Management and Corporate Planning* (2nd edition), London, Leonard Hill.

English, J. *et al.* (1976) *Slum Clearance*, London, Croom Helm.

Environmental Health Officers' Association (1977) *A National Housing Policy—the Environmental Health Officers' Association's Views*.

Fagence, M. (1977) *Citizen Participation in Planning*, Oxford, Pergamon.

Ford, J. (1975) 'The Role of the Building Society Manager in the Urban Stratification System: Autonomy versus Constraint', *Urban Studies*, 12, 3.

Gibson, M. S. (1972a) 'A New Approach to Urban Renewal?', *West Midlands Grass Roots*, No. 3.

Gibson, M. S. (1972b) 'Urban Renewal: Some Recent Developments', *West Midlands Grass Roots*, No. 4.

Gibson, M. S. and Langstaff, M. J. (1972) 'Community Action and Housing Policy: Possibilities in Birmingham', *Community Action*, No. 2.

Goodman, R. (1972) *After the Planners*, Harmondsworth, Penguin.

Green, G. (1975) 'The Leasehold Problem in Saltley' in Lees, R. and Smith, G., *Action Research in Community Development*, London, Routledge and Kegan Paul.

Green, G. (1976) 'Property Exchange in Saltley', Political Economy of Housing Workshop of the Conference of Socialist Economists.

Hadden, T. (1978) *Compulsory Repair and Improvement*, Centre for Socio-legal Studies, Wolfson College, Oxford, Research Study No. 1.

Hain P. (ed.) (1977) *Community Politics*, London, Calder.

Hall, P. *et al.* (1973) *The Containment of Urban England, Vols. I and II*, London, George Allen and Unwin.

Harloe, M. (1977) 'Will the Green Paper Mean Better Housing?', *Roof*, Vol. II, no. 5.

Harloe, M. (1978a) 'The Green Paper on Housing Policy', Brown, M. (ed.) *Yearbook of Social Policy*, 1978, London, Routledge and Kegan Paul.

Harloe, M. (1978b) 'Housing and the State: Recent British Developments', *International Social Science Journal*, Vol. XXX, no. 3.

Harloe, M. *et al.* (1974) *The Organisation of Housing*, London, Heinemann.

Harrison, A. (1977) 'The Valuation Gap: a Danger Signal?', *CES Review 2.*

Harvey, D. (1974) 'Class-monopoly Rent, Finance Capital and the Urban Revolution', *Regional Studies*, No. 3.

Harvey, D. and Chatterjee, L. (1974) 'Absolute Rent and the Structuring of Space by Financial Institutions', *Antipode* 6.

Hatch, S. (1973) 'Estate Agents as Urban Gatekeepers', Paper to the British Sociological Association, Urban Sociology Group, University of Stirling.

Hindess, B. (1971) *The Decline of Working Class Politics*, London, Paladin.

Hirst, P. (1977) 'Economic Classes and Politics', in Hunt, A. (ed.) *Class and Class Structure*, London, Lawrence and Wishart.

Hooper, A. (1978) 'The Political Economy of Housing in Britain', *International Journal of Urban and Regional Research*, 2, 1.

Howick, C. (1978) 'Corporate Planning—Theoretical Perspectives', unpublished paper.

Jacobs, M. (1977) 'Save our Cities', *International Journal of Urban and Regional Research*, 1, 2.

Karn, V. A. (1975) 'Priorities for Local Authority Mortgage Lending: a Case Study of Birmingham', Research Memorandum No. 52, Centre for Urban and Regional Studies, University of Birmingham.

Karn, V. A. (1976) 'The Operation of the Housing Market in Inner Urban Areas: Final Report to the SSRC', unpublished report available from the National Lending Library.

Karn, V. A. (1977/8) 'The Financing of Owner-occupation and its Impact on Ethnic Minorities', *New Community*, Vol. VI, Nos. 1 and 2.

Karn, V. A. (forthcoming) 'Low Income Owner Occupation in the Inner City', in Jones, C. (ed.) *Perspectives on Urban Deprivation and the Inner City*, London, Croom Helm.

Kelly, F. and Wintour, J. (1977) *The Housing Crisis Nationwide*, London, Shelter.

Lambert, C. (1976) 'Building Societies, Surveyors and the Older Areas of Birmingham', Working Paper No. 38, Centre for Urban and Regional Studies, University of Birmingham.

Lambert, J., Paris, C. and Blackaby, B. (1978) *Housing Policy and the State*, London, Macmillan.

Langstaff, M. J. (1972) 'Housing Improvement and Community Action in Birmingham: a Study Based on Institutional Urban Theory', M. Soc. Sci. thesis, Centre for Urban and Regional Studies, University of Birmingham.

Marx, K. and Engels, F. (1973 edition) *Collected Works*, London, Lawrence and Wishart.

Mason, T. (1977) 'Community Action and the Local Authority: a Study in the Incorporation of Protest', Harloe, M. (ed.) *York Conference 1977, Urban Change and Conflict*, London, Centre for Environmental Studies, Conference Series no. 19.

Means, R. (1977) 'Social Work and the Undeserving Poor', Occasional Paper no. 37, Centre for Urban and Regional Studies, University of Birmingham.

Mellor, J. R. (1973) 'Structure and Process in the Twilight Areas', *Town Planning Review*, 44, 1.

Mellor, J. R. (1977) *Urban Sociology in an Urbanized Society*, London, Routledge and Kegan Paul.

Millar, E. (1972) 'Report on the Health of Birmingham in 1972', City of Birmingham.

Miller, M. (1978) 'The Recapitalization of Capitalism', *International Journal of Urban and Regional Research*, 2, 1.

MOHLG Circular 65/69, *Housing Act 1969: Area Improvement*, London, HMSO.

Murie, A. (1975) 'The Sale of Council Houses: a Study in Social Policy', Occasional Paper No. 35, Centre for Urban and Regional Studies, University of Birmingham.

Murie, A. and Forrest, R. (1976) 'Social Segregation, Housing Need and the Sale of Council Houses', Research Memorandum No. 53, Centre for Urban and Regional Studies, University of Birmingham.

Murie, A., Niner, P. and Watson, C. (1976) *Housing Policy and the Housing System*, London, George Allen and Unwin.

Mustoe, N. E., Eve, H. B. and Anstey, B. (1960) *Complete Valuation Practice*, London, The Estates Gazette.

Needleman, L. (1968) 'Rebuilding or Renovation?: a Reply', *Urban Studies*, Vol. V.

Nevitt, A. (1966) *Housing, Taxation and Subsidies*, London, Nelson.

Nevitt, A. (1978) 'Issues in Housing' in Davies, R. and Hall, P. (eds.) *Issues in Urban Society*, Harmondsworth, Penguin.

Newton, K. (1976) *Second City Politics: Democratic Process and Decision Making in Birmingham*, Oxford University Press.

Norman, P. (1971) 'Corporation Town', *Official Architecture and Planning*, Vol. XXXIV.

Offe, C. (1975) 'The Theory of the Capitalist State and the Problem of Policy Formation', Lindberg, L. N. *et al.* (eds.) *Stress and Contradiction in Modern Capitalism*, Lexington, Mass., Lexington Books.

Pahl, R. E. (1975 edition) *Whose City?*, Harmondsworth, Penguin.

Paris, C. T. (1977) 'Housing Action Areas', *Roof*, 2, 1.

Paris, C. T. (1978) '"The Parallels are Striking" . . . Crisis in the Inner City? GB 1977', *International Journal of Urban and Regional Research* 2, 1.

Paris, C. T. and Lambert, J. R. (1979) 'Housing Problems and the State—the Case of Birmingham, England' in Herbert, D. T. and Johnson, R. J. (eds.) *Geography and the Urban Environment*, London, Wiley.

Pickvance, C. G. (ed.) (1976) *Urban Sociology: Critical Essays*, London, Tavistock.

Pickvance, C. G. (1977a) 'Some Aspects of the Political Economy of French Housing', Paper to the Conference of Socialist Economists Housing Workshop, Birmingham, September 1977.

Pickvance, C. G. (1977b), 'From "Social Base" to "Social Force": Some Analytical Issues in the Study of Urban Protest', in Harloe, M. (ed.) *Captive Cities*, London, Wiley.

Political Economy of Housing Workshop of the Conference of Socialist Economists (1975) *Political Economy and the Housing Question*, London.

Political Economy of Housing Workshop of the Conference of Socialist Economists (1976) *Housing and Class in Britain*, London.

Power, C. N. (1965) *The Forgotten People*, Evesham, Arthur James.

Rex, J. R. (1968) 'The Sociology of a Zone of Transition', Pahl, R. E. (ed.) *Readings in Urban Sociology*, Oxford, Pergamon.

Rex, J. R. and Moore, R. (1967) *Race, Community and Conflict*, Oxford University Press.

Roberts, J. T. (1976) *General Improvement Areas*, Farnborough, Saxon House.

Samuel, R., Kincaid, J. and Slater, E. (1962) 'But Nothing Happens', *New Left Review*, January 1962.

Saunders, P. (1978) 'Domestic Property and Social Class', *International Journal of Urban and Regional Research*, 2, 2.

Seabrook, J. (1971) *City Close Up*, Harmondsworth, Penguin.

Select Committee on Race Relations and Immigration (1976/77) *1977 the West Indian Community*, London, HMSO.

Shelter (1974) *Slum Clearance*, London, Shelter.

Shelter (1975) *Evidence to the Housing Finance Review*, London, Shelter.

Sigsworth, E. and Wilkinson, R. (1967) 'Rebuilding or Renovation?', *Urban Studies*, Vol. IV.

Sigsworth, E. and Wilkinson, R. (1970) 'Rebuilding or Renovation?: a Rejoinder', *Urban Studies*, Vol. VII.

Simmie, J. (1974) *Citizens in Conflict: the Sociology of Town Planning*, London, Hutchinson.

Spencer, K. (1970) 'Older Urban Areas and Housing Improvement Policies', *Town Planning Review*, Vol. XLI.

Spencer, K. and Cherry, G. (1970) *Residential Rehabilitation: a Review of Research*, Research Memorandum No. 5, Centre for Urban and Regional Studies, University of Birmingham.

Stones, A. (1972) 'Stop Slum Clearance Now', *Official Architecture and Planning*, Vol. XXXV.

Sutcliffe, A. and Smith, R. (1974) *Birmingham 1939–1970*, Oxford University Press.

Thornley, A. (1977) *Theoretical Perspectives on Public Participation*, Oxford, Pergamon Press.

Townsend, P. (1975) *Sociology and Social Policy*, Harmondsworth, Penguin.

Ungerson, C. (1971) *Moving Home*, Occasional Papers on Social Administration, no. 44, The Social Administration Research Trust.

Watson, C. J. (1974) 'The Housing Question', Cherry, G. E. (ed.) *Urban Planning Problems*, London, Leonard Hill.

West Midlands Grass Roots: various issues 1972–5, Community Action Journal, Birmingham.

Westergaard, J. and Resler, H. (1976) *Class in a Capitalist Society: a Study of Contemporary Britain*, Harmondsworth, Penguin.

Whitehead, C. (1977) 'Where Have all the Dwellings Gone?', *CES Review 1*.

Williams, P. (1976) 'The Role of Institutions in the Inner London Housing Market: the Case of Islington', *Transactions Institute of British Geographers*, NS 1.

Williams, R. (1973) *The Country and the City*, London, Chatto and Windus.

Wintourt, J. and Van Dyke, S. (1977) 'Housing Action Areas but Where's the Action?' *Roof*, Vol. II, no. 4.

Index